D0519646

MOTOR TRADE
–MANAGEMENT & FINANCE–

AN INSTITUTE OF
THE MOTOR INDUSTRY
STUDENT GUIDE
by
John Banks M.Sc (Warwick) FCCA

First published in 1992 by
The Institute of the Motor Industry
Fanshaws
Brickendon
Hertford
SG13 8PQ

© 1992 The Institute of the Motor Industry
Revised edition 1998

Typesetting by
Tradeset Photosetting Ltd
10 Garden Court Business Centre
Tewin Road, Welwyn Garden City
Hertfordshire AL7 1BH

Printed in Great Britain by
Black Bear Press Ltd
King's Hedges Road
Cambridge CB4 2PQ

ISBN 1 871880 02 5

CONTENTS

PREFACE

This students' guide, has been written to assist with the studies of The Institute of the Motor Industry's Certificate of Management. The text has been developed from the syllabus of the Institute's course and acts as a useful study guide for the Management and Finance modules. To assist the student it has been written in the same easy to use 'question and answer' format as its sister publication *Motor Trade Law*.

August 1992

PART 1: MANAGEMENT

Section A

MANAGEMENT PRINCIPLES

The Theory of Management

What do we mean by management?

There are almost as many definitions of management as there are managers. Definitions tend to be either short, vague and meaningless, or long, involved and easy to forget. Some definitions stress the scientific nature of a manager's job and talk about planning, regulation, decision-making, performance, control, integration, supervision and motivation. Others see management as more of an art – the art of getting work done by others. Neither type of definition is wrong, but instant definitions of this sort fail to give a realistic impression of what managers actually do. One manager described his job in this way:

'Being a manager is the most frustrating, infuriating and demanding job anyone could ask for. You don't get time to yourself, and you're constantly "on call". You always have to watch out for everyone else. For these reasons I wouldn't do anything else.'

(From Robert C. Dailey, *Understanding People and Organisations*.)

What do managers do?

If management is difficult to describe in one sentence, is there any agreement on what managers actually do, or on how they spend their time? The sort of things that managers do are:

- Daily routines and administration

- Monitoring the performance of the business

- Sorting out problems and dealing with crises

- Planning for the future

- Managing the necessary changes

- Time management

Why is 'Time Management' included? Because part of a manager's skill is in creating an effective balance between all these tasks. A poor manager may be overwhelmed by the demands of day-to-day routines and minor disasters while ignoring the need for planning and change. Another may dream about a perfect future while paperwork and chaos pile up in the present. A good manager has the ability to stick to priorities and at the same time remain flexible enough to respond to the unexpected. Examining the conflicting demands that confront a manager is what we turn to next.

Administration and management

The terms 'Administration' and 'Management' tend to be used interchangeably, and there is no hard and fast rule about where one starts and the other finishes. The popular understanding is that administration is a part of management, and consists of responsibility for the routine running of the business. It does not include the big decisions about where the business is going, but does include the responsibility for carrying out those decisions after they have been taken.

Specialist skills and management

Many managers spend some of their time using a specialist skill. An accountant for instance may be a member of a management team, but may spend time preparing financial statements and reports. When doing this sort of work, the accountant is using a specialist skill and is not being a manager. Similarly, when the sales manager is actually selling a car to a customer, he or she is not acting as a manager. It is only when the accountant and sales manager are directing and co-ordinating the efforts of others in achieving the aims of their departments, that they are managers.

In small businesses, managers tend to spend more time carrying out specialist activities. And in almost all businesses, the lower down the management scale, the more time is spent using technical skills. Supervisors for instance may spend only a third of their time managing. Departmental heads such as service managers may spend around half their time managing. Managing directors spend almost all of their time on management tasks. The proportions vary of course, but it's important to recognise that technical skills as a specialist are very different from management skills.

Fire-fighting and planning for change

Coping with the day-to-day problems and crises that face every manager is sometimes known as 'fire-fighting': . . . Tony the mechanic is off sick and a customer is calling to collect his car at lunchtime. Brenda in accounts is threatening to leave if she is not upgraded. The photocopier is on the blink again. . . . It's easy for a manager to be overwhelmed by these everyday mishaps, to concentrate on today and to let the future take care of itself. That way lies real disaster. A business has to change and adapt, to plan and direct its own future. Managers are responsible for the possibilities of tomorrow as well as the problems of today.

How do people become managers?

To cope with these conflicting demands, a good manager needs to be knowledgeable, determined and wise, as well as having the skills of a juggler and patience of a saint. So how do people get to be managers? In the USA and Germany, managers are usually professionally trained. In Britain there is much less emphasis on formal training. Managers 'emerge' by some mysterious process in the tradition of the great British amateur. People who have spent years of training in the purely technical side of their jobs are often propelled into positions of responsibility with little or no training in management itself. Being a good mechanic does not necessarily mean you will automatically be a good supervisor, just as brilliant footballers can sometimes fail spectacularly as club managers.

But does this mean that you can be a poor mechanic and a good supervisor? Most emphatically it does not. In a highly technical industry like the motor trade, supervisors and middle managers in particular need a high level of technical expertise, as well as managerial skills.

Before we begin to examine these skills in greater detail, perhaps you should pause and consider that you are not leaving your future success to chance. By studying for The Institute's Certificate of Management, you are approaching the task of management in a business-like and professional way.

What is management theory?

We have seen that management is difficult to define and seems to consist of a bewildering variety of tasks and responsibilities. Is there a theory to explain the process of management? There are, as you might have guessed, quite a number. Management theory developed as a response to the increasing size of factories and organisations towards the end of the nineteenth century. The beginnings were simple but spectacular, and theories of management have been developing ever since. The main approaches that we shall look at are:

- Classical

- Human relations and systems theory

- Human resources

- Humans as complex

We shall examine each of these in turn.

What are the classical theories of management?

The two people who best represent the early, or classical theories are an American, Frederick Taylor, and a Frenchman, Henri Fayol. Taylor was an engineer and developed, by practical experiment as well as writing, what came to be known as scientific management. Fayol, from the mining industry, looked for the first time at the general principles of management.

Taylor and the science of shovelling

In 1898 Taylor was hired by the Bethlehem Iron Company to improve work methods. Gangs of men were employed to load pig iron onto railway trucks, which they did at a steady rate of twelve and a half tons a day. Taylor took the best man, Schmidt, and promised a big increase in wages if he worked for a day in exactly the way he was told. Schmidt followed his instructions, earned his extra wages, and loaded 47 tons of iron during the day. Over the next three years, Taylor revolutionised the work methods of all the manual workers with a similarly spectacular effect.

How did Taylor do it?

Taylor's results were obtained by taking a systematic approach to the production process. He used four basic elements:

- The separation of manual work from mental work.

- Developing more efficient methods of organising work.

- Systematic selection, training and development of workers.

- Planning work in accordance with these systematic principles rather than allowing workers to use their individual methods.

Scientific management today

Much of this sounds commonplace today, but at the time the ideas were truly revolutionary. They were also, despite the extra wages, unpopular with manual workers, wholesale redundancies usually following in the wake of scientific management. Taylor also saw manual workers as merely machines, their human feelings and desires as rather a nuisance if anything. Despite this, there is much of value in the way that he saw the need to organise work in a systematic way. And a glance through the door of any factory with a production line shows that many of Taylor's ideas form the basis of how work is organised even today.

Fayol and the organisation of management

Important though Taylor's work was, and still is, he was looking mainly at how manual work is organised, rather than how managers should go about their business. Henri Fayol, a French mining engineer, used his accumulated experience as a manager to create a theory of management covering the whole organisation. Taylor concentrated on the manual worker in a 'bottom up' approach, Fayol started at the top and worked down.

The six operations in business

First he suggested that every business had six operations:

- Technical – production, manufacturing etc.

- Commercial – buying and selling.

- Financial – finding capital and using it.

- Security – protecting goods, people and ideas.

- Accounting – stocktaking, costs, accounts etc.

- Management – planning, organising, co-ordinating, commanding and controlling.

He was the first person to see management as separate from other activities. Who carries out these operations in your business and how do they do it? The jobs may not be so neatly divided up, but you can probably see that all of them get done.

Fayol's general principles

He also suggested that there are certain general principles that should be applied in the management of any business:

- Division of labour – specialisation means people are more productive.

- Authority – managers have the right to give orders.

- Unity of command – each person should receive orders from only one superior.

- Common goals – everyone should be working towards the same objectives.

- Centralisation – the manager should have final responsibility, but should delegate some of the work.

- Order – people and materials should be in the right place at the right time.

- Equity – people should be treated in a just and fair way.

- Stability – long term job security.

- Initiative – employees should be given the freedom to use it.

- Esprit de corps – keeping people happy and united through teamwork.

This was the first attempt to give a set of guidelines to managers in running a business. From your own experience you can probably see that some of the principles are a bit over-simplified. For instance, people who specialise in one job may be efficient, but in a small business particularly, it may be more useful to have someone who can adapt to a number of tasks.

What is a hierarchy?

The way in which managers view those working for them, and the way the work itself is organised, affects the way in which the organisation is structured. For instance, scientific management and Fayol's principles needed the solid foundation and order provided by what is known as a **hierarchy**. A hierarchy is a chain of command in which everyone knows what their job is and to whom they are responsible. It's best illustrated with a diagram:

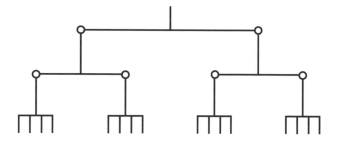

You will all be familiar with this sort of arrangement – it's the sort of chart you see on the wall in the general manager's office. The army is organised into this sort of structure. Privates are responsible to a corporal, a number of corporals to a sergeant, a number of sergeants to a lieutenant, and so on and so on up to general and field marshal.

The classical school comes under criticism

We have used Taylor and Fayol as the two most important pioneers of classical theories of management. There were many others who developed and improved on their ideas, like the colourful Frank Gilbreth who practised time and motion study on his wife and twelve children. These theories were looked on by many as universal rules that could be applied in all circumstances. But others began to realise that one essential ingredient was missing – *people*, and the way they behaved in practice.

Work and human relations

Classical theory had seen people in a rather mechanical way – as machines who would respond to the directions of management. But you know from your own experience when you go to work that you don't leave your own aims and desires behind when you go through the door. You also relate to other people in the organisation in a variety of ways. You may be friendly, hostile, or share common interests. Most of these relationships and alliances do not show up on the neat organisation chart on the managing director's wall. The attempt to explore the 'missing link' in the classical theories became known as the **human relations school**.

What was the problem?

The industrial revolution had produced large factories, scientific management had found the most efficient way to organise work, and Fayol and others had discovered the secrets of effective management. Nothing could possibly go wrong – but unfortunately it did. The problem was that employees had lost control over their work, the work itself had been deskilled, they had low status, little interest in their jobs and no reasons to work hard except for limited financial ones. Managers could see the problem but had few ideas about how to solve it. They turned to a group of people who specialised in the study of human behaviour – psychologists. The search for a solution was on.

The Hawthorne studies and Elton Mayo

The most famous early experiments took place in the 1920s and 1930s at the Hawthorne Western Electric plant in the USA, and were made popular by a Harvard professor called Elton Mayo. A group of workers were put in a separate room and closely observed while different working conditions were tried. First the lighting was increased. Production went up. It was increased several more times and production went up every time. The experimenters then reversed the process and reduced the lighting. To their surprise (and probably yours) production kept on rising. Other conditions were changed, such as rest breaks and wages systems, and all major changes led to an increase in production. What were the psychologists to make of this? They had only been trying to test the effects of lighting and other conditions but had stumbled on something quite different. After eliminating every other possibility they decided that the reason for the increase was that the workers felt recognised and valued because they had been chosen for this experiment. And this social recognition was more important to them than the other changes that had been tried.

Social needs

It may sound as though they had discovered the secret of increased output, but in further experiments of a similar kind output remained stubbornly low. Had they got it wrong first time? What they decided was that social forces were at work again, but this time in an agreement to keep production at the same level.

What these and other experimenters eventually uncovered came as a great shock to managers – a mass of social needs and relationships that were more important to workers than either a bigger pay packet or keeping the manager happy. The assumption of scientific management that people were a series of individuals motivated only by money was just not true.

People as social animals

The conclusions that Mayo and others came to was that:

- People are basically social.

- If jobs are meaningless, employees will look for satisfaction in social relationships at work.

- Work groups have more influence on individuals than the incentives and controls of management.

- Managers will be successful if they can satisfy their subordinates' social needs.

You may recognise the importance of some of these points from your experience as a subordinate. You will also have to acknowledge them in your behaviour as a manager.

How does this apply to the motor trade?

Dealerships and garages are no different from other organisations in that informal relationships and groups exert a strong influence on the way people behave. Have you observed the way some people 'don't fit in' with a group and how they are treated? Or how a group can show more loyalty to itself than to the management?

All organisations have a complex mass of social relationships just under the surface. The motor trade, however, has certain characteristics that should reduce some of the negative effects.

- Most garages are, by organisational standards, relatively small. Managers are not remote authority figures and good ones may inspire loyalty and friendship that cut across barriers. Poor managers of course can still have a big effect on a small business.

- The majority of jobs in the motor trade are in themselves quite interesting. Mechanics for instance have a wide variety of tasks, problems to solve and a high degree of control over their own work. In the pre-scientific management tradition they even provide their own tools. Anyone not convinced that a mechanic's job is basically an interesting one should spend a week shovelling pig iron, or try working in a modern biscuit factory.

A good manager in the motor trade will still have to be aware of the importance of these social factors, particularly when making changes or dealing with 'personnel problems'. All of this of course makes the job of management far more difficult and at times impossible. You should console yourself with the fact that nobody gets it right all the time. And that's the reason why the job is so fascinating anyway.

Is human relations the answer?

The human relations approach was such a startling change from the assumptions of scientific management, that for a time it dominated management thinking. Groups in particular were assumed to be the key to success. Nowadays we can see that human relations did provide some answers, but by no means the whole story. Managers did, on the whole, become more sympathetic to their workers, and more aware of their feelings and needs. But problems remained. It was proven that people were not just motivated by money, but money was still of great importance. And looking after people's social needs could not disguise the fact that many of them found little meaning in the work itself. It was time for managers and psychologists to go back to the drawing board.

The systems approach to organisations

Before we move on to the next 'revolution' in management thinking, we should briefly take a look at how the human relations approach changed the way in which organisations were viewed. The classical theory had relied on the straight-forward hierarchy that we illustrated earlier. It now became clear that organisations were much more complex and untidy than this simple structure allowed. Instead of connections between various levels in the hierarchy going up and down the chain of command vertically, there were all sorts of connections between people and departments going horizontally and diagonally as well. In a large garage for instance, the managers of the workshop, service and parts department may form a working group. The roles that people take on are also more complicated. The supervisor of a work team is not just a manager, but is also part of that team.

What is a 'system'?

The idea of a **system** is very simple, a system has an input, a processing system, and an output. A car factory has inputs of steel, components, paint and the other raw materials necessary to make a car. The processing system includes the factory, equipment, and all the employees. And the output is of course finished cars. A simple system can be shown like this:

There's slightly more to it than this of course. Consider the output of a garage. There are cars, parts and petrol sold and vehicles repaired. But there is another important output for a successful garage – satisfied customers. Customers who are not satisfied will go elsewhere and they will not therefore be future inputs. Inputs will fall, there will be less to process, and output will also fall (less customers = less sales = less profit). So outputs also affect inputs. We can show this on our diagram by including what is known as a feedback loop:

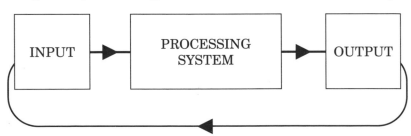

Systems theory can become very complex and mathematical in practice. Fortunately we do not have to go into any greater detail in this book. But even this simple description is useful in showing how one part of an organisation is bound up with and dependent on others. A mechanic's rudeness to an awkward customer can cause the loss of a future car sale. Workshop efficiency is dependent on the co-operation and effectiveness of the parts department. Systems theory can help managers to see how their role affects the achievements of the business as a whole.

The next step forward

The human relations approach had been a big breakthrough in seeing employees as much more than machines. The problem remained that many of them were still doing machine-like jobs, and no matter how sympathetically they were treated, there was no disguising this fact. The time had come to grasp the nettle and look at what people actually did.

Human resources

Psychologists observed that people seemed happier, healthier and more fulfilled when they were achieving some sort of personal growth towards their true potential. People felt better running in top gear than straining away in second. The psychologist Maslow called this 'self actualisation'. Another psychologist, Herzberg, in a study of engineers and accountants, discovered that what made them feel good about their jobs was achievement, challenge, responsibility and recognition – all factors related to the work itself. The factors that made them feel bad were not directly concerned with the work but with the work environment – salary, working conditions, supervision etc. The things that motivated them

were different from the things that made them dissatisfied. The real way to get people to give their best
was to provide them with challenging and interesting
work and to use their abilities to the full. This approach
was called **human resource management.**

What is job satisfaction?

The human resources approach tended to look at the
satisfaction that could be derived from the job itself.
Terms like **job enrichment**, **job enlargement** and
job rotation have become common as managers have
come to realise that monotonous and repetitive jobs create fatigue, boredom and hostility. The result is often
absenteeism, high labour turnover, sabotage and an
increase in accidents. The personnel department of one
USA car plant explained that the 70% turnover of staff
on their assembly line was no problem because anyone
on the street could be trained to do the job in one and a
half hours. Other employers took a different view.

A job at Volvo

Sweden has a low population, a high level of education,
and high wages. Working on a production line is not
popular. Volvo, the car manufacturers, wished to increase output in the 1970s and in their new factory
made a number of radical changes:

- Instead of the car passing along the line being
  'chased' by the workers, the car remained stationary
  while each group of operations was carried out.

- Instead of workers being isolated from each other,
  they worked in small groups, responsible for one particular set of operations, such as the wiring, doors and
  so on.

- The way the group organised the work was up to
  them.

Although not all Volvo plants were organised in this way, the lessons were learnt. Wages were high, the changes were popular with workers, and Volvo remains a successful and profitable car maker. Other well-known companies like IBM, Philips and Shell have also made similar changes.

So is the human resources approach the answer?

Like scientific management and human relations it's certainly part of the answer and it has affected the way in which managers think. But the fact remains that most jobs are still designed according to scientific management principles, and many employees still find that the influence of their own work group is more important than the wishes of management. Workers are also suspicious of new methods, having learnt from experience that increases in productivity are often followed by redundancies. Redesigning work to give people jobs that will satisfy them and the aims of the organisation is by no means a cheap option. There is certainly a long way to go. But as the level of education increases along with people's expectations, the long-term trend is likely to be away from assembly line production. Managers will increasingly have to look at the way in which work itself is organised in order to get the best from their staff.

Human resources management today

We have introduced human resources management, or HRM, as one of the latest developments in management theory. HRM has become increasingly popular as a general term to describe a new and more professional approach to employees, although some people see it as nothing more than personnel management by another name. It's true that work design is changing slowly, but there are signs that the attitudes of many managers are changing more quickly. For the remainder of the book we shall use the term 'human resource management' to cover anything connected with the management of people at work.

Which theory is the right one?

All of them and none of them. Each of the three broad theories which we have discussed gives a partial answer to the problem of managing an organisation. But none of them is sufficient as a simple and comprehensive explanation of human beings at work. Scientific management is right in assuming that people do work harder for more money. Human relations is correct in pointing out that social factors have an influence on productivity. And people with interesting and meaningful jobs are happier and do work harder, as we saw in the human resources approach. During the 1960s, managers and researchers began to think that reality was a bit more complicated than the existing explanations suggested.

Humans as complex

Human beings, as usual, turn out to be more complicated than the theories about them. What motivates Cliff may not motivate Gary. It may be right to treat Jill in a particular way in one situation, but if the circumstances change, the same approach may be all wrong. You know from your own experience at work that you don't always feel the same, or react in the same way to what goes on around you. Sharp words from an irritable and harassed boss may wash over you one day, but make you angry on another occasion.

How to manage people

The theory that the best way to manage people is dependent on a whole variety of circumstances is called **con-**

tingency theory. It means that a manager has to combine all the skills of a scientific manager, a human relations manager and a human resources manager. This is a tall order and all managers, including the best ones, make mistakes. But managers, like everyone else, can learn from their mistakes. As you gain experience and learn from the pioneers of modern management over the last hundred years, you will gradually discover the secrets of effective management.

Is that the end of the story?

Theories and ideas about management and organisations will continue for as long as there are organisations to manage. In fifty years time, the latest developments may appear as old-fashioned and unsophisticated as some of the assumptions of scientific management do now. One thing is certain however, management will still be as interesting and demanding as it is today.

The Process of Management

Managing the future

Why managing the future? You have enough to do dealing with the present – that is when you are not being praised or blamed for things that happened in the past. But think about it – the effects of your actions as a manager will all be felt in the future. As a manager you are trying to make things happen. A top manager may be trying to make things happen in one, two or five years time; a supervisor may have a shorter time scale of a day or a week. But both are primarily concerned with getting the outcome they want, whether it's a bigger and more profitable business, or a repaired car and a satisfied customer. You can learn from the past of course, and you would be foolish not to do so, but only as a guide to your actions in the future.

How do we go about managing the future?

The process of deciding what we want and working out the best way of getting there seems at first to be quite complicated. There are a number of steps involved and a few new terms to consider. But there is nothing difficult or illogical about the stages that have to be passed through. We go through a similar process all the time when we make decisions about our personal future. The problem is that some of the terms used can be confusing – objectives, policy, planning, and strategy for instance, all of which seem to deal with similar sorts of things. What do they all mean and how can we tell them apart? The purpose of this section of the book is to explain the meanings of these terms, to put them into some sort of context, and to show how they all relate to each other. We are not trying at this stage to give a detailed explanation of each stage in the process – that will come later when we look at managing the future in more detail.

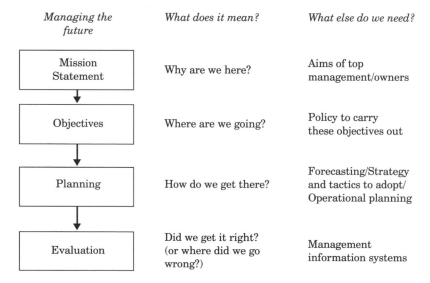

Managing the future	What does it mean?	What else do we need?
Mission Statement	Why are we here?	Aims of top management/owners
Objectives	Where are we going?	Policy to carry these objectives out
Planning	How do we get there?	Forecasting/Strategy and tactics to adopt/ Operational planning
Evaluation	Did we get it right? (or where did we go wrong?)	Management information systems

What do all these terms mean?

If you go to any business meeting or seminar, you will hear terms like policy, planning and strategy used a great deal, and not always in the right context. A further problem is that there is sometimes genuine disagreement over the exact meaning of some of them. The diagram gives an overview of many of the terms we shall be using and shows how they fit together.

We shall now look briefly at each part of the process in turn. Remember that this is only an overview – we shall examine each stage in greater detail later.

What is a mission statement?

In order to set the ball rolling, it's first necessary to decide what the overall aim or purpose of the business is – 'why are we here?', in fact. The most obvious thing that people think of first is to make a profit. While this is certainly important, in the case of smaller businesses in particular, profit may not be the main aim of the owner or manager. More often than not, a person setting up in business will not do so primarily to make a profit. Personal fulfilment, interest and a desire to be their own boss are likely to be more important.

As a business gets bigger, profit tends to become more important, but even in the largest companies profit is not the only reason for existing. It is now generally accepted that the managers of a business have aims and responsibilities beyond providing profit for the owners, or shareholders. They should also be aware of the interests of employees, consumers and the community, and increasingly their responsibility to the environment. Many of these aims have been forced on a sometimes reluctant management by the actions of government, unions and pressure groups.

A mission statement is therefore likely to contain much more than financial aims, and will include things such as growth, reputation, good industrial relations and excellent service to customers. All these things are important in the survival of the business, because if it does not survive, none of the aims in the mission statement can be met. Larger businesses will prepare a written mission statement. With smaller ones the aims may be understood, rather than formally written down.

What are objectives?

An **objective** is an end result or goal that you are trying to achieve. Objectives may be personal ones (I want to be a better manager), or business objectives (the company intends to expand).

Objectives can be more specific than this (I want to be general manager by the time I'm thirty), or (the dealership intends to increase its share of the used car market in the area to 15% in five years). They are all statements of where you, or the business, want to get to at some time in the future. You, as an individual, have to set your own objectives. It is up to the managers and owners to set the objectives of a business.

Objectives are based on the mission statement

The contents of the mission statement, as you saw, are not very specific, but they do make the foundations on which more detailed objectives can be built. At a personal level, your overall aims might be 'to be happy and to have an interesting life'. Not a very controversial choice, but having decided on it you can then start to look at your personal objectives. Where am I going? What success do I wish to achieve in my job? How would I like my social life to develop? Do I have any sporting ambitions?

A business must also decide where it's going. How will it fulfil its overall aims shown in the mission statement? By setting objectives, both long-term and short-term, management can set goals for the business to attain. Objectives are much more detailed than the overall aims, and will often include target figures and percentages, for example, 'to increase sales by 20% per year for the next three years'. We shall return to objectives soon.

What is policy?

Objectives look at what is to be achieved, **policies** examine how they are to be achieved. Policy decisions are taken by top management, although there may be advice taken from lower down the organisation. One of the major problems in understanding what policy means is that it seems to cover two sorts of things. There are the big policy decisions that determine the whole way in which the business will attain its objectives – for example 'growth will be achieved by taking over other garages'. At the other end of the scale are the relatively minor items of policy such as 'cheques will only be accepted if accompanied by a cheque guarantee card'. One type of policy decision affects the whole management philosophy, the other creates a set of rules for employees to follow in particular sets of circumstances.

'Minor' policy decisions?

All these apparently minor policy decisions do however set the tone for the way in which a business relates to its customers. The policy decision of Marks and Spencer's to give cash refunds without question has had an enormous effect on customer relations and sales.

One thing common to all policy is that it tends to have a feeling of permanence about it. Policy can and should be changed at times, but change it too frequently and not only will employees and customers be confused, but much of the effort that you have put into the next stage of the process will have been wasted.

Planning – the future in detail

Having decided on our objectives (our destination), and sorted out a set of guidelines and rules that we intend to adopt in getting there (our policy), we can now set about planning out our route in detail.

Why plan?

At the start of the book we looked at what managers actually do, and compared the tasks of 'fire fighting' and the day-to-day running of the business with planning for the future. Without planning, a business will lurch from one crisis to the next and have no idea where it's heading. Success or failure will depend largely on chance. It's like going on a journey without a map – you may reach your destination, but you are equally likely to end up in Blackpool or Bognor. Despite this, many businesses do no forward planning at all.

We shall devote a whole section to planning later in the book, but for the time being you should be aware that planning is either long-term or short-term depending on the time scale involved. One of the essential steps in planning is **forecasting**, which we shall briefly introduce next.

Predicting the future

We may have clear objectives and a sound policy to work to, but we need another ingredient before we can begin to plan in detail. We have to make predictions about what is going to happen in the future. We are all familiar with forecasting through the national pastime of the weather forecast. In fact we often incorporate the weather forecast into our personal plans. If we are planning a picnic, we listen to the weather forecast before planning what clothes to wear.

A business has to forecast what is going to happen in the world at large, the state of the national economy for instance, or the demand for small cars. It also has to predict what will happen inside the business, the date for the launch of a new product or the possibility of industrial relations problems for example. Forecasting what will happen next month is of course much easier than trying to predict what will happen in a couple of years' time. Weather forecasts are usually not bad for the following day, but hopelessly inaccurate for more than a week ahead. Long-term business forecasting is not as unpredictable as the weather, but still has to rely on a certain amount of informed guesswork. Once the forecasts are complete, planning can begin, and managers can start to assess the best **strategy** and **tactics**.

What are strategy and tactics?

Sports commentators constantly talk about strategy and tactics, but not always with a great deal of accuracy. Strategy is more long-term than tactics. For instance, the manager of a football team will decide on strategy for the team for the following season – the general formation, style of play, whether new players are needed. In the short term it will be difficult and probably foolish to try to change the strategy.

Tactics are more short-term. For a particular game the manager may insist that the opposing centre-forward is marked very closely. Or the out-of-form goalkeeper may be dropped for a game.

In business, strategy is decided by top management and, although it can be changed, is always long-term. An example of strategy might be a decision to sell only high quality used cars less than three years old. Tactics are also determined by senior managers, but with more help from managers at a slightly lower level. They will try to find the most effective ways of carrying out the strategy. A tactical decision might be to offer a free sunroof on all new cars during the month of June.

What is operational planning?

Top and middle management are usually concerned with strategic and tactical planning. The time-scale involved in strategy may be measured in years, in tactical planning it may be years or months. But there is also a great deal of planning that takes place in a business that has a time-scale of days and weeks. This normally involves supervisors and departmental managers, and is concerned with day-to-day operations – who does what and when? This is not an easy task as the managers involved have to react to the ever changing needs of customers, and to adjust to the different tactics adopted by senior management.

Policy, strategy, tactics and operational planning

To clarify how all these tasks relate to each other, we can say that:

- Policy can be changed, but is usually quite long-lasting. A major change in policy will mean changes in strategy, tactics and operational planning.

- Strategy is long-term, but can be changed without affecting policy. It will however trigger changes in tactics and operations.

- Tactics are more short-term than strategy and can change without affecting either policy or strategy. Changes will usually be necessary at an operational level.

- Operational planning is on the shortest time-scale and will not affect policy or strategy. But short-term problems at an operational level may prevent or delay a change in tactics.

What does evaluation mean?

You have put a great deal of effort into setting objectives, and planning the best strategy and tactics for reaching them. It would be foolish to forget to compare what actually happens with what you planned and hoped would happen. The process of comparing actual results with what you planned is called **evaluation**. It's asking the questions 'did we get it right?', and 'where did we go wrong?'. Unless we look at successes and failures in the past, it's unlikely that we shall get our plans right in the future.

How do we find out?

Not by waiting till the end of the year and seeing if we made a profit. Too many things may have gone wrong by then. Management needs to monitor constantly whether things are going to plan, to make minor adjustments, change tactics if necessary, and even, if thing are going badly wrong, to change strategy. How do we find out? A football manager has no problem, a glance at the league table gives a weekly and often painful update on progress. The management of a business needs something more sophisticated – something that deals with all the different strands of the plan. They need information about sales, orders, costs, production, money in the bank and a whole range of items. What they need is a **management information system**.

A management information system should give managers the information they need, in the right form and the right quantity, and at the right time. Fast enough to be able to do something about the deviations from plan which will always occur, even in the best run business.

Managing change in practice

This section has attempted to put the whole manage-ment of the future into some sort of context. We have tried to show what the terms we shall be using mean, and how they fit in with each other. You can see that the distinctions between some of the activities are blurred, even in theory. You will see later that in practice, and particularly in small and medium sized businesses, this is even more so. What is important, whatever labels we use, is to understand the process that is going on as a business tries to work out what it wants, and how to get it.

We have touched only briefly on many of these activities. In the following sections we shall look at all of them in more detail, and attempt to relate them to your own experience of the motor trade.

Section B

MANAGEMENT PRACTICE

Managing the Future

Setting objectives

We saw in the last section that an objective is an end result or goal that we are trying to achieve. Most people in their personal lives set objectives because by doing so they maintain at least some control over where they are going in life. To illustrate how important objectives are, it's best to imagine what life would be like without them. Instead of directing our efforts towards what we want, we let chance and other people decide our future. We may have some interesting experiences on the way, but we shall have no idea where we are going. It's no way to live a life, and as we shall see, certainly no way to run a business. The very fact that you are reading these words is proof that you have one particular objective – to complete successfully the The Institute's Certificate of Management.

Achieving personal objectives

Just because we set ourselves objectives does not necessarily mean that we shall achieve them. They may have been too ambitious in the first place. Your objective of playing football in the first division may be a non starter if you are of only average ability. On the other hand your objectives may be quite realistic but you may not achieve them for some other reason – an injury for instance, or a change in personal circumstances. You may just change your mind about what your objectives are, or even go for more ambitious ones. We may fail to reach our objectives or we may change them, but they are still useful because they give a direction to our lives, something to work towards and to strive for.

Do business objectives work in the same way?

Yes. Ideally, business objectives should be realistic and possible to attain with imagination and hard work. But quite often objectives are too ambitious, or there is a change in conditions outside the business which makes the objectives impossible to achieve. And, as with some people, some businesses have no clear objectives at all. The business *may* survive, but leaving the future to chance is a dangerous option.

What about the 'mission statement'?

You will remember that we started looking at business objectives by preparing a mission statement – the 'why are we here?' question. Asking 'why are we in business?' is the first step we have to take before we can attempt a more detailed look at our objectives. The answer to this question depends on the philosophy of managers right at the top. Do they:

- Have a purely economic outlook?

- Have a social outlook?

- See themselves as 'stakeholders'?

We shall look at each of these in turn.

Are we in business to make a profit?

Of course we are. Managers who take a purely economic view see this as the *only* reason for being in business, and want as much as possible. Profits are certainly important, and a business will not survive for long without them. The Finance part of the book discusses profits in some detail, and you will see that profit does not mean champagne and fast cars, but having a bigger and healthier business at the end of the year than at the start.

Profits are important, but managers who see profits as their only aim are ignoring the wider needs of employees, the environment and the community. This purely economic view also ignores the fact that many managers are controllers of the business, but not necessarily the owners. They may benefit from profits, but they may also have their own agenda of what they want to get out of the business.

The social view

In the same way that the 'human relations' school of management thinking took a less mechanical view of workers, the social view of managers setting the overall objectives takes into account the needs and desires of the managers themselves. Managers, it is assumed, will make enough profit to keep the owners of the business satisfied and then think about what *they* want out of the business. A sixty-year-old manager for instance may be much more concerned with job security than with maximising profits. The problem with the social view is that, like the economic outlook, it fails to show the whole picture.

What is the stakeholder theory?

As the economic view fits with classical management theories which we discussed in the first section, and the social view with the human relations approach, so the **stakeholder theory** fits with the more complex view of human organisations described in contingency theory.

In other words, it's a bit more complicated than either the economic or the social view allows for.

Quite simply, the stakeholder theory argues that the aims of managers are both social and economic. They have to make a profit in order to survive and grow, but they also have to safeguard the interests of employees (including themselves), customers, the community at large, and the environment. Some of these aims may well lead to increased profits, at least in the long term. Others may be forced on a reluctant management by legislation or by the actions of pressure groups. It makes the preparation of the mission statement an interesting balancing act.

How far ahead do we set objectives?

Having set out its aims in the mission statement, a business will obviously want to set out more detailed objectives as clearly as possible. How precisely they can be worked out depends on the time scales involved. Objectives can be:

- Long term – anything over five years.

- Medium term – two to five years.

- Short term – less than two years.

The further away the objective, the more difficult it is to set in detail. Long-term objectives are really ambitions or aspirations, rather than precise expectations. An example might be 'To be the biggest garage in Gloucester in terms of new car sales within the next ten years'.

Short-term objectives can be set more easily, and the business should realistically be able to achieve them. For instance, 'To increase sales of new cars by 8% within the next two years'. Medium-term objectives fall somewhere between the other two.

What influences the setting of objectives?

When managers sit down to work out objectives, they are influenced by three things:

- The mission statement.

- The *opportunities* that the business is likely to encounter in the future.

- The *resources* that will be available to them in terms of people, money and products.

Opportunities will depend on a variety of factors, some within the control of managers and some not. Managers can influence the effectiveness of sales staff, workshop efficiency, or the attitude of employees towards customers. But they have little influence over the design or quality of the new cars that they will be expected to sell, or over the general economic conditions in which they will have to operate.

Managers also have to bear in mind what resources they have available. Do they have the staff capable of carrying out ambitious objectives? Do they have the financial backing? And what about buildings? Many dealerships in town centre sites are unable to expand purely because of lack of space.

Why are some objectives difficult to achieve?

For the same reasons that you and I sometimes fail to achieve our personal objectives – because we were unrealistic in setting them, or because we don't work as effectively as we should. A business consists of a collection of individuals who are only human, make mistakes, are too ambitious or too timid, and sometimes have other things on their mind apart from work.

But no matter how perfectly people perform *inside* the business, conditions *outside* the business can change and make it more difficult for a business to achieve its objectives. New laws or increased taxes on vehicles or petrol can reduce demand. Customers' expectations also tend to increase over time. And the health of the economy in general affects the motor trade more than most, new car sales in particular being hard hit in a recession. We shall see when we look at forecasting that some of these events and changes can be predicted and should therefore be incorporated in realistic objectives. This is not always easy, as experts and politicians are unable even to agree on the health of the economy in the present, never mind the future. But just because there are difficulties does not mean that we should not set objectives. It does mean that objectives should be regularly reviewed to take into account both the performance of the business and changes in the environment.

Do objectives affect everybody in the business?

Overall objectives may be set by managers at the top, but they affect everyone from managing director to new apprentice. We saw in the previous section how objectives affect planning, and how planning is at a strategic, tactical and operational level. The effects of a change in objectives are felt all the way down the line. For example:

- An objective to increase the efficiency of a workshop by 15% over two years might result in changes in the flow of work through the shop, in the purchase of new equipment, in staff training and incentives. All these things stem from the original objective and need to be planned in great detail if the objective is to be achieved.

- An objective to improve the safety record of a department will mean planning the changes in working practices, and training and education for staff.

Objectives are set at two levels – the principal objectives of the whole business and the secondary objectives of each individual department. The objectives of each department have to be co-ordinated so that the efforts of every part of the business are directed towards achieving overall objectives. Some organisations go even further than this and set objectives not just for departments, but for individuals as well.

Objectives for individuals?

In the USA in the 1960s, management experts asked the question, 'If objectives are useful for the business as a whole and for each department, why not for individuals?' If there was some way of co-ordinating and controlling individuals and groups so that everyone worked towards the same goal, wouldn't this be an effective way of managing the organisation? In theory at least the answer seemed to be yes. The method they developed is called **management by objectives**.

What is management by objectives?

Management by objectives (MBO) is a method of control which measures individual performance against individual objectives. It can apply to anyone in the organisation, although it is more frequently limited to managers, from supervisors upwards. For the purposes of illustration, it may be best to imagine MBO applying to a middle manager. Individuals are asked what they do and why they do it, in an attempt to find what the key parts of the job are. This alone is a useful exercise as it enables people to focus on the real priorities of their work which are often lost in a jumble of day-to-day pressures.

Objectives are then set by a process of consultation between the individual and his or her manager. This should have three main results:

- Motivation – the manager should be highly motivated to achieve the objectives.

- Individual goals should be co-ordinated with the goals of the business.

- There should be a high degree of job satisfaction.

How does MBO work in practice?

After overall and departmental objectives are set, the following procedure takes place:

- All managers agree with their immediate superiors a set of objectives and targets to be achieved. These should be realistic but at the same time challenging.

- Each manager has the responsibility of planning out how his or her targets will be achieved.

- There should be some agreed method of evaluating and reviewing actual performance against targets, and of modifying objectives, plans and targets if necessary.

The emphasis is always on participation and consultation. MBO will not work if it is imposed from above.

MBO and the Motor Trade

The motor trade has a number of features that make MBO a realistic option. Each department has clear responsibilities and should be able to work out sensible objectives for managers. And targets to aim for are not too difficult to quantify. Examples of the sort of objectives that might be set in a dealership are:

- For a service manager – to increase the number of labour hours sold by 5% in the next twelve months using the existing staff.

- For a parts manager – to reduce the number of slow moving items to less than 22% of the total value of stock.

- For a workshop supervisor – to improve the safety of staff by reducing the number of accidents by 25% from its present levels.

These are examples of the sort of objectives and measurable targets that might be set. Each manager would have a number of these focused on the six or eight key areas of their job.

What are the problems with MBO?

For a time after it was developed, management by objectives was very popular. It was seen as the answer to the problems of motivating and controlling middle and lower managers in particular. Like many of the other breakthroughs we have examined it provided some answers, but not the whole solution. It is very useful for instance for managers to analyse critically what they do, and to focus their attention on the key elements. But there are a number of problems:

- MBO fails to deal with the conflicts between the objectives of the business and of the individual. Just because top managers would like everyone to be working towards the same goals does not make it happen.

- It's often difficult to set measurable targets, and unrealistic ones may have to be changed.

- MBO only looks at what managers do, not how they do it. Managers can continue to work inefficiently providing they achieve their objectives.

Policy Making

What is policy?

Remember what we said about policy earlier? We compared our objectives to our destination, and said that policy was a collection of rules and guidelines to adopt in getting there. We also pointed out that policy can cover the big items that determine the major ways in which a business sets about achieving its objectives, and a series of minor rules that enable employees to act in a sensible and consistent way. We can now look at policy in more detail.

Why have a policy at all?

The best way to illustrate why policy is necessary is to imagine what running a department would be like without one. What would you do if a customer returned a part and demanded a cash refund? What would you do if a customer asked for credit? What action would you take if Mark was absent for a week without producing a doctor's note? What if Sandra asked for maternity leave? How long would you allow on full pay? How long on half pay? Managers are constantly presented with situations of this sort. If they have to take a new decision every time, they are likely to be inconsistent over time, and certainly different managers will take different decisions. The result would be an unfair and chaotic mess of unhappy employees and customers.

This is why every business works out a series of policy decisions – so that managers can be fair, just and consistent in their dealings with staff and customers. Not everyone will be happy with the decisions a manager takes, but at least they will know that the same rules apply to everyone.

How is policy made?

Policy is decided by managers at the top, usually the board of directors. It is unlikely however that they will be experts in all the necessary areas, so it is usual for policy committees to be formed from managers lower down the business. Using their experience and expert knowledge they will recommend what policies should be adopted, but it is the function of top managers to make the final policy decisions. The situation in a very small garage is much simpler. The owner/manager will decide on policy and may not in some cases even write it down. But everyone working in a business has to be made aware of what the policy is, however formally or informally this is done.

What factors need to be considered in setting policy?

When setting policy, managers need to take into account the following:

- The aims and objectives of the business.

- Where the policy will apply – the sales department, service, accounts, or the whole business.

- The type of situations that will arise in the normal course of business and which the policy is meant to cover.

- The type of policies normally adopted in the motor trade. Policy does not need to be be identical to that of competitors, but managers should be aware of what is considered the norm.

- What laws or regulations apply in the area under consideration.

What are the rules of good policy making?

When policy is made, it is attempting to anticipate the sort of situations with which managers will be faced in the future. This is not always easy to predict, so policy should be so worded that managers can take decisions within company policy using their initiative in the changing situations that arise in practice. Managers in other words need helpful guidance and not a strait-jacket.

Policy should wherever possible apply equally to everyone. This may not always be possible where different departments have differing needs. But too complex a policy will cause error and confusion.

What is a policy framework?

A policy framework sets out the areas that policy should cover. Overall policies will be set first, usually by the board of directors. This will lay down the attitude of the business in trying to achieve its objectives and will largely depend on the contents of the mission statement. The vast majority of policy decisions will come next and will relate to the functional areas of the business as follows:

- Financial – where to raise funds and how to use them. The attitude to borrowing, investment and expansion.

- Marketing – what are we going to sell (products, services, range, quality, after sales service), where are we going to sell (who are our customers), how are we going to sell (promotion, advertising, publicity), and at what price are we going to sell (price levels, discounts, payment terms)?

- Production – what premises and equipment do we need, what sort of output are we aiming for, what about quality control? What is our buying policy and how much stock do we need to carry?

- Personnel – recruitment and selection, who do we need and where and how shall we get them? Pay and conditions, how much do we pay, bonuses, pensions and health and safety? Industrial relations, unions, grievance and disciplinary procedures. Training and staff development, technical and management training, promotion policy.

- Customer care – attitude to the customer, improvements in service and facilities, complaints procedures.

Policy as you can see is very wide ranging and detailed, and entails a huge amount of effort. Much of it is however quite long-lasting, and the effort will certainly save both time and confusion in the future.

Who is affected by policy?

Every single employee and every customer is affected by policy decisions. The wrong personnel policy will result in poorly motivated staff, a high turnover of employees, and industrial relations problems. Inappropriate production policies will add to the problems of employees and result in disappointed and fast disappearing customers. And in the intensively competitive environment of the motor trade, customers who are not properly valued by an effective customer care policy will soon go elsewhere.

How flexible should policy be?

Although we have said policies often tend to be fairly long-lasting, some policies are not particularly difficult to change. A change of objectives on the other hand may cause a massive amount of disruption and reorganisation. Many policies are quite flexible and should be altered and updated if conditions change. The last few years have seen major changes taking place in customer care policies in the motor trade as garages have tried to improve their image. Financial policy may change if the business is experiencing a shortage of cash – imposing stricter limits on customer credit for instance.

It is important however not to change policy so frequently that those people who are affected by it become confused, or feel that they are being unfairly treated.

How do external influences affect policy?

We have just described improvements in customer care policy that come about by pressure from consumers. All businesses are subject to changes in their environment, and some of these changes will affect policy. The actions of government in making laws and setting taxes relating to the motor trade, together with local and national economic conditions will all contribute to a reassessment of present policy.

The efforts of competitors to gain an advantage can also force a change of policy. For instance, if a competitor offers free transport or a courtesy vehicle to service customers, then if that is not your policy, your business could suffer. While you may have to react to this sort of external influence, it would be much better to make policy innovations yourself, and let your competitors react to you.

In the motor trade, personnel policy is particularly affected by the recommendations of the National Joint Council for the Motor Vehicle Repair Industry (or NJC), which negotiates matters relating to pay and conditions (see Finance, Section D). New cars of course are largely marketed by the manufacturers, and individual dealerships will usually tailor their own policy on advertising and promotions to coincide with the manufacturer's policy.

How do you know what policy is?

No matter how good the policy it has to be effectively communicated. It is important that employees are aware of any aspect of policy that relates to them either as personnel policy or in their dealing with customers. A policy manual that can be easily updated is important, as are clear operating procedures, particularly for staff who deal directly with customers.

Customers should also be clearly aware of how policy relates to them, and this is normally done by printing them on invoices and documents which the customer receives. Important items of policy can also be prominently displayed in a department as a constant reminder to staff and customers.

Should policy making be by consent?

We saw in the first section of the book that it is very difficult to impose conditions on employees that they consider to be unjust or unreasonable. Although it is the responsibility of managers at the top to make policy, they must do this with the consent of those affected by it. An unfair policy on promotion for example, will cause discontent and disruption. Imposed policies will be unpopular and may be unworkable. Policies that are negotiated and agreed are likely to be much more effective.

Forecasting

What is forecasting?

We saw in Section A that forecasting is trying to predict what will happen in the future. Despite the fact that looking into the future with any sort of accuracy is extremely difficult, we all spend a lot of time doing it. A shopping list is based on a forecast of our need for food and drink. Before planning next year's holiday we have to forecast whether we shall have enough cash in the bank to pay for it.

A business also has to predict what will happen in the future before it can begin to plan out in detail how it will achieve its objectives. What will be the demand for new cars? How many trained mechanics will we need? What changes will there be in technology? Is the country sliding into recession or about to experience a boom? A business can't begin planning until it has examined questions like these. To answer them it needs to look at what happened in the past, what is likely to happen in the short term, and what may happen in the long term. We shall start by considering the sort of information that we need.

What do we need to know from short-term forecasting?

Short-term (or short-range) forecasting refers to forecasts of a year or less. Because we are not trying to look too far into the future, these should be reasonably accurate. We need information from inside the business and from outside as well.

What information do we need from inside the business?

Internal information will be about the following:

- The past performance of the business. The past is often a good guide to the future, and it is usual to start by scrutinising the management information system to see what the business has achieved in the past. The information can come from accounts, sales returns, details of service and repair etc. Managers will also attempt to answer the following questions:

- Is the business keeping its share of the market?

- What products and services will be sold and how up-to-date are they? Will any new vehicles or other products and services be launched?

- Are there any plans to move to new premises, or to buy new equipment?

- Human resources – what staff will be needed, and what wage and salary increases are likely? What is the industrial relations situation likely to be for the next twelve months?

- Cash – what will be needed in the way of money? When will cash come in and when will it have to be paid out?

What information do we need from outside the business?

The information we would need from outside the business is about:

- Demand for our products – is it growing or declining?

- Our competitors – what will they be up to? Do they have new products to launch? Are they increasing their share of the market at our expense? Have they recently made any changes in technology? How do their prices compare with ours?

- Does the business borrow money, or need to in the future? If it does, managers will need to know if the cost of borrowing (the amount of interest paid) is likely to go up or down.

- How government actions will affect the business. Demand in the motor trade is always being influenced by decisions about the level of taxes – the tax on new cars, petrol, VAT, and road fund licences. Governments often introduce laws which affect garages – MOT regulations, seat belts, exhaust emissions etc. Although the contents of the Budget are secret, it is sometimes possible to spot the trend and anticipate changes.

What information do we need from long-term forecasting?

Ideally we would like to know about all the things we considered under the heading of short-term forecasting. The problem is of course that the further into the future we look, the less confident we are about how accurate our forecasts are. Predicting the state of the economy, or what our competitors will be up to in five years time is impossible with any sort of accuracy. But the motor industry in general has to make long-term predictions because of the time it takes to design and manufacture a new product. The launch of a new car will have been planned several years earlier, and motor traders will have to sell it in an environment very different from the one in which the new car was first discussed.

From the motor trader's point of view, this means that they can predict with some confidence the sort of products they will be selling for several years ahead. But they will still have the difficult job of forecasting how many vehicles they will sell, the state of the economic environment, and what national transport policy will be in the years ahead.

How accurate are forecasts?

Just because making predictions about the future is difficult and we rarely get it completely right does not mean that forecasting is a waste of time. There is a great ideal of guesswork involved, but it is informed guesswork. Even a hazy idea of the future is better than being totally in the dark.

What we can say with reasonable accuracy is that a forecast for three months ahead is likely to be more accurate than one for three years. But even short-term forecasts can sometimes be hopelessly wrong if some unforeseen event takes place. The most spectacular example of this occurred in 1974 when the price of oil rose dramatically. The motor industry was affected more than most as the cost of petrol went through the roof. Motoring habits changed overnight and the demand for bigger cars was much reduced.

Anticipating changes in technology

Changes in technology are usually easier to predict than those relating to demand, or to general conditions for the business. The question is not normally if something will happen, but when? We have mentioned this already in relation to the development of new vehicles, but there are other technological changes which affect the motor trade, for example:

- The use of computers in automating procedures like stock control, service paperwork, and accounts.

- The use of electronic equipment for diagnosing and correcting faults, or in the sale of petrol.

- Improvements in vehicle specifications that lead to changes in service and repair methods and equipment, for example the use of special plastics to replace steel.

Motor traders have to forecast these changes so that they can plan how to deal with them. Will they for instance have the right staff to cope?

Human resource forecasting

The motor trade needs a high degree of technical skill to adapt to changes in technology. Most independent forecasts predict that there will be a shortage of skilled labour in the coming years. Human resources forecasting is therefore crucial in the motor trade, and managers must try to assess:

- The number and type of staff needed.

- Likely wage and salary levels.

- Training needs to cope with the rapid changes in technology.

- Training and development for managers and other personnel.

Cash flow forecasting

The most important financial forecast is called the cash flow forecast. This estimates how much money will be flowing into the business and how much will be flowing out. And, just as important as how much, it also looks at when the cash will come in and go out. Like other forecasts it will be more reliable and show more detail for the next twelve months than for longer periods. Finance, Section B discusses cash flow forecasts in great detail.

Does forecasting affect objectives and policy?

A forecast can often lead to a change in objectives. If a recession is predicted it may lower expectations of sales. On the other hand if a boom is forecast, objectives may become more ambitious.

Policy can also be affected. For example, a change in consumer habits can force a rethink in existing policy. If a rapid expansion in DIY car repairs were predicted, instead of regarding DIY as competition, managers might reorganise the parts department, start to hire out specialist tools, and try to make some profit from the expanding DIY market.

Where does forecasting information come from?

We have already discussed one of the most important sources of information on which to base short-term forecasts – the management information system. This will provide information on what has happened to the business in the past, its strengths and weaknesses, and the trends that show up over time. We cannot rely on the past repeating itself, but it would be foolish to ignore the rich source of information and clues we can find there.

Other useful sources of information for short and long-term forecasting include the Department of Trade and Industry, local government plans and statistics, and larger libraries which have information on trade and business, social trends and predictions, much of it now held on computer files. The motor industry itself is another good source of information on which to base forecasts, the Retail Motor Industry Federation (RMIF) and the Society of Motor Manufacturers and Traders (SMMT) amongst others. Your own 'intelligence service' should of course be keeping an eye on the competition.

Planning

Using those forecasts

We know what our business is trying to achieve (our objectives), we have a set of rules and guidelines to help us (our policies), and we have a number of predictions about the future to rely on (our forecasts). Now we are in a position to make some definite plans about how we are going to reach those objectives. Forecasts, on their own, are worthless to the business. Their value only becomes apparent when we start to plan – if the forecast is accurate, then the more reliable the plan, and the better chance there is of achieving objectives.

What is planning?

Life is so full of planning that we rarely think of it as a separate exercise. We plan shopping trips, holidays, jobs around the house, even what we are going to do tomorrow. We may do it in a formal way by writing the plan down, or just plan things in our heads – but however we plan we are working out in advance how we shall accomplish something. We look at what resources we have (money for shopping, paint and brushes for decorating), and at the most systematic way to achieve the end result we want. After we have finished planning we carry out the plan, and then look at the end result. Is it what we want? Could we have done it better? How successful were our plans in other words? In business there will be more detail, decisions will be more difficult, and certainly there will be more formality. But the process will be just the same. Decide on objectives, plan out how to achieve them, carry out the plan, and finally evaluate the results of the plan.

Planning for the short term

Most of the planning activity that goes on in a business is short-term, that is for less than one year ahead. Middle managers and supervisors concentrate on even shorter periods, days or weeks, for the majority of the work. A service manager is usually concerned with planning service and repairs for up to a week ahead. A non-routine event like reorganising the stores will have to be planned on a longer time scale, but will still be comparatively short-term.

Most short-term plans can be carried out exactly according to plan. But things *can* go wrong, and plans should always be flexible enough to cope with the unexpected. If the electrics specialist is off sick when a particular job has been planned, then someone else will have to cover. Minor disasters like this are so common that they should be anticipated. Totally unforeseeable circumstances are rare in short-term planning.

Planning for the long-term

The long-term means anything more than one year. It is usually the concern of top managers, and the period covered by planning varies according to the type of business. The fashion industry can rarely plan anything more than a year ahead, oil companies frequently think in terms of twenty or thirty years. Motor manufacturers may not plan for as long as this, but need to think many years ahead. A large, well-managed garage should be considering long-term plans for the next three to five years.

Long-term planning differs from short-term planning in that unforeseeable circumstances are almost bound to occur. No matter how good the forecasting has been, things will not go according to plan. *Flexibility* is the keyword. To stick rigidly to a plan when conditions have changed is worse than having no plan at all. The plan should be tuned to the new circumstances, and if conditions change drastically, completely overhauled. A deep and unexpected recession may change a plan for rapid expansion into a plan for survival until things improve.

Strategy, tactics and operational planning

In Section A we looked at three levels of planning:

- Strategy – always long-term and linked to long-term overall objectives. It almost always relates to the whole business.

- Tactics – may be long or short-term, but are always on a shorter time-scale than strategy. They may relate to the whole business, but usually apply to an individual department.

- Operational planning – always short-term, mostly very short-term. It is always at departmental level.

We shall discuss each of these aspects of planning in turn.

What goes into strategic planning?

Strategy is decided by senior management and is about *what* should be done. The following ingredients are needed:

- Clear objectives for the business as a whole, including sales and profit targets.

- A detailed analysis of where the business is *now*. Its financial position, marketing effectiveness, capacity of workshops, showrooms etc., human resources, existing customers – all its strengths and weaknesses in fact.

- An assessment of the competition, their products, services and prices.

- Forecasts which have been prepared on both the internal and external factors affecting the business.

What is a SWOT analysis?

Many businesses take these factors into account by undertaking a **SWOT** analysis. SWOT stands for (S)trengths, (W)eaknesses, (O)pportunities and (T)hreats.

- Strengths – what advantages does the business have going for it? Customer loyalty? Good reputation for service and repair? Sound finances?

- Weaknesses – it is much more difficult to honestly assess the problem areas. Lack of space through poor location? Poorly organised and over-stocked stores? Top management dependent on one key person with no effective delegation? Poor cash flow?

- Opportunities – mostly outside the business. Is the market for any product or service likely to expand? Can the management team be strengthened by taking on a new sales manager? Is a new model about to be launched?

- Threats – again largely coming from outside the business. Is competition becoming more fierce? Is there danger of the business being taken over? Are government regulations going to make life more difficult? What about changes in technology? A management that is too complacent about these sort of threats may find themselves in trouble – like for instance the British motor-cycle industry who were too slow to react to Japanese innovation.

A SWOT analysis enables managers to take a systematic look at all aspects of the business in carrying out strategic planning.

What comes out of strategic planning?

The ingredients are there – all the strategic management team have to add is hard work, imagination, flair and experience, and they will produce a plan to lead the business towards its objectives. It will normally cover the following areas:

- Financial – planned sales, costs and profits. These are shown in budgets (see below and Finance, Section C).

- Marketing – what products and services will be sold and at what price levels? What potential customers will be targeted?

- Human resources – numbers of staff required and levels of skill. Broad plans for staff training and management development.

- Development and growth – this is to some extent covered by the previous three headings but, in a fast changing industry like the motor trade, is often treated separately. What major changes are planned – a move to an out-of-town location for instance?

What about tactical planning?

Strategic planning is about *what* should be done. Tactical

planning is about *how* it should be done. Tactics are still the responsibility of managers at the top, but department heads will take a more active part. The starting point is to accept the strategic plan, and then to work out how to carry it out. Tactics are both shorter term and more flexible than strategy. It's quite possible to change tactics without altering the basic strategy – although a change in strategy would inevitably lead to different tactics.

A tactical plan for the used-car sales department for example, would examine how the available resources could be used to fulfil its part in the strategic plan. It would look at space, staff and the money available for stock, and see how each could be used to attain sales and profit targets set.

Planning operations

The third level of planning is the responsibility of department managers and supervisors and is concerned with who does what and when? The smooth running of a business depends on it and, if it is not done well, it is unlikely that the tactics and strategy will work out as planned. The time scale involved is usually measured in days, weeks and months.

Workshop loading – an impossible task?

One of the most difficult operational planning tasks in a busy garage is workshop loading. The service manager and workshop supervisor have to deal with customers who are not always reliable, cars that refuse to be repaired in the time allocated, spare parts that are not immediately available, and mechanics who are sick or on holiday. Despite all these potential delays, most customers collect their vehicle at the promised time, along with a completed bill. This is not because service managers are members of the Magic Circle, but due to their systematic approach to the job and because their operational plans are very flexible.

Each job is given a job card, a multi-part document which accompanies the vehicle, and is used in the issue of parts and in the preparation of the bill (job cards are described in detail in Finance, Section D). The progress of the job may also be recorded on a wall chart or computer screen. The key to success however is to expect a certain number of customers not to turn up, some repairs to prove stubborn, parts to be unavailable and staff attending funerals – and to be able to do something about it. Included in all operational plans should be the 'what happens if?' question. It turns a day of potential drama and crisis into something more manageable.

What are budgets?

Most plans have at some point to be turned into hard figures. What income do we expect to receive from parts sales? What will be the wages bill for the service department? How much will the sales department spend on advertising? A budget expresses the plan in financial terms and will be in great detail for the current year, and less so for following years. For each department and for the business as a whole, the budget will show what planned sales are, and what we plan to spend on each type of cost (vehicles, parts and materials, wages, advertising, electricity, stationery etc.). Until the budget is worked out, we cannot know if the plan is a viable one.

Budgets are not just useful at the planning stage. They also enable managers to *control*. If you know what sales you *should* make in the month of August, then you can compare this with what you actually *do* make. Similarly, if you have planned to spend £1,500 on promotions in the first three months you can compare this with actual spending of £2,300. Where things have gone to plan, you can forget about them. Where they have not, like the £800 overspending on promotions, you can look at the reasons why and take action if necessary. Planning and control go together.

Planning in the form of budgets *enables* you to control. Budgets are covered in detail in Finance, Section C.

Human resources planning

Not all plans can be reduced to financial terms – although all plans have financial implications. Planning the human resources that the business will need is vitally important in the motor trade. Many tasks are highly skilled and require years of training. Hiring and firing cannot be done on a casual basis, and getting the right people in the right place at the right time takes careful planning.

One problem that most garages experience is the conflict between having staff who are specialists in a particular skill, and staff who can turn their hand to anything. Specialists are quicker, but make operational planning more difficult. Distributing the work, and dealing with unexpected demands and staff absenteeism, is much more complex. Managers should try to get the right balance, by planning for recruitment and training well in advance. This will be at a strategic and tactical level, and will be based on the level of activity and targets predicted.

The marketing plan

How are we going to bring our products to the attention of potential customers? And how are we going to keep those customers once we have got them? These are the questions that the marketing plan is trying to answer. A good starting point is to concentrate on the 'four Ps' of marketing – **product, price, promotion** and **place**.

- Product – exactly what products and service are we trying to sell? What advantages do we have over our competitors?

- Price – how do we price our products compared with our competitors?

- Promotion – how shall we get our products to the attention of customers? How shall we advertise and what promotional activities shall we use? How can we build on the marketing efforts of the manufacturers?

- Place – where are we selling from? In town or out of town? What geographical areas can we expect to attract our customers from?

The answers to these questions will depend on the forecasts we made of changes in customer demand, local and national economic conditions, and the availability of new products.

Increasingly important in the motor trade is an aspect of marketing called 'customer care management'. So important that it often has a section of the overall plan to itself. Customers expect a far higher level of service than they did in the past, and the garage that can provide it will have a definite edge over its competitors. Customer care makes the customer the focal point of the business. Only by satisfying the customers' needs will sales be made, wages paid and profit earned. Marketing and customer care management are discussed in detail in Finance, Section C.

What makes a good plan?

No matter what sort of plan is being prepared, there are certain principles which should be adopted:

- The plans should be based on clear objectives.

- The right ingredients should be used – data on past performance, relevant forecasts, and the experience and imagination of managers.

- Plans for each department must be co-ordinated. This is done continuously with operational planning on a day-to-day basis. Co-ordinating longer term plans is more difficult to achieve, although the relatively small size of

most motor trade establishments means that good communication between managers at all levels should make
this much easier.

- Targets should be quantified and given a financial value
  where possible. What the plan is trying to achieve
  should be clear and unambiguous.

- Plans should not be over-ambitious. If targets are impossible to achieve, the effect will be to discourage people
  from even trying.

- Plans must be flexible so that if they are too ambitious
  or too timid, or if conditions change, the plan can be
  suitably modified.

- Plans should be communicated to everyone who is
  affected by them.

- Plans should be evaluated and compared with what
  actually happens. Much of this monitoring of performance can be done through budgetary control.

What is a contingency plan?

We have seen that if a plan is too rigid it is unlikely to be
successful. Flexibility is essential, and a way of building
this into plans is called 'contingency planning'. Contingencies are events or conditions that may or may not
occur. Part of your personal planning for the winter may
be to carry a shovel in the boot of your car so that you can
dig yourself out of a snowdrift. It may or may not snow,
but your plan is flexible enough to deal with bad weather,
should that particular contingency arise.

A business has to deal with an uncertain future and must
include some contingencies in its plans. For instance, a
plan to reorganise a workshop over a period of a month
may be planned for a slack period. If activity is higher than
expected, the reorganisation may take longer. A more flexi-

ble approach would be to set a target time of three to six weeks.

Plans for expansion may be dependent (or contingent) on attaining sales targets and having sufficient cash in the bank. If the business fails to achieve one part of the plan, another may have to be delayed or cancelled.

Who does the planning?

At an operational level, most planning is carried out by department managers and supervisors. Strategic planning is the responsibility of managers at the top, and tactical planning is usually carried out by senior managers and departmental heads working together. It depends of course on the size of the business. In a large dealership group, only the managing director of each dealership might be involved in strategic planning for the group as a whole. In a small garage all managers may be involved in every aspect of planning.

Top-down or bottom-up planning?

We have seen that in most cases long-term planning is decided by top managers and then passed down the management line. This can mean that managers who will be responsible for carrying out the plan have had no involvement in the process and may be hostile to it, or may not fully understand how the plan was worked out.

An alternative way is to use 'bottom-up' planning, where plans are drawn up by each department separately. These are submitted to the senior management team, who can then modify them where necessary and co-ordinate them into a plan for the whole business. This method has the advantage that departments are more committed to plans they have helped to devise. The disadvantage is that if top managers decide to ignore the 'bottom-up' plan, it will be even more difficult to persuade departmental managers to carry out the 'top-down' alternative.

Evaluation – or 'did we get it right?'

There is little point in going to all the trouble of preparing plans, trying to carry them out, and then ignoring what actually happens. An essential part of the process is to carefully compare the actual performance of the business with what was planned. By looking at where actual performance differs from the plan, managers can focus their efforts on the areas that need attention. For instance, if we plan to sell 3,000 hours of service and repair in the month of March, and we actually sell 2,950 then things have gone more or less to plan, and no further action is necessary. If however only 2,300 hours are sold, then managers will want to know the reason why so that action can be taken to improve performance in the future.

Focusing on things that are not going to plan is called **management by exception**. It is a particularly efficient method of managing any business that is too big to be completely controlled by one person. It means that managers can *delegate* responsibility but still retain overall control. Since many plans are in financial terms, the most important tool that managers have to measure performance is the budgetary control system. This will compare actual results with the plan and show up any differences (or variances).

Actual results cannot always be shown in figures or financial terms, and managers will have to compare plan with performance in other ways – for example, a plan to change working hours may have to be evaluated by asking customers and staff if they prefer the new arrangement.

The business plan

As you can see, plans are wide-ranging and detailed, covering every aspect of the business. It is common to have a summarised version of the plan, showing the most significant elements, including sales targets, major developments and the more important budgets. This is called 'the business plan' and can be shown to existing or potential investors, and to people like the bank manager.

A warning about the use of terms

In this section on managing the future, we have used terms like 'objectives', 'policy', 'strategy', and 'tactics', and given them quite specific meanings. In your dealings as a manager, you may find that some people use different terms, or the same terms in a slightly different way. This does not necessarily mean they are wrong (although they may be), but it does reflect the fact that there is no universal agreement on the use of business language. Older managers for instance may not use terms like 'the mission statement'. Some people include the setting of objectives as a part of strategic planning, rather than something that comes before it. Labels do not matter too much, providing you have a clear understanding of the process involved in ensuring a successful future for the business.

Section C

MANAGEMENT STYLES AND RELATIONSHIPS

Leadership

What is leadership?

When we look at leadership we tend to think first of famous leaders like Elizabeth I, Napoleon, Gandhi, or the current Prime Minister. Unusual people in other words. But most leaders are far from unusual and have to use their leadership qualities quietly and with little hope of fame or glory. They are managers of course, and every manager has also to be a leader. Not all the time – sometimes (as we saw in Section A) managers use specialist skills, sometimes they are dealing with managers at the same level or with superiors. But where they are dealing with people who work for them, trying to get them to do something, or sorting out their problems, then they are acting as leaders.

Managers as leaders

Leadership is about influencing people to act in a particular way. Managers can sometimes get people to do what they want purely because they are managers. Because in other words they have power over them – they may have influence over pay and promotion, choice of work, even the job itself.

But there is another dimension to leadership. You know from personal experience of people who have managed you that some rely purely on their position to get things done. Others do not need this formal sort of authority in order for you to carry out work – you do it willingly because they give you support, help and encouragement, look after your interests and the interests of your fellow workers, create a happy working environment and for a variety of other reasons. They are, in other words, good leaders.

What makes a good leader?

Since it is fairly easy for us to recognise, from our own experience, those people who have led us well and those who have done it badly, it has been surprisingly difficult to analyse the factors that go into making a good leader. Managers and psychologists have been working on the problem for a long time, and what they have discovered is the subject of this section.

The trait theory – searching for 'the great man'

Early research looked at good leaders and tried to find what personal qualities (or traits) they had which set them apart from everyone else. It was assumed that 'great men' would emerge because of particular attributes whatever situation they found themselves in. Hundreds of studies were done and lists drawn up of the ideal traits of a leader. Intelligence, initiative, health, age, even height and eye colour were put forward in the search to identify leaders. The results of the studies were not very satisfactory. Even the vague list of qualities that most leaders did seem to share was not very useful because plenty of other people who were not leaders seemed to possess them as well.

The trait theory also assumed that people were either leaders or followers. As most middle managers discover, there are times when you have to lead, and other times when you need to follow. The search for 'the great man' seemed to be getting nowhere, and researchers turned their attention away from what people *are*, and began to look at what they *do*.

Is the answer in leadership style?

Are some managers good leaders because they behave in a certain way? The attention of managers and researchers now turned to this question. Is a manager who tells you what to do without allowing any discussion more or less effective than one who asks for your opinion first? Different researchers put managers into a variety of categories – dictatorial, authoritarian, autocratic, paternalistic, democratic, consultative. Fortunately you do not need to know the exact meaning of each one as they all boil down to two broad styles – **directive** and **participative**. There is another style called 'laissez–faire' (let things take their course), which in effect means no management at all. We do not need to consider it further.

What is a directive leader?

This is the traditional view of the way in which a manager should behave. Managers issue an order and expect it to be carried out. It worked for Frederick Taylor at the Bethlehem Iron Company (see Section A), and works well in strictly disciplined hierarchies like the armed forces. A directive leader is not necessarily an unfriendly one, but he or she will decide what is to be done, who will do it, and how it will be done. This may have been successful in the past, but a leader who always adopts this style will find it increasingly difficult to manage in today's world.

What is a participative leader?

At the other end of the scale are leaders who allow their subordinates to participate in making decisions about work. Participative leaders see themselves as part of the working group, rather than above it. Discussion of how things are to be done is encouraged and there is often free-dom to divide the work up as the group thinks fit. Despite this supportive and democratic approach, it is still the responsibility of the manager to take the final decision. Subordinates are usually happier with this sort of leader, and staff turnover and industrial relations problems are reduced.

Which style is best?

What do you think? It sounds like no contest – a participa-tive leadership style must be best. It is certainly true that in recent years there has been a move away from the direc-tive styles of the past, but to change style completely does not seem to be the answer. It has been impossible to prove that people work harder with participative leadership, and in certain situations and for certain people, a more direc-tive approach seems more effective.

The managerial grid

One of the main problems for managers is that they have to worry about *production* and about the *people* working for them. Keeping both customers and workers happy is not always easy. Two researchers called Blake and Mouton devised an approach to this problem by using what they called 'The Managerial Grid'. They asked managers to rate themselves on two scales:

Scale A – (from 1–9) is that of 'Concern for People'.
Scale B – (from 1–9) is that of 'Concern for Production'.

Imagine rating your performance as a manager on these two scales. If you are the sort of manager who is really keen to get the work out, but not overly sympathetic to the needs or problems of your staff, you might perhaps rate yourself at 3 on Scale A (people) and 8 on Scale B (produc-tion). You would be a '3,8' manager, and would be able to see how your management skills might be improved.

How would you rate yourself? At the extremes you could be a '1,9' manager for instance, who shows very high concern for people, but is much less concerned about production. Or a '9,1' manager (similar to Frederick Taylor), who thinks that production is all important, but that the social needs of people are largely irrelevant? If you are a '1,1' manager I'm afraid you are not really managing at all, but if you rate yourself at '5,5' you are performing adequately on both counts. A high score on both scales is what you should be aiming for, and if you rate yourself at '9,9' you are either the best manager in the world, or being a little unrealistic.

Is the management grid the answer?

It's certainly part of the answer, and a useful way of analysing a manager's performance. How do you think you score as a leader? The Management Grid has been used successfully in management training, and if you do eventually become a '9,9' manager, you can be sure that you are an excellent leader. The trouble is that it's a bit like the search for the 'great man' – nobody is that good. And it's still assuming that there is one best way to behave, and that once you have discovered the secret you will be the perfect manager. Life, as your experience as a manager has already taught you, is not quite that simple.

The conflict between production and people

As a manager, you will experience times when there is a conflict between the needs of the people who work for you and the needs of a busy production schedule. And no matter how perfect a manager you are, you will not be able to keep everybody happy. For instance, Terry the mechanic is going through a rough patch at home and is getting on badly with his workmates. One afternoon he asks to see you to talk about a transfer to another workshop. As a good manager, concerned about your subordinates, you know what you need to do – give him some time, be supportive, let him discuss his problems, and try to find a solution that is fair to everyone.

But you are also concerned about production, and you have a lot of customers arriving to collect their cars later that afternoon. What do you do? You have to make a choice between people and production. Most managers would put the customer first and try to deal with Terry on another occasion. But if Terry's problems are bad enough you might have to put his needs first. You might have to be a '9,1' manager on one occasion and a '1,9' manager on another. It all depends on the situation.

Matching style to situation

Managers began to see that a management style that worked in one set of circumstances was not appropriate in another. A style that is effective with a group of workers on a car factory production line may be completely wrong if used by a sales manager attempting to lead sales staff in a dealership. Managing a highly trained group of mechanics is different from managing a supermarket. It's that word 'contingency' again – and the theory that the right style varies according to the situation is called **'contingency theory'**.

What is contingency theory?

Contingency theory takes a more complex view of the circumstances likely to face a manager. It looks particularly at the relationship between the leader and the group, the task that has to be accomplished, and the position of the leader in the group.

A researcher called Fiedler looked at leaders in a variety of organisations. What he found was that a directive style worked best either when the situation was *very favourable* to the leader, or where it was *very unfavourable*. In between, where it was only moderately favourable to the leader, a participative style was best. What does this mean?

What situation favours the leader?

Fiedler said that situations favourable to the leader were:

- Where the leader was popular and trusted by the group.

- Where the task to be accomplished was clear and well defined.

- Where the leader had a lot of power over the group – the ability to reward and punish and the backing of top management.

Fiedler found that where all these factors were present, then a more *directive* style of leadership was effective. He also found that where a leader was unpopular, managing ambiguous tasks and not very powerful, a directive style was *still* most effective. But somewhere in the middle, where a manager is neither popular nor unpopular, where the task is neither completely clear nor totally ambiguous, and where a manager has a moderate amount of power, then a *supportive* style is best. This is a position that many managers find themselves in.

How does this relate to the motor industry?

Despite the fact that these are quite complicated ideas to grasp, Fiedler has been criticised for taking too simple an approach. But managers do have lessons to learn from contingency theory, the main one being that they have to take a flexible approach according to the situation they find themselves in. The motor trade is no different from any other business in that the same manager might manage different departments in an alternative way. And the same department might be managed by different managers adopting different leadership styles. Let us look, as an example, at a service department.

What is the right style for a service department?

Let's look at managing a service department in terms of Fiedler's three situations. Firstly, service managers themselves can be popular, unpopular, or anywhere in between (a). Secondly, the task itself is in some ways quite clear – to repair or service a vehicle. But the job is far from simple and repetitive and mechanics have to work on their own initiative to a large extent (b). Thirdly, how much power does a service manager have? It varies of course, but most are neither powerless nor completely powerful (c).

So what does this mean in terms of management style? You can see that as soon as we begin to discuss a real situation even the most complex theories fail to give precise answers. But there are some clues. The task itself (a), and the amount of power the manager has (b), seem to fall somewhere in the middle of Fiedler's scale, and point to a participative style being the most effective. The big *difference* between service departments will most likely be in the degree of popularity and trust in the manager. We could probably go as far as to say that:

In most service departments, a manager would be most effective adopting a generally *participative* style – but:

- a very popular manager could afford to be slightly more directive,

- an unpopular manager might *have* to be slightly more directive.

Look at your own workplace – do any of the managers conform to Fiedler's theory of leadership?

What is an assertive manager?

As you can see, theories about management style can be confusing and at times contradictory. It's important to know that managers need to be flexible in different situations, but is there some practical way in which managers can improve their leadership? One of the latest techniques in management development is assertiveness training. The idea is that a manager shows four broad types of behaviour – **aggressive**, **manipulative**, **passive** or **assertive**:

- Aggressive managers usually get their own way, but at a cost. They will create hostility and resentment because they are only considering their own needs. They will probably be tense and angry a lot of the time.

- Manipulative managers are really being aggressive by other means. They are never direct and get results by making people feel guilty or inadequate, or using emotional blackmail. Subordinates often feel frustrated, confused and unhappy.

- Passive managers try to please everyone, to be popular, and to put their own needs last. This avoids conflict in the short term, but stores up trouble for the future. Health and confidence also usually suffer.

- Assertive managers express their own needs, but also allow other people to do the same, to say what they want, and to state their opinion – to be assertive themselves in other words. When trust has been built up, this should result in open and honest relationships between managers and their staff. Confidence within the department should increase as people begin to take the initiative.

Sounds easy? Unfortunately it's not. It's always much easier to get your own way by being aggressive or manipulative, or keep out of trouble by being passive. Learning to be assertive requires confidence and training, and means taking risks. Many managers are finding that the rewards, at a business and a personal level, are worth the effort involved.

Leadership – a two way process

It's important to remember that the people who work for you are not passive objects who will respond in predictable ways to your style of leadership. They will, sooner or later, let you know what they think about the way you manage them. Are they happy or unhappy? Do they respond and co-operate? Is there any team spirit? The best lessons you will get on leadership are the ones you get from the people you lead. Leadership is a two way process and you need to understand how your actions are affected by them, as well as the other way round.

The best style of leadership for you

Looking at the theory and practice of leadership should enable you to adopt good habits, drop bad ones, and to understand the effects of your actions on your staff. It should not, however, encourage you to behave in a way that seems to you false or hypocritical. The best type of leadership is the one that works for you and the real test of leadership is in results rather than style.

Motivation

What is motivation?

A visitor from Mars would wonder what on earth we are all up to. Why do we stand in factories, sit in traffic jams, dismantle gearboxes, operate computers? Why do we work at all? Is it because we need to, or because we want to? Theories of motivation look at why people do what they do, and how much effort they put into it. If you as a manager can understand what motivates the people working for you, then you may be in a position to improve their performance. For instance, if people are motivated by money, then you can get them to work harder by promising more money for greater effort. If someone is motivated by status, you can get them to work harder by giving them a new job title, a bigger desk, or their own parking space. Motivation is not only about how well people work, but also about loyalty and commitment to the business.

Does motivation explain good performance?

If you can find out what motivates your staff, can you guarantee they will perform well? Unfortunately not – there are many other factors that contribute to effective performance. Do they have the right equipment? Are they well organised? Do they have the ability? No amount of motivation can get someone to rebuild an engine if they lack the basic ability. But, everything else being equal, a person who is highly motivated will certainly perform better than someone who is less motivated.

What motivates you?

Before we look at the research that has been done in the field of motivation, take a few minutes to think hard about what motivates you. What motivates you in your place of work? What motivates you in your social life? What motivates you to study for The Institute's Certificate of Management? And how are these things different from the factors that might have motivated you if you were living a thousand years ago? What do you think would have motivated you then? Try writing down your answers and see how they compare with the research – and if you have changed your mind by the end of the section!

Do you remember Frederick Taylor and Elton Mayo?

In Section A we began to examine the question of what motivates people at work. Of the early pioneers you may remember Taylor and his pig-iron shovellers, and Mayo and the Hawthorne experiments:

- Taylor made an assumption about what motivates people. He assumed that they were only motivated by the need for money – promise more and they will work harder.

- Mayo believed that they were also motivated by social factors – recognition, group loyalty and a whole range of things that had nothing to do with money. Mayo thought that if these were satisfied, then people would perform better.

Although Mayo had found something quite startling, it wasn't until 1943 that a serious attempt was made to analyse the factors that did motivate people at work.

Maslow and his hierarchy of needs

An American psychologist, Maslow, argued that we have five basic needs. When we have satisfied the first need we start worrying about the second, when that is satisfied we go on to the third, and so on. His 'hierarchy of needs' is shown below, starting with the most basic need of all:

- Physiological needs – literally what we need to live and survive at a physical level. The need for air, food, water and so on. A starving human will risk any danger or ignore any social taboo for food. Survivors of shipwrecks and air crashes have resorted to cannibalism in order to stay alive.

- Safety needs – after physiological needs are satisfied, we next want things like freedom from harm, shelter and security.

- Social needs – next comes the need for love and affection, the need to be with other people and to be accepted.

- Esteem needs – the need to be recognised by others, to feel confident, appreciated and respected.

- Self-actualisation needs – do you remember self-actualisation from Section A? This is the need we have to develop our talents to the full, the need for challenge and achievement.

What does this mean to a manager?

In the normal work situation a manager is not concerned with the first two levels. These needs are usually satisfied – and according to Maslow, once a need is satisfied it is no longer a motivator. Once we have enough food we start wanting the next thing in the hierarchy. Once we are safe and secure we start to be motivated by social needs. If Maslow is correct, a manager should know that a need is not a motivator until the lower needs have been satisfied. For example, we would not think about our social needs if confronted by a charging rhinoceros.

Was Maslow right?

Like so much else we have discussed, Maslow gave us some answers, but not the whole picture. He had a great influence on the way we think about motivation and was certainly right to say that humans are motivated by a variety of factors. He has been criticised for a number of reasons:

- The theory is too vague for a practical manager to apply to a real situation.

- It is by no means certain that levels of motivation progress in such a neat and orderly way. People are much more complicated than this and may have a variety of needs at any one time. An artist for instance may put self-actualisation needs before social needs.

- Maslow's evidence for his theory came from looking at a very narrow selection of people (white, middle-class American males), but suggested that it applied to human beings as a whole.

Theory X and Theory Y

In the 1950s, and building on the work of Maslow, Douglas McGregor suggested that there were two different ways of looking at people at work. He called his two assumptions Theory X and Theory Y:

- Theory X assumed that people will avoid work and responsibility wherever they can. They are not very bright and need to be closely supervised.

- Theory Y assumed that people are not by nature passive and lazy, and only behave in this way because of their experience of work. Basically, they see work as a natural activity, will accept responsibility, and in the right conditions do not need close supervision.

You can see that the assumptions behind Theory X are completely opposite to the ones underlying Theory Y. Which of these extreme positions fits closest to your own experience as a manager? Does this necessarily tie in with your experience as a subordinate? Frederick Taylor was certainly a Theory X fan, and managers from the human resources school would subscribe to Theory Y. You can see that the assumptions you make as a manager will affect the way in which you try to motivate your staff to perform well.

How would a Theory X manager succeed?

A Theory X manager would attain the goals of the business by:

- Very close supervision and control, modifying people's behaviour to fit the needs of the business.

- Using rewards and punishments to ensure that people do what is needed. A directive style of leadership is necessary.

A Theory X manager essentially sees people as machines to be programmed to produce the desired outcome.

How would a Theory Y manager succeed?

A Theory Y manager would attain the goals of the business by:

- Recognising that people have the ability and motivation to accept responsibility, and are capable of directing their efforts towards attaining those goals.

- They must therefore arrange conditions and methods so that the objectives of the business are reached through individuals attaining their own goals.

- This can only be done through co-operation and adopting a participative leadership style.

A Theory Y manager takes a generous view of people and expects a great deal from them.

Theory X and Theory Y in practice

Few managers take these extreme positions, but you can all probably recognise these assumptions from your own experience of managing and being managed. Which theory works best? Most people prefer Theory Y – after all, it's not very nice to think of people as mere machines. It's also true to say that there has been a move away from Theory X management over the last few decades. But there are some uncomfortable facts that often make it impossible to adopt a Theory Y style, however much a manager would like to. Consider the following situations:

- On a production line where the work is boring and repetitive, there is little opportunity for development, responsibility or self-fulfilment.

- During a recession when redundancy and cut-backs prevent agreement and participation.

In both cases a more directive, Theory X style tends to be the only option. As we saw in the section on leadership, however, there are many factors in the motor trade which suggest that a more participative style, using Theory Y assumptions, is likely to be most effective.

Affiliation, power and achievement

Another person to be influenced by Maslow was McClelland, writing in the early 1960s. He proposed that people have three types of need in relation to work. Everyone has some of each, but not the same levels of each:

- The need for *affiliation* (or friendship) – everyone has this need, but if it is particularly strong, the individual will put social relationships before the needs of production.

- The need for *power* – managers usually have a strong need for power and probably will not succeed without it. Having power, however, does not guarantee success.

- The need for *achievement* – combined with a high need for power this can be a potent combination. People with a high need for achievement want responsibility and need feedback on their progress. High achievers sometimes tend to work on their own too much, and to be unaware of the needs of the team and the business.

How do you think your needs, and the needs of your staff fit in with this theory? If you rate yourself highly on the need for power, you will probably not wish to know that in a 20-year follow-up study of Harvard graduates who scored high on the need for power, 58% had high blood pressure or had died of heart failure. (From D. C. McLelland, Power: the inner experience.)

Satisfaction and dissatisfaction at work

Another way of looking at motivation is to find out what satisfies people in their work, and what dissatisfies them. If you can find the answer to these questions, it must help you in your job as a manager to get the best out of people. A psychologist called Herzberg (whom we introduced briefly in Section A) asked a group of engineers and accountants what aspects of their jobs satisfied them and what dissatisfied them. What was interesting about their responses was that the things that satisfied them in their work were not the opposite of the things that dissatisfied them.

What dissatisfies people at work?

Let's examine the things that caused dissatisfaction first. They were all to do with the *conditions* of work – the salary, supervision, company policy and administration, interpersonal relationships and physical working conditions. Herzberg called these **hygiene** or **maintenance factors**. If any of these were wrong, individuals felt dissatisfied. Nothing surprising about that. What *is* surprising is that when all these things were right, they did *not* cause satisfaction. Why not? Because when conditions are right, people just don't notice them. You have probably experienced this yourself. Imagine for instance that you work in an area with inadequate lighting. Like most people you will probably grumble about the fact constantly until something is done about it. But if the lighting is perfect, you won't even be aware of it. Bad lighting dissatisfies. Good lighting fails to satisfy.

So what does satisfy people at work?

Herzberg found that the things that satisfied people were achievement, recognition of that achievement, interesting work, responsibility and advancement. He called these motivating factors. What is interesting about them is that they are all connected with the work itself, and not the conditions surrounding the work. They were about what Maslow called 'self actualisation'.

What does all this mean for a manager?

Herzberg pointed to the fact that there is a great difference between job context (all the things that surround the job), and the nature of the work itself. Maintenance factors such as salary and physical working conditions may explain (in the words of Charles B Handy) 'Why work here?', but only the motivating factors deal with 'Why work harder?'. The lesson for managers is that they must get the maintenance factors right, but these on their own are not enough. To motivate, they need to look at the work itself.

How can a manager motivate through work?

A word of warning. Along with almost all other management theories, Herzberg's findings have been criticised. He based his studies on interviews with engineers and accountants, two groups of people who had highly paid and relatively interesting jobs. The same responses might not be forthcoming from workers on a production line where the work is repetitive and boring. Other research has shown that, even for executives, financial rewards are also an important motivating factor.

Even so, the ideas of Herzberg, and the other advocates of the human resources approach that we introduced in Section A, have had a powerful influence on the way in which managers think. There have been bold experiments such as the reorganisation of work that we described at some Volvo factories, but still many jobs are designed closer to the principles of scientific management than to the ideals of human resource management. Where work is designed along the lines of scientific management, managers do not have much scope to motivate people through the task itself. They have to rely on the 'carrot' of money, together with close supervision, to get the work out.

What about the motor trade?

As we have stated before, many jobs in the motor trade do not conform to this pattern. They have variety, are quite challenging and some require problem solving. The scope for a manager to motivate staff through the work itself is much higher than in many types of business. The techniques that can be used are:

- Job enlargement – this effectively means that jobs are designed to be less specialised. There is more variety in the work and a greater range of activities.

- Job rotation – job 'swapping', so that people get experience of a wider variety of jobs. This has the additional advantage for a manager that the unexpected absence of one member of staff will cause less disruption.

- Job enrichment – this is the most powerful means of providing job satisfaction. It includes job enlargement and job rotation, but also means giving people more responsibility and power to organise their own work. It is the most difficult for the manager because it means that people have to be trusted to work on their own initiative.

What is positive motivation?

The sort of motivation we have been discussing so far is **positive motivation**. It means that people work hard because you are giving them something they want, or fulfilling some need. We have described positive motivation through money and security, social needs, esteem and recognition, and in terms of satisfaction through the work itself. There is one very simple form of motivation that is effective, costs absolutely nothing, and which in general we are not very good at. What is it? Simply giving praise where praise is due. The simple act of saying, 'Thank you, you did a great job', to a service receptionist who has taken over when the manager is ill. On the whole, British managers find it easier to criticise than to praise. And as any psychologist will tell you, constant criticism is a very ineffective way of motivating people.

What is negative motivation?

You are negatively motivated to do something if by doing it you avoid some consequence that you don't want to happen. You may pay your taxes for instance because you wish to avoid going to prison. Traffic wardens are good examples of negative motivators. You don't park on the yellow line because a warden with a notebook may be lurking round the corner. Negative motivation only works well where positive motivation would be impractical – it's impossible to reward a motorist for not parking in the wrong place. Negative motivation may work in upholding the law, but is not a good way of motivating people at work.

How does loyalty to a company affect motivation?

Loyal employees are those who are most committed to company goals. They feel that they have a stake in the business and are less likely to be absent or to leave. Someone who claims 'I only do the job for the money', will leave if a better paid job comes along. But although people who are committed to the organisation are likely to be more dependable, and less likely to take time off or to leave, there is little evidence to suggest that they work any harder. Research on the connection between loyalty and commitment is confusing and contradictory. People in higher positions, however, are likely to be more committed, and the longer a person has worked for an organisation, the longer he or she is likely to stay.

Communication

Why is good communication important?

Dealing with problems, planning for the future, writing letters, sitting in meetings, talking to customers – managers spend most of their time communicating in some way or other. The communication system in a business is like the oil in an engine. You need the right amount of the correct type, and it needs to flow to all the places that need it. Too little and the business will not run smoothly, too much and you will gum up the works altogether.

The problem with communication is that it seems to have a built-in tendency to go wrong. You know this from your personal experience. How many times have you made an arrangement with someone such as, 'I'll meet you at the end of Bridge Street at nine'? Even assuming that the person turns up on the right day, the chances are that they will be at the wrong end of Bridge Street, and possibly at nine in the morning when you meant nine at night. The message was absolutely clear and unambiguous as far as you were concerned, but left plenty of scope for misunderstanding by the receiver.

How is information communicated in a business?

There are channels of communication in a business along which information flows. It flows downwards from the top, through department managers to supervisors, and then to their staff. This is the sort of communication of which Frederick Taylor would have approved. Managers today are also concerned that, to keep a well-motivated and effective workforce, information must also flow in the opposite direction, from bottom to top. Communication up and down the organisation is called **vertical communication**. Information also has to flow across an organisation, between different departments. This is crucial in the motor trade where departments are so dependent on each other. In the average garage there is a constant two-way flow of information between sales and service, sales and parts, and service and parts. This is called **horizontal communication**.

Formal and informal communication

All businesses have a mixture of formal and informal channels of communication. A very small garage will rely heavily on informal channels – a diary, notepad, and continuous face-to-face communication may be sufficient for an organisation employing three or four people. A large dealership could not run efficiently without a more formal system of forms, reports and memos. But, however big the organisation, there will still be some informal communication to keep things running smoothly. For instance, if the parts department is experiencing a problem with the paperwork from the service department, a quiet word from the parts manager to the service manager may be all that is required to improve the situation.

Communications within a business can usually be classified into three types:

- Formal and routine – information that flows from one part of the business to another on a regular and routine basis. This may be on standard forms such as customer orders, parts requisitions or employee time-sheets (see Finance, Section D). It may also be by routine reports, sales returns or monthly budgets, for example.

- Formal and non-routine – information in the form of memos, special reports, notices etc., that do not recur on a regular basis.

- Informal – face-to-face spoken communication, the use of the telephone, or removable self-adhesive notes for messages.

'I heard it on the grapevine'

There is one type of informal communication that everyone is familiar with – the 'grapevine', or unofficial channel of communication. Every organisation has a network of information that by-passes the official channels. Genuine information and rumours both true and false can be transmitted on the grapevine with astonishing speed, but not always great accuracy. A good manager will use both official channels and the grapevine to communicate, but the best way to avoid rumour and speculation is to keep all staff as fully informed as possible about all the things that affect them.

Communicating with the outside world

So far we have looked at communication inside the business, but many of the same considerations apply to communication with people and organisations outside the business. These include customers both potential and actual, car manufacturers and other suppliers, and other organisations such as the Inland Revenue. Communications can be formal and routine (purchase orders, sales invoices), formal and non-routine (letters, sales advertising), or informal (the service manager having a chat to a customer). Whether the information is for inside or outside the business, the rules of good communication are the same.

The process of communication

All communication goes through the same basic process shown below:

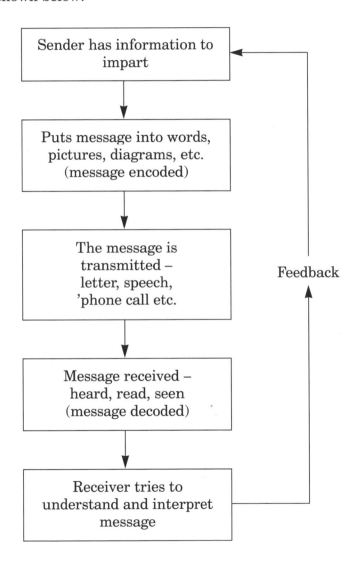

Most messages are in the form of words, but figures, pictures and diagrams are also used. And don't forget that with face-to-face contact, many messages are transmitted without any of these, by gestures and facial expressions. If the process is so clear, what can possibly go wrong? Most problems with communication occur around the last stage of the process, where the receiver fails to understand what the sender is trying to communicate.

What are the causes of poor communication?

The most common problems that hinder communication are:

- The sender may express the message badly. It may be unclear, in an inappropriate form, or capable of being interpreted in more than one way. The use of business jargon can be woolly and misleading – it often looks impressive, but can mean almost anything.

- The receiver may be biased or selective. We only tend to hear or see the good news, and to avoid the bad. We have no difficulty in remembering praise, but may ignore or distort criticism. We also tend to select the parts of a message that suit us – an accountant receiving a report may consider only the financial issues and ignore areas such as customer care or health and safety.

- The receiver may have too much information or not enough time. This sort of information overload may lead to the receiver ignoring some messages altogether, as for instance many people ignore junk mail. Computer systems can sometimes provide managers with more information than they can effectively use.

- If there is a lack of trust between the sender and receiver, the sender may be less than frank and open, and the receiver will interpret the message with suspicion or hostility because of his or her previous experience. In a business with poor industrial relations, the workers will not take communications from the management at face value.

- 'Noise' or the wrong environment may be the problem. A poor 'phone line may cause misunderstanding, or trying to discuss staff problems in a noisy workshop.

With so many things to go wrong, it's surprising that communication works at all. A business can certainly improve its communication network by trying to eliminate all the barriers we have described. But it can also actively encourage good communications.

How can communications be improved?

How can a manager actively improve communications? There are a number of general rules:

- Choose the most effective way of getting the message across. Remember that some people respond best to the written word and some to the spoken word. Use the most appropriate channel – formal or informal, official or unofficial. Use more than one channel if necessary.

- Encourage two-way rather than one-way communication. One-way may be quicker, but two-way allows for questions, discussion and clarification. A manager who gets feedback can see if the message is getting through. In face-to-face communication, a manager can learn a lot from body language.

- Have as few links in the communication chain as possible. The more links in the chain, the greater the possibility of the message being distorted.

- Develop your listening skills. It's much easier for a manager to talk and take charge of a discussion than to listen to the contributions of others. Remember what we said about assertive managers – say what you have to say, but allow others to do the same. Your staff will be happier and you will learn more than you imagined. As Richard J. Ferris, the Chairman of United Airlines once put it: 'People are given two ears and just one mouth, so they can listen twice as much as they talk.' (From Ray Wild, How to Manage.)

- Remember also that, as a manager, you are in a powerful position. The people who work for you see you as a figure of authority and may find it difficult to keep you fully informed. If you can break this barrier down (and you are the only person who can), then you will not be kept in the dark about what is really going on.

- In written communications, avoid jargon and use plain language as clearly as possible. Be brief and to the point but make sure that all the essential information is included.

Communication in the motor trade

We have looked at a general list of the dos and don'ts of effective communication. It's now time to examine in greater detail the different types of communication that a manager in the motor trade is likely to use. We shall cover:

- Routine and standardised communication – forms, invoices, time-sheets etc.

- Written communications, including memos, letters, reports and other common types.

- Spoken communications, including face-to-face discussions, interviews, the use of the telephone, and meetings.

- Modern developments involving computers, faxes etc.

Communication through routine paperwork

The vast majority of communication, both inside a business and with the outside world, is done on pre-printed stationery which is hand-written, typed, or produced by a computer. Internal documents include estimates, job cards, service loading charts, time sheets, and wages slips. External documents include orders to suppliers, bills to customers and statements of account to credit customers at the end of the month. Most of these standard forms are multi-part documents which are used for more than one purpose.

Section D of Finance looks at routine paperwork in some detail, so it is not necessary to expand on this now. But it is important to realise that most communication is at this routine level, and it is therefore important to get the system right, and to make sure that it operates smoothly and effectively.

Letters

A business letter communicates with the outside world and it is important that it creates the right impression with the person receiving it. The general rules that we outlined above for all written communications should be adopted, but in addition it is vital when writing to people outside the business to:

- Eliminate any errors of spelling, typing or grammar.

- Select the right tone in terms of friendliness or formality according to the circumstances. A letter to a long-standing customer whom you know personally will adopt a different tone from a letter to a distant supplier who has failed to deliver on time.

- Use the appropriate form of address. Formal letters to someone you do not know usually start with 'Dear Sir' or 'Dear Madam', and end with 'Yours faithfully'. Less formal letters begin with 'Dear Mr Smith', or Mrs, Miss, or Ms if the letter is to a woman. Such a letter would end with 'Yours sincerely'. There has been a tendency in recent years to write letters in a less formal way. Because word processors make it possible, even circulars can be 'personalised' and addressed to an individual.

- Your business may use its own particular style for letters (usually called the 'house style'). Although conforming to this style may sometimes be frustrating, it does ensure that letters are prepared quickly according to an established pattern.

- A business will often use standard letters to deal with situations which arise on a regular basis, for example the late payments of accounts.

Memos

A memorandum, to use the full name, is an internal document often on a simple standard form. It is usually typed, although some businesses prefer the speed and informality of hand-written memos. The advantage over a verbal message is that there is a permanent record. A memo should contain the name of the sender and of all the recipients, a title to indicate the subject matter, and the date and a reference number. Because it is an internal document, the style is less important than in a letter, but the same considerations concerning clarity, brevity and the avoidance of jargon apply. In the last few years, many businesses have begun to use self-adhesive 'post-it' notes as a fast and effective means of passing written messages that do not need to be permanently filed.

Reports

Discipline, accidents to people or property, customer complaints, faulty parts, reorganisation – all may be the subject of a report. The preparation of a written report can be a daunting task for a young and inexperienced manager. But there are a number of simple rules that can be adopted. Reports should of course be as brief as possible, but by their very nature they are much longer than the average letter. For this reason a report needs to be organised in the following way:

Title / Introduction / Main body / Conclusions

A busy manager reading the report needs the introduction and conclusion to draw out the main points. It is the job of the writer, and not the reader, to clearly show what these main points are. In the words of a famous Hollywood producer: "Tell'em you're gonna tell'em. Tell'em. Then tell'em you've told'em."

What should each section of the report include?

Most reports will include:

- Title – brief and simple, the reader should identify immediately exactly what the report is about.

- Introduction – include why the report is being written, what the aim of the report is, and how you have organised the report.

- Main body of the report – this will contain all the information you have gathered, organised into a logical sequence, and using 'headlines' to help the reader (and writer) split up the longest part of the report into manageable pieces. The main body of the report should contain the evidence which supports your conclusions.

- Conclusions – restate the aim of the report and state your main conclusions as briefly as possible. Do not introduce any new information in the conclusion – you are merely emphasising the major points already covered in the main body of the report.

- Recommendations – some reports require recommendations for action, others do not. Check carefully on what is required and include recommendations after the conclusions if necessary.

- Appendix/annex – if a report is particularly long, or if some of the information that would normally be included in the main part of the report will only be of interest to some readers, it may be appropriate to include some detailed information in a appendix or annex at the end of the report.

Other written communications

There are many other types of written communication, including:

- Policy manuals – all managers, and staff who deal with customers, should have access to an up-to-date manual of company policy.

- Staff handbook – every employee should be aware of the conditions of employment, holiday and other entitlements, bonus agreements etc.

- Notice boards – useful for brief messages concerning meetings, social events etc. Notices are likely to be ignored if the board is too crowded or out-of-date notices are not taken down.

- Staff magazines – a good way of encouraging a feeling of belonging, particularly in a dealership group spread over a large area. Producing a good quality magazine is however time-consuming and expensive.

Spoken Communication

We have already discussed what can go wrong with spoken communication, and how it can be improved. Spoken communication is different from written communication in that 1) it leaves (usually) no permanent record, and 2) it is much more of a two-way process. It is also a much richer and more subtle form of communication because the listener can not only hear the words, but can also hear the way they are said. And in face-to-face communication there are all sorts of non-verbal elements involved – facial expressions, gestures and other body language.

Using the telephone

All but the smallest businesses use the 'phone for internal and external calls. The following suggestions for effective use of the 'phone apply to all calls, but are particularly important when talking to customers:

- Give your name and department when answering the 'phone.

- Be polite, calm and patient – even when you feel the opposite.

- When making a call, prepare beforehand by getting together all the information you need.

- Be brief and to the point, especially when the customer is paying for the call.

The face-to-face interview

Managers are constantly in this situation, usually dealing with one other person. The occasion may be a selection interview, dealing with a grievance, counselling, reviewing progress, a disciplinary matter, or, most unpleasant of all, termination of employment. Alternatively a manager may be dealing with someone from outside the business, a customer or supplier for instance. Whatever the situation, in addition to avoiding the problems and adopting the strategies of good communication already outlined, a manager should:

- Choose the right time and place – try to ensure privacy, avoid interruptions and allow enough time.

- Prepare carefully – make sure you have the right information and plan what you intend to do.

- Explain clearly at the start what the purpose of the interview is and what you hope to achieve.

- Don't forget the rules of good communication – particularly those concerning putting people at their ease and listening carefully to what they say.

- Decide on what action to take and make sure your decision is clearly understood by the other person.

Meetings

Part of a manager's time can be taken up in meetings and some managers resent this. But meetings are an essential part of communication and of co-ordination between different departments. If you think about it, a meeting has, potentially at any rate, all the advantages of spoken communication with the additional bonus of a permanent record in the form of minutes. The problem with many meetings is that they are not well organised and are poorly chaired. Good organisation, chairing and minute-taking require a great deal of skill and experience, which we shall not attempt to deal with here. Managers at the start of their careers are in any case more likely to be ordinary members of a meeting. All participants should remember the following:

- Prepare well – make sure you have the information you need in an appropriate form. You will have limited time and need to be 'on top' of your subject so that you can respond to questions. Read any information circulated beforehand.

- Be prepared for conflict – although meetings are often friendly, they are excellent forums for resolving conflicts between departments. Put your point of view assertively but try to remain calm – if you lose your temper you will lose the argument.

Staff meetings may be formal, with an agenda and minutes, and with the purpose of negotiating working conditions and practices. Alternatively, they may be simple discussions to give out information and to allow staff to ask questions and put their point of view in an informal way.

Computers and Fax

Developments in computer technology have revolutionised communication in terms of the amount of information available and the speed at which it can be transmitted. This has not changed the basic rules of good communication, but it has the job of selecting what information is appropriate more difficult. Information overload has increased as the problem changes from what information to provide, to what information to leave out. Computer applications in the motor trade are so important, that a separate half-module is part of the core syllabus of The Institute's Certificate. However we can briefly mention here that:

- Information can be transmitted almost instantaneously between computer terminals within the business, or outside the business, to another branch for instance, using external telephone lines. This vastly speeds up two-way communication.

- Communication by fax has also speeded up the transmission of important letters and documents. Anything that can be photocopied, including drawings and diagrams can be fed into a fax machine and transmitted immediately via telephone line to any other fax machine.

- Telex and teleprinter messages are transmitted in a similar way, but can only print out a simple written message.

Developments in this sort of information technology move so rapidly that a book on the subject becomes out-of-date almost as soon as it is printed. A manager needs to be aware of any developments that may make communication more effective.

Section D

MANAGEMENT RESPONSIBILITIES

Functional Management

What is functional management?

We have looked at management theory, management skills, and management styles, but we should always bear in mind that every manager is managing a functional area of the business – making sure that cars or parts are sold, or that service and repairs are carried out effectively. We have said that managers spend part of their time using specialist skills and the remainder being a manager. In the motor trade, the job of management would be impossible without a background of solid technical skills. The most common difficulty for a new manager is in broadening out from a narrow speciality into the wider perspective needed by someone who is managing a task, rather than doing it. The purpose of this section is to examine briefly the functions of a business, and how to manage them.

What functions need to be managed?

You may remember Henri Fayol and his management functions from Section A. We now tend to use the following functions:

- Production – including the layout of workshops, tools and equipment, production planning and control.

- Marketing – selling cars, spares, repairs and petrol. Identifying the demand for products and services, finding customers and keeping them satisfied.

- Finance – finding sources of money and investing them in the business wisely. Accounting for money coming in and going out, and providing managers with financial information.

- Purchasing – making sure that the right materials are available in the right quantity, at the right price and in the right place.

- Personnel – getting the right people with the necessary skills. Recruitment, training, development, promotion, pay and conditions, industrial relations, health and safety, equal opportunities.

Some of these functions are covered in other parts of the book, or in a different part of the syllabus. We shall examine each one briefly.

The production function

The organisation of production is a major part of the syllabus in the Administration and Organisation module. Here we shall merely highlight the major tasks faced by managers involved in service and repair work. Industry uses three types of production – **mass production**, as used in car manufacture, **batch production**, where items such as car components are made in economical batches, or lastly **job production** where each job is different. This is the type of production used in the motor trade, where although there are similarities between jobs, each job has its own specification. It is the task of those involved in the management of production to:

- Organise the layout and flow of work through a department, and to decide on what staff, equipment, jigs and tools are needed.

- Plan when jobs are to be carried out.

- Ensure that the right staff are available to carry out the work and that they have the necessary materials and parts.

- Monitor and control production to make sure that plans are carried out efficiently.

- Carefully control the quality of output. This is of the utmost importance in the motor trade where a mechanic's error can not only affect the reputation of a garage, but can also put a customer's life at risk.

The marketing function

Production and marketing are put first because without them, the other functions would have no meaning. Providing products and services, and selling them, are the central functions of any business. Marketing is about identifying the needs of potential customers, and then trying to satisfy those needs. Some people argue that marketing also tries to create new needs. For instance, thirty years ago, motorists were unaware that they needed electrically operated windows and in-car stereo. Did marketing just uncover this need, or was the need created by car manufacturers? Whatever the answer to this question, it is certainly the job of marketing to find out what people want and to try to sell it to them.

What does marketing include?

You can see from this that marketing is much more than just selling. Car salespeople like to give the impression that making a sale is all down to their skill in selling. Their skill is essential, but the actual sale is only the tip of the marketing iceberg. Marketing is included in Finance, Section C, but we should briefly state here that the marketing function consists of:

- Market research – who are your potential customers, where are they, and what do they want? Who are your competitors and what products and services do they provide? Market research tries to find the answers to these questions.

- Advertising and promotion – how are you going to bring to the attention of your potential customers (your market), the products and services you provide? And how can you do this in such a way that they actually buy? The motor trade of course relies heavily on the publicity of the manufacturers with their large advertising budgets – but each individual garage or dealership still has a lot of control over its own success or failure in this area.

- Distribution – the customer can't buy it if it's not there. Largely because of the efforts of marketing people, customers today are unwilling to wait patiently if something is not immediately available. Your competitors may have it if you don't. Part of the marketing function is to ensure that products and services are available at the time they are required.

- Making the sale – the skill of sales staff in showing the advantages of your particular products and services in the best light is a vital one, and this is reflected in the commission that they earn for selling new or used cars.

- Customer care management – in the competitive world of the motor trade the search is on for 'added value', something that will give your business an advantage over your competitors. The image of many garages is changing rapidly in order to provide customers with what they want – a good product, pleasant surroundings, and a personal service.

The finance function

We shall discuss the finance function only very briefly as

financial management is the subject of the other half of this book. It is included here as a reminder that financial management is not just the responsibility of financial specialists like the chief accountant. All managers should be aware of the financial implications of their actions and take a full part in the financial management of the business. The finance function includes:

- Making sure that funds are available to buy equipment, pay wages, and to settle all bills.

- To keep proper and accurate accounts of all the financial dealings of the business.

- To monitor performance and control costs – usually through a system of budgetary control.

- To provide fast and effective financial information for managers.

The purchasing function

Few organisations in the motor trade have their own purchasing department, so why is the purchasing function shown separately? Purchasing used to be thought of as part of the production function, but since the size of businesses has increased enormously, the task of efficient and sensible buying has become of critical importance. Imagine the complexity of purchasing for a motor manufacturer for instance.

In the motor trade, there are some unusual conditions, in that the prices of many purchases are effectively fixed by the manufacturer or oil company. But there are still a great many supplies where the price can be negotiated. The quantity to buy and the amount to keep in stock is also of crucial importance. Buy too many spares for instance, and customers and workshop managers will never have to wait. The business will, however, have far too much money tied up in stock sitting on the shelves. Buy too few spares, and the amount of money tied up is fine – but you will hold up production and may lose customers. The purchasing function is a tightrope act – the consequences of losing the correct balance can be disastrous.

In the motor trade, purchasing is usually done by each department, rather than by a central buyer. But because of the interdependence of departments, it is absolutely vital that purchasing requirements are co-ordinated for the whole business.

The personnel function

The personnel function is like the financial function in that, although much of it is seen as a specialist area, the responsibility for personnel matters is shared by managers at all levels. In large organisations there may be a separate personnel manager who will co-ordinate all the necessary functions, but in smaller businesses, department managers will take on the responsibility. The main personnel functions are:

- Human resources planning – many jobs in the motor trade are highly skilled. Advance planning is needed to get the right people in the right place at the right time.

- Recruitment and selection – how will the business recruit applicants for jobs, and then make the right selection between them?

- Training – a properly trained workforce and a properly trained management are essential to the future success of any business. The technical nature of the motor trade means that training is of particular importance.

- Staff development – whereas training is concerned with the acquisition of skills and knowledge, development attempts to ensure that each member of staff is able to reach his or her true potential. As the business grows and develops, so should each individual. (Recruitment, training and development is covered shortly.)

- Pay – one of the most difficult tasks is in setting fair levels of pay that satisfy employees and the need to make a profit. Wages and salaries in the motor trade are covered in Finance, Section D.

- Health and safety – part of the personnel function is to protect the health and safety of employees. This is of course a moral responsibility, but it also makes sound financial sense – accidents are expensive and inconvenient as well as painful. There is a great deal of government legislation on health and safety matters, including the Health and Safety at Work Act 1974. Managers are legally responsible for implementing the laws which are relevant to their departments. Clean and hygienic refreshment areas, adequate medical attention and, for larger organisations, recreational facilities should also be provided.

- Industrial relations – this is a huge and complex area which this book does not attempt to cover. It encompasses the relationship between management, the workforce and trade-unions, and government, and is concerned with the negotiation of pay, working conditions and practices. In the motor trade many of these matters are negotiated at a national level by the National Joint Council for the Motor Vehicle Retail and Repair Industry, or NJC (see Finance, Section D). Some issues may be sorted out at a national level, but all managers have a responsibility towards promoting good industrial relations with their own staff.

Recruitment and Selection

Why is recruitment important?

We have said before that jobs in the motor trade are technical and demanding, and that the people who fill them need a high degree of skill and good qualifications. If a business is to prosper, they need other qualities as well, like honesty, drive, enthusiasm, and the ability to work in a team. Success depends on recruiting the right people. There is also a more mundane reason for making the right decisions when recruiting. It's much easier to hire someone than to fire them. Mistakes in recruiting can be expensive and the results can be with you for a long time.

What is the job?

A job becomes vacant either because an existing member of staff leaves, or because the business is expanding and a new job is being created. In either case the first thing to do is to work out exactly what the job consists of, the purpose, tasks and duties involved, responsibilities, and standards of work expected. This is called the **job analysis**.

Having done this, the next step is to prepare a **job description**. This should consist of the following headings:

- Job title and department.

- Brief summary of the main purpose of the job.

- Detailed description of the duties involved.

- What responsibilities go with the job, and who is the holder of the job responsible to?

- Hours of work and working conditions.

Who do we need?

We have used the job analysis to prepare a job description. We can also use it to establish what skills and qualities the person doing the job is going to need. This is called the job specification. One useful way of approaching this task is to break down the specification into the sort of characteristics that people possess. Professor Alec Roger of the National Institute of Industrial Psychology (NIIP) suggested that there were seven of these (often referred to as the seven point plan):

- Physique – health, appearance, vision and other physical attributes.

- Attainments – education, qualifications and experience.

- General intelligence – the ability to reason and perform complex tasks.

- Special aptitudes – particular talents and the inclination to be good at certain things such as figures or mechanical tasks, or with people.

- Interests – activities outside work such as social and leisure pursuits.

- Disposition – in terms of characteristics such as honesty, reliability, enthusiasm and leadership qualities. What sort of personality and temperament does the job require?

- Circumstances – Age, place of residence, mobility and other relevant personal circumstances.

The above categories are not only useful in setting out a job specification, but also as a means of giving structure to an interview, as we shall see shortly.

Recruitment – where from?

Depending on the type of job, there are a variety of sources from which to recruit people:

- Internal promotion – a fast, effective and inexpensive method of filling management vacancies, providing there are suitable candidates.

- Schools and colleges – a useful source of apprentices and trainees.

- Employment agencies – including government Job Centres (no charge), and local private agencies (a percentage of starting salary). Useful for manual, clerical and specialist jobs.

- Recruitment consultants – for management and specialist jobs. There are a number of specialist consultancies who deal exclusively with the motor trade.

- Press advertising – usually at a local level. Relatively inexpensive with a wide audience over a small area.

- Trade and professional journals – such as Motor Industry Management. Good for management and specialist vacancies as it reaches a specific audience over a wide area.

- Local commercial radio – reaches a wide audience very quickly, but is much more expensive than local newspaper advertising.

- Informal methods – such as the recommendations of existing staff, or a notice on the forecourt, may be appropriate for some jobs and is certainly low cost. It may, however, exclude people who are even better able to do the job.

Designing the right advertisement

A job advertisement in a local newspaper or a journal

should ideally produce just enough candidates of the right ability and experience. If an advert is too vague, you will have to sort through hundreds of applications. If it's too demanding or dogmatic you may put off perfectly good candidates from applying.

Preparing a successful advert is a skilled operation and some businesses use professional help. Local newspapers often offer free (if biased) advice on setting out an advert. A glance at a local paper will show that most adverts are dull and uninspiring. Remember that your business is on show even in a job advert, and try to create an eye-catching and interesting style. Use the company logo if you have one.

What should the advert include?

A job advert should include details of:

- The name and address of the business, and the person to whom applications should be made.

- A brief description of the job that tries to encourage the right people and discourage poorer candidates. The general state of the labour market will be relevant in deciding the exact wording.

- Qualifications required in terms of experience, academic background, or for instance a clean driving licence.

- The location of the job and any unusual or unpopular factors such as working away from home or unsociable hours.

- Details of salary and benefits – although it is not always necessary to include exact figures.

- Details of how to reply to the advert.

Internal promotion or new blood?

Which is best, promoting someone from inside the business, or an external candidate? This will depend on the recruitment policy of the business and the circumstances at the time, but:

- Internal recruiting – will encourage staff loyalty and motivation by providing a career structure. Applicants will know the business and the business will know them. It is inexpensive. It does, however, limit the choice of candidates considerably. At a time when the motor trade is adapting to new conditions and changing demands, internal candidates may sometimes be conditioned to the ways in which things have always been done, which may not always be appropriate.

- External recruiting – introduces a wider variety of candidates with new ideas and a fresh approach to the problems and possibilities of the organisation. It is potentially fairer as internal candidates can also apply, although bringing in an outsider can sometimes be disruptive, and the process of recruitment time-consuming and expensive.

A policy used by some businesses is to promote from within, and to recruit external candidates at a lower level. This will encourage commitment and provide a career structure, but still allow a fair and open recruitment procedure.

What information can we get about a job applicant and where from?

The information we need can be based on the NIIP seven point plan shown earlier. The information can come from the following sources:

- Application form – a well designed standard form will show details of education, previous employment, circumstances and outside interests. Bear in mind that the form is filled in by the applicant who is trying to create a good impression.

- References – from former employers or teachers. Written references rarely say anything negative about the applicant, but by 'reading between the lines' and looking at the things that the referee does not say, it is often possible to gain a more accurate picture.

- Interviews – a short-list of candidates will be interviewed, and the way in which they perform will usually be the main factor in deciding on who gets the job. This is despite the fact that research has shown that performance at an interview is not a reliable guide to how effective people are at the job. Interviewing is examined in detail below.

- Testing – for mental or mechanical ability, or to assess personality. These have been widely used in large organisations, although to be effective, the tests themselves need to be scientifically proved against the job. This is so complex and expensive that it is rarely done properly, and the use of 'off the shelf' tests is quite controversial. The popularity of tests has declined in recent years.

- Internal candidates – a vast quantity of much more reliable information is available on candidates from inside the business. This 'warts and all' information can sometimes prejudice decision-makers against internal candidates in favour of outsiders who only show their good points. Alternatively, selectors may be prejudiced in favour of safe but uninspiring insiders.

Selection by interview

Most people have been interviewed for a job and the experience is not always a satisfactory one. Often candidates come away feeling that they have not done themselves justice. They are confident that they could succeed in the job, but somehow they have 'failed' the interview. In fact a great deal of research suggests that interviews are a poor way to predict how someone will perform when it comes to doing the job. Despite this, interviews remain the most popular means of selection. A survey by a recruitment agency found that 81% of its clients in the motor trade used interviews as the main means of selecting employees.

It's all very well to say that interviews are unreliable, but the problem is that none of the alternatives (such as testing) are in practice any better. What are managers to do, faced with the task of selection? Interviews are in general unreliable – but good and well structured interviews are much more reliable than sloppy and unstructured ones. The most effective answer for a manager is therefore to increase his or her skill at interviewing. We shall now look at how this can be done.

What types of interview are there?

The most familiar type of interview is the one-off, one-to-one interview between a manager and a job candidate. Interviews for many non-managerial jobs are conducted like this. Other types of interview include:

- Interviews with a series of managers one after each other. In this way impressions of a candidate can be pooled.

- An interview panel of several managers. This can be off-putting for candidates who are unlikely to be relaxed and show their usual behaviour. It does, however, show how a candidate reacts under pressure and is frequently used for managerial appointments.

- A group interview in an informal setting. Questions are asked but more in the form of a discussion, during which managers can observe the candidate's behaviour and responses.

Who should interview?

Who will interview will depend on the type of job and the method of interview used. Applicants for junior and unskilled jobs may be interviewed by a single manager – the service or parts manager for instance. More senior appointments will involve more interviews and more interviewers as the consequences of a poor choice are more serious. Many businesses involve professional recruitment agencies in the process of selecting senior managers.

Where should the interview take place?

Most interviews take place in the manager's office, in which case it is essential that the room should be quiet and free from interruption. Chairs and tables should be placed in such a way that the candidate can be as relaxed as possible in the circumstances. It is also essential that the candidate can see the area in which he or she will be working.

How to prepare for an interview

Just as a candidate has to prepare for an interview, so should the person conducting the interview. As an interviewer you should:

- Have a clear idea of what is needed in the person carrying out the job – characteristics such as mechanical ability, enthusiasm, initiative, or the ability to communicate with customers.
- Study any information you have already, such as application forms or references.
- Work out what you are trying to find out, possibly in the form of a check-list based on the seven points we discussed earlier. The questions should relate only to the skills, attitudes and knowledge defined as a job requirement by the job specification. Don't forget, to be fair to all candidates you should ask each of them the same set of questions.

What makes a good interview?

Think about interviews where you have been the candidate. Which were good, which were bad, and why? Have you come across the stiff and formal chap who never smiles? Or the one who doesn't let you get a word in edgeways? Getting the most out of an interview is a highly skilled process which all managers need to work at. What are the important things to remember?

- In the first few minutes candidates should be put at ease with a few informal exchanges which should get rid of any initial nervousness. Candidates should be encouraged to speak as early in the interview as possible.

- Don't make up your mind on first impressions or on the basis of prior information. Keep an open mind throughout the interview.

- Be a good listener. Only speak to guide the interview along the lines you want, or to answer the candidate's questions. A rule of thumb some interviewers use is to only speak for a quarter of the time. This is far more difficult than it sounds. Encourage the candidate to talk freely by asking open-ended or neutral questions. 'Tell me about your education' is much better, and much more revealing, than a series of quick-fire questions about schools and GCSEs. Fill in any missing information with more direct questions. Give sufficient feedback (occasional nods, smiles, or words of encouragement) so that candidates know what information you are looking for.

- When the candidate is feeling more relaxed, you can ask more difficult and demanding questions. Try to do this in a non-aggressive way. 'Why did you leave your last job?' may make the candidate defensive. You might find more out by asking what they liked about their last job, and what they disliked. Follow up on any unsatisfactory answers.

- After you have assessed the performance of the candidate, put the spotlight on yourself – how did you perform? And more important, how can you make the next interview a more successful and revealing one?

Why should I avoid bias and discrimination?

As far as you and your business are concerned, there are two reasons, one negative and the other positive. The first reason is that it is illegal to discriminate against people on the grounds of race, sex, or marital status, and an aggrieved candidate can claim damages from your business at an industrial tribunal. The second reason is a much more positive one. The idea of the selection process is to find the best person for the job. If you exclude people on grounds other than their ability to carry out the job, you may end up with the second best. Recruiting the second best may be a luxury that your business cannot afford.

How can I avoid bias and discrimination?

Bias, discrimination and prejudice of one sort or another are very deep seated and difficult to get rid of. It may not even be something that a manager is consciously aware of. But managers have a duty to themselves, to job applicants, and to the business to eliminate it from the selection process. They can concentrate on the following areas:

- The job analysis which you prepared tells you what the job consists of and what characteristics and abilities the ideal candidate will need. The selection process should focus on these essential factors and not on the sex, race, marital status, or any other factors that do not affect the candidate's ability to do the job.

- Try to avoid general assumptions about particular groups of people – 'this is men's work', or 'that's a job for a woman', for instance. Operating a typewriter keyboard was for years seen as women's work, but since the advent of computers, men working in a parts department seem quite equal to the task. It is this sort of generalising, called **stereotyping**, that is so deep seated and difficult to eliminate. Anyone involved in selection should be aware of the dangers of stereotyping and realise that these sort of generalisations tell us nothing at all about an *individual*.

The motor trade has a traditionally male image, and although there are signs that this is changing, the process is very slow. Managers who are seriously interested in fair and efficient selection will have to work hard on themselves and on their colleagues. Free booklets on how to avoid discrimination in selection are available from the Equal Opportunities Commission, the Commission for Racial Equality, and from local Training and Enterprise Councils.

Equal opportunities in the 1990s

Many businesses are now realising that equal opportunities at work are not just desirable in terms of social justice and freedom of choice, but are justified in economic terms as well.

In the changes that will come about in the 1990s, in the law, in Europe, and in the labour market, it will no longer be possible for business to ignore the skills and talents of whole sections of the population.

Having variety in the workforce and in management also makes a business more responsive to the needs of society as a whole. Since women and ethnic minorities are big customers of the motor trade, it makes sense to ensure that they are properly represented inside the business as well.

Developing an equal opportunities policy should be a priority of those businesses that wish to survive and succeed in the 1990s. As Sir John Moores, Chairman of Littlewoods, put it, 'Equal opportunities is not only fair: it makes good business sense'.

Training

Why is training important?

Effective recruitment and selection is vital, but is only part of the process of getting people with the right skills and expertise into the business. Recruitment and selection provide the raw materials. Training and development turn those raw materials into the finished product. Every new employee, from a sales manager to a sixteen-year-old apprentice, needs some training. And the process does not stop there. Changes in technology, methods and attitudes now occur so quickly that it is unlikely that one period of initial training will equip an individual for a lifetime of work. Training is increasingly seen as an activity that extends throughout a person's working life.

What do we mean by training?

It's important that we do not start off with too narrow a definition of what training is. Training is often thought of as applying to manual workers only. If you are studying for The Institute's Certificate of Management you will not need to be reminded that it applies to managers too. All employees need some training, including clerks, sales staff, managers, people who operate computers, and anyone who deals with customers. And training is not restricted to formal training courses at colleges. Training goes on inside the business, outside the business, on-the-job, off-the-job, formally, informally, and in a whole variety of ways.

Training in the UK

Listening to politicians and public figures, you might assume that training is one of our highest priorities, taking up a hefty slice of the economic 'cake'. In fact, we have a rather suspicious attitude to training, and spend much less than our industrial competitors in Europe, the USA and Japan. The need for training has never been greater, and population changes in the 1990s will lead to a shortage of skilled workers and make the situation even worse. Despite this, many people receive only the briefest training when they start a job. And if there is a recession, the training budget is often one of the first to be cut.

The motor trade depends on the skills and knowledge of its employees, and has a much better training record than many other industries. But there is no room for complacency, or for hoping that someone else will pay for training from which you will benefit. If the motor trade is to rise to the challenges of the future, each business, and each individual manager, must take their share of responsibility for making sure that all employees are properly trained.

Investing in training

Germany and Japan do not spend money on training out of duty or generosity. They do it because it pays them – because training is not an ordinary overhead like rent or insurance – it is an investment. They pay out now and reap the benefits in the future. The investment in training they made in the past is one of the main reasons for their economic success now.

What is the difference between training and development?

Training and development can easily be confused because it is difficult to talk about one without referring to the other. However, the essential difference is that:

Training is about the *job*, and equipping people with the skills and knowledge to be able to carry out that job.

Development is more concerned with the *individual*.

Attention is concentrated not on a particular job, but on the needs, abilities and potential of individuals. It's about getting the best out of someone, for their own sake and for the benefit of the business. It may of course involve the person undertaking some training, in order to develop their potential. We shall discuss development in the next section.

How do you identify the training needs of a department?

What factors influence training needs in a department?

- The human resources plan – this will show the long and short-term needs of the business for staff at all levels, and with varying degrees of skill and competence.

- The abilities and skills of the present staff. Try asking them what abilities and skills they have that would contribute to the development of the department. You might get some surprises.

- How can the present staff be utilised and developed in order to fulfil the needs of the human resources plan? What ideas do *they* have on the sort of training they need? If their needs fit in with the needs of the department, and the suggestion has come from them, they will be much more committed to the training.

- A programme of recruitment to fill any gaps between the plan, and the potential of the present staff to carry it out.

- Changes in technology and methods of work which will lead to the need for training for existing and new staff.

Working out a training plan

In an ideal world, after training needs have been assessed, the total cost can be calculated and this amount can be allocated to the training budget. In practice of course, training has to compete with other things that the business needs to spend money on, and difficult decisions have to be taken about spending priorities. A business may end up with the training that it can afford, rather than the training that it needs. Saving money by cutting back on training is always an easy short-term option. Managers are used to asking the question 'Can we afford to spend this money?'. With training, sometimes they must ask a more difficult question – 'Can we afford *not* to spend this money?'.

When you have assessed the training needs of your department and how much money you have got, then you can work out a training plan. The plan should include details of:

- What the objectives of the training are. Unless you state these clearly at the outset, you will not be able to judge how effective the training has been.

- Who is to be trained, for which jobs, and what sort of training they need.

- Who will do the training, where it will be done, and when.

- What training methods will be used.

- A system of monitoring and evaluating how successful the training has been.

A training programme for each individual

There is little point in training someone who does not wish to be trained. It's a waste of their time and your money. The possibility of training should be discussed with people from the earliest stage, as part of assessing their potential. When the training plan for the business as a whole has been worked out, it can next be converted into a training plan or programme for each individual. This should again be discussed with each individual to ensure that the training is right for him or her. Each person's training programme should include details of where, when and how the training will take place.

Choosing the best type of training

You know from your own experience of learning that in some situations and with certain teachers you learnt things quickly and thoroughly. On other occasions you may have lost interest, or failed to understand what was being taught. For instance, learning about book-keeping can be dry and boring, but it doesn't have to be. In terms of the learning process, what is being taught is less important than how it is taught. For example:

- The best way to learn how to change spark plugs is by practising on a real engine – backed up by classroom theory on why it is necessary to do so.

- Learning about Theory X and Theory Y managers can be accomplished better by reading, classroom discussion, or role playing.

- First aid training often uses trainees as 'guinea pigs' to supplement classroom learning.

Choosing the best methods and techniques is of crucial importance in effective training. And because money for training is strictly limited, making the right choices is doubly important.

Why is motivation so important in training?

We saw earlier that an understanding of what motivated people was important to a manager. Do you remember Maslow's hierarchy of needs, and Herzberg's motivating factors? Training involves a lot of hard work, and people will only put in that sort of effort if there is something in it for them, in terms of money, status, or self-actualisation. Motivation at the start of a training programme is usually quite high. The difficult thing is to maintain good motivation throughout the training process. How can this be done?

● By using a variety of approaches and techniques. People learn best in different ways, some from the spoken word, some from the written word, others by diagrams or visual images. Alternate theory and practice and use methods that allow trainees to participate. Learning by doing is better than learning by watching someone else doing.

● Give trainees plenty of feedback on their progress. Remember that praise and positive feedback for things they have done well are more effective than blame for mistakes they have made.

● Choose good trainers, and if you want to know who the best trainers are – ask the trainees!

What is the learning curve?

We spend most of our lives learning – as a baby, at school, learning tasks at work, learning to play games. It's important for anyone involved in training to understand how we learn. In the early stages of learning any task, we make very fast progress. But after this initial burst, we tend to reach a plateau where progress seems to slow down, before faster progress is resumed. This pattern seems to happen most of the time, whatever the task, and you can probably recognise it from your own experience of learning to play a new sport for instance. Do you recall learning to drive? Most people learn what all the various bits are very quickly – brake, accelerator, clutch, mirror, indicators, steering wheel. Then comes the terrible moment when all the components have to be put together and used simultaneously. Progress, and possibly the car, seem to come to a halt. After a time there is a breakthrough, and learning once again takes off. This process is called the **learning curve**, and can be shown in a simple graph.

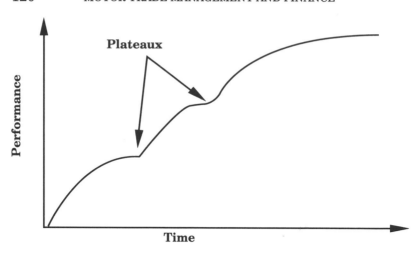

Recognising when a trainee has reached a plateau on the learning curve is important in terms of motivation. He or she will need particular encouragement at a time when it feels as though little is being achieved.

Where should training be carried out?

There are two alternatives:

- On-the-job training which is carried out in the normal job location – in the parts store, service bays, or accounts office. The training is carried out by more experienced employees or supervisors.

- Off-the-job training which is carried out away from the normal workplace, at a college, trainers' premises, hotel, or even on the business premises but away from the job location.

What are the advantages of on-the-job training?

Most training tends to be on the job itself. The main advantages are:

- The training is absolutely relevant to the task being learned, and is done in a real work situation.

- The training may be linked to an NVQ qualification.

- No special trainers or facilities are needed and therefore the training is inexpensive.

- Trainees can begin to make a contribution immediately.

On-the-job training is relevant and economic, but it is not always effective. Supervisors may have little experience of training techniques and may be too busy to devote sufficient time to the task. The growth of the NVQ system has done a great deal to make on-the-job training more professional and successful.

What are the advantages of off-the-job training?

A combination of on-the-job and off-the-job training is probably the best option for most employees. The advantages of training away from the job are:

- Where a group of trainees is involved, it becomes more economic.

- It does not cause disruption to the normal work of the department.

- Professional trainers can be used.

- For some training, such as health and safety, or a management course, being away from the demands of the job is a positive benefit.

The disadvantages of off-the-job training are that it is expensive, and trainees may not always see the relevance of what they are learning. A business also has little control over the quality of the training.

What is induction?

The process of introducing new employees to the business is called **induction**. This initial training can last from a few minutes to a day or even longer. The purpose is to familiarise new employees with the policies of the business, with the physical layout of the place, to introduce staff with whom they will come into contact, and to show how the department operates. Health and safety regulations, first aid facilities, and welfare provisions such as a canteen should also be included. Short talks and video presentations may be incorporated into the induction process in larger organisations.

This initial training is of particular importance in enabling new people to fit in to the business quickly and effectively. The time when employees are at their most vulnerable and are most likely to leave a job is just after they have started. A well thought out induction process can help to reduce this waste of resources.

Keeping records of training

It is important to keep comprehensive records of training both for the business as a whole and for each individual. These will be kept by the training officer or personnel manager in larger businesses, or otherwise by departmental managers. Records should include space to record the results of training and any comments. These will be particularly useful when it comes to a review of an employee's performance and an appraisal of his or her prospects for development and promotion.

How can you monitor training?

The short answer is with great difficulty. Finding out just how effective training has been is not easy, and many organisations don't even try. But we said at the start of this section that the justification for training was that it is an investment – so some effort ought to be made to find out if the investment is worth while. How can it be done?

- By asking the trainees themselves. Since motivation is so important, the opinion of the people receiving the training is valuable. Bear in mind that it is a subjective view and not scientific, but, particularly if questionnaire forms are anonymous, it should at least be honest.

- By assessing if the objectives of the training have been successfully attained. This can be done by:

  1) Testing the trainees before and after the training. Make sure that any tests are directly connected to the training.

  2) Measuring if performance on the job has improved. Make sure that nothing else has changed to explain any difference in performance.

Staff Development

Why do staff need to be 'developed'?

We have seen in the last section that staff need to be trained. Isn't that enough? Training looks at the requirements of the business, and tries to ensure that people with the right skills and qualifications are in the right place at the right time. The aim of staff development is not dissimilar, but instead of looking at the needs of the business, it takes as its starting point the needs, ambitions and potential of the individual employee. The key to staff development is its focus on the *individual*.

Staff development in practice

Staff Development, like training, is another area where there are usually more words than deeds. Many businesses pay only lip service to staff development, and it is generally acknowledged that the formal schemes operated by a lot of organisations are poorly thought out and badly implemented. Despite this, in theory at least, the rewards of effective staff development are high, both for the individual and the business. What are these rewards?

- For the individual – we have seen in earlier sections that most people feel happier, and more committed to the business, if their talents and abilities are used to the full. Staff development may lead to promotion and increases in salary and status.

- For the business – human resources are the most valuable assets of a business and the aim of development is to get the best out of them. You would not dream of deliberately using an expensive machine at half of its capacity – but businesses throughout the country are full of people whose talents are often only half used.

Who will take over from the Service Manager?

A problem faced by all businesses is one of succession. All employees eventually retire, some move on to other jobs, and some may even be run over by a bus. Someone has to take over, and the business that does not plan for this will lurch from one 'unexpected' crisis to another. What happens if the service manager is promoted to general manager? It may be good news for the assistant, but not if he or she has had no preparation and development. The gap may have to be filled from outside the organisation by expensive and time-consuming recruitment for the manager's post. And the assistant may well feel resentful and less committed to the business than before. One of the main purposes of staff development is to tackle the problem of succession.

What is staff appraisal?

To appraise someone is to estimate their worth in some way. Staff appraisal is often carried out in the form of **performance appraisal**, particularly as part of a bonus scheme. The sort of appraisal we are interested in here is **development appraisal** to try to assess the potential of the employee for increased responsibility. This may include a reference to an employee's performance, but is quite separate from performance appraisal itself. It is carried out in two ways:

- Information gathering on the employee's record to date. What jobs have they done, what responsibility have they had, what training and qualifications, what is their attendance and timekeeping record? This information forms the 'homework' for the next stage of the process.

- A yearly appraisal interview with each member of staff. The usual rules of good interviewing apply as people may feel nervous and apprehensive. If criticism of staff is involved, this feeling of anxiety may be shared by the manager. It's important to build on the relationship already established, and to try to see things from the point of view of the employee.

What is the appraisal interview trying to achieve?

The appraisal interview is one of the most sensitive situations a manager has to handle. Get it wrong, and confrontation and hostility will outweigh what you are trying to achieve. The aim is to create a plan for an individual which develops the skills and potential they have. To do this, the person's achievements should be discussed, any gaps in their skills or knowledge should be highlighted, and their strengths and weaknesses explored.

Most importantly, the interview should draw out the ambitions and hopes of the employee. These may be unrealistic of course, or they may not be compatible with the needs of the business. And not everyone will want to be developed. A manager should realise that some people are quite happy with the job and responsibilities they have at the moment, and there is no sense in pushing them where they don't want to go.

One useful technique is that of self appraisal. Get people to assess how they think they have done, and what improvement they can suggest. Subordinates tend to be more critical of themselves than you are (or would dare to be).

Who appraises the managers?

Some large organisations are going one step further than staff appraisal or self-appraisal. They are asking the staff to make an appraisal of their manager. Staff in general have been surprisingly fair and measured in assessing their boss, although the process has been extremely uncomfortable for some managers. How do you think your staff would appraise you?

A development plan for an employee

The end result of the appraisal process should be a **development plan** for each employee. This should look at the following areas:

- Career planning and development – how can an employee's career goals and ambitions be met within the business?

- Skill and knowledge development – what training does the employee need, and how and when can they get it?

- Counselling needs – are there any particular problems inside or outside the business that the employee needs to overcome in order to develop?

We shall look briefly at each area in turn.

Career planning and development

Not everyone has the same attitude to their career, and some people change their attitude as they grow older and circumstances change. Helping employees to plan and develop their careers happens at any time, but the annual appraisal is a good time to take stock of the needs of the employee and of the business. How can an employee's career be developed? The main possibilities are:

- By promotion – what path does the employee want to take – more responsibility for technical matters, to become a specialist, or to move into a more general area like management? Are there likely to be any suitable vacancies in the near future?

- By job enlargement, job rotation, or job enrichment. These techniques will give an employee more experience and responsibility.

- By acting as understudy to a manager. This will give an employee experience of the manager's role, and may solve the problem of succession.

- By giving an employee special tasks or assignments, such as solving a technical problem, preparing a report, or representing the department at a meeting. This is a good way for a manager to assess the capabilities of a subordinate without risking any long-term commitment.

Developing skills and knowledge

The close relationship between development and training can be seen when it comes to assessing what additional skills and knowledge an employee needs in order to develop. These improvements usually come through training. Any sort of training may be involved, either to fill gaps or to introduce an employee to a completely new area. One type of training that is particularly associated with staff development is **management development training**. This is becoming an increasingly popular way of introducing the theory and techniques of management to people starting on a career in management, and of improving the performance of those who are managers already. The Institute's management courses are tailored to the requirements of the motor trade. Less specialised, short residential courses are also popular with more senior managers, although these can be expensive.

Development through personal counselling

Whether you like it or not, as a manager you will spend a lot of time listening to the problems of your staff. Difficulties at work and at home can hinder an employee's progress and block the development of their full potential. Helping them to deal with these problems can be, at the same time, the most frustrating and the most rewarding part of the job. Remember that employees will only open up if they see you as being on their 'side'. You are unlikely to be able to sort out miraculous solutions at an appraisal interview, but it may be a good time to take an overview of an employee's problems and to explore ways of moving forward for everyone's benefit.

How do you know if staff development is working?

The aim of staff development is to assist individual employees to develop their full potential and to progress as far as they can in the business. Do managers do this because they are do-gooders whose sole concern is the welfare of their staff? Managers may possibly be kind and generous people, but that is not the reason that they operate a staff development programme. They do it because their staff will become more skilled, more ambitious for themselves and for the business, and less held back by personal problems. This should result in greater commitment, more dependable performance, and the use of initiative and imagination. Staff development pays in other words.

But how on earth can the results of staff development be evaluated? A business never stands still, and it is impossible to measure what improvements in output, sales or profit are a direct result of staff development. The annual appraisal is a time when the effect of development on an individual can be assessed. For the business as a whole, it is clearly impossible to measure improvements in quantifiable terms. But in terms of the attitude and commitment of people at work, the morale, the way in which staff work as a team – all these indicators can be recognised and experienced. The motor trade needs staff of high quality. Staff development is a search for just that.

What is a Middle Manager?

This section examines management responsibility and authority, and how managers delegate. Although most of what is said applies to all managers, the focus is on the middle manager in particular. So what is a middle manager? We have just looked at the functions of management – the need to manage marketing and finance for example. This takes a *horizontal* view of managers in a business. We now need to take a *vertical* perspective and look at the different levels of managers. Most organisations have three levels:

- Top managers – who have ultimate control of the business, usually a small group of managers, or even one person, such as the managing director or general manager.

- Middle managers – the largest group, responsible for implementing the policies and plans of top managers. Includes people like department managers, works managers, the chief accountant, and personnel manager.

- Supervisors – first line managers who control and co-ordinate the activities of non-management staff such as mechanics or clerks.

In some ways middle managers and supervisors have the hardest task of all. While top managers only have to give orders and workers only have to take them, the people in the middle have to do both – take orders from above, and hand out orders to those lower down the line. This section tries to make sense of this difficult balancing act.

Authority, responsibility and accountability

Before we go any further, we have to define a few of the terms which we need to use in the remainder of the section. As with many other terms in management, '**authority**', '**responsibility**' and '**accountability**' are sometimes used incorrectly, or often in a confusing way. Responsibility and accountability are often used to mean exactly the same thing, by managers in practice, and in textbooks. We shall show below the definitions we are going to be using in this section – but this does not mean that other definitions are necessarily incorrect. They may be, but it might just be that the English language is being used in a slightly different way.

What do we mean by authority?

Fortunately there is no confusion over what we mean by authority. 'Authority is a form of power which orders the actions of others through commands which are effective because those who are commanded regard the commands as legitimate'. (From A Dictionary of Sociology, edited by G. Duncan Mitchell.) In a parts department for instance, staff will carry out tasks and duties assigned to them by the parts manager because he or she has the authority to direct them and they agree to that authority. The important things is that authority should be clearly defined, and everyone, particularly the manager, should be aware of its limits. For example, does the parts manager have the authority to terminate the employment of parts staff?

What do we mean by responsibility?

Most of the confusion and disagreement is over the word 'responsibility'. The problem is that you can be responsible *for* something (a task or duty), and you can be responsible *to* someone (your immediate boss). In this section, when we talk about responsibility, we mean responsibility *for* carrying out the tasks and obligations that are part of our job description. When we are using the word in the sense of being responsible *to* someone, we shall use the term 'accountable' – for example, sales staff are accountable to the sales manager.

What do we mean by accountability?

In an organisation, we mean that each person is clearly accountable for his or her actions to an immediate superior. It requires that each member of the management team accepts responsibility for carrying out certain tasks and duties, and is answerable for the discharge of those responsibilities to the person who has authority over them in the management structure. Authority flows downwards in an organisation, accountability flows upwards, as we shall see in the organisation charts we shall be examining shortly.

The right structure for the organisation

Imagine you have the unlikely task of setting up a completely new medium-sized business. How would you work out what departments you needed, what managers and staff were necessary, and how they all related to each other? To set up a successful organisation you would have to:

- Determine the functions to be carried out – selling cars, spares, repairing and servicing etc.

- Decide what departments you need to carry out these functions – service, parts, sales, accounts etc. – and how these departments will relate to each other.

- Appoint leaders for each department and clearly set out what authority they have and what their responsibilities are.

- Appoint the staff that will be needed and clearly lay down what tasks and duties they will perform. How will they fit into the departmental structure and to whom will they be accountable?

- Provide the equipment the business needs.

- Provide a system of communication within and between departments and between different levels of management.

- Install a system that will give management the information they need to control all aspects of the business.

When you have sorted out these problems you will have devised an **organisation structure**, and can then draw up an **organisation chart**. Of course you are much more likely to have to deal with an existing organisation chart, which may sometimes be out-of-date or poorly structured. Organisation structures and charts need to be modified or replaced to reflect the changes that occur in every business.

What is a line relationship?

To illustrate organisation charts we shall show how the common forms of structure are represented. The simplest structure is the line relationship which exists between a manager and a subordinate. Look at the chart below:

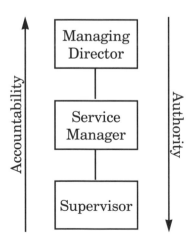

The relationship is very clear – the managing director has authority to direct the activities of the service manager, the service manager has authority over the supervisor. The authority in other words flows down the chart. In the opposite direction, the supervisor is accountable to the service manager, and the service manager to the managing director. Accountability flows back up the chart. You will see that this is important when we discuss delegation shortly.

What is a staff relationship?

If for instance a managing director needs help with routine functions, an 'assistant to the managing director' may be appointed. The assistant would be accountable to the managing director, but would have no authority over the managers further down the line. This is called a staff relationship, and can be shown as follows:

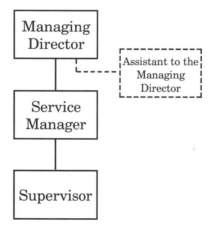

Alternatively, an expert may be appointed to advise all managers on a particular subject – the use of computers for instance. If the expert can only *advise*, and does not have the authority to insist that the advice be taken, then this is still a staff relationship.

One word of warning – be careful of the distinction between 'assistant' and 'assistant to'. An assistant service manager would normally be part of the line management and have authority over the workshop supervisor. An assistant *to* the service manager would be in a staff relationship.

What is a functional relationship?

If an expert is appointed to provide a service – personnel for instance – and managers are bound to accept that service, then this is called a functional relationship. An accountant for example usually has authority over accounting procedures within the service manager's department, because the line manager of both (the managing director) has delegated that authority to the accountant:

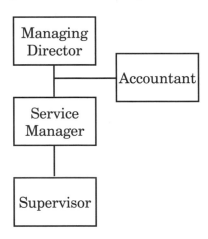

Organisation charts in practice

Most businesses have a combination of line, staff and functional relationships. Look at your own organisation chart – can you see what the relationships are? Bear in mind that functional relationships are sometimes assumed, otherwise the chart would be a mass of confusing lines. A typical chart for a medium sized dealership might look something like this:

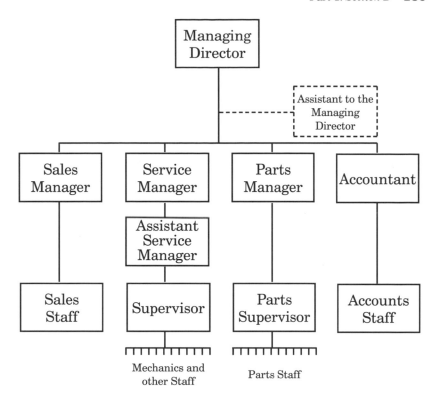

Line and staff relationships are shown, but the functional relationship between the accountant and the other three managers is assumed.

What are the advantages of an organisation chart?

The main advantage of an organisation chart is in its preparation. This entails a clear analysis of lines of authority, of who is responsible for what, and who is accountable to whom. Charts can be modified in the light of changes, and are useful when introducing new employees to the business.

What are the disadvantages of organisation charts?

Apart from the fact that charts become quickly out-of-date, the main problem is that they show an over-simplified and inflexible view of the relationships that occur in practice in any organisation. One thing you should have learnt from the preceding sections is that people and the relationships between them are more complicated than can be shown on a simple chart. Sticking rigidly to the lines on the chart would be difficult in a dealership where there is so much communication between departments. Charts are useful in settling disputes over authority, responsibilities and accountability, but tend to fade into the background in the day-to-day co-operation that gets the work done.

What is the span of control?

The span of control refers to the number of subordinates that can effectively be supervised by a single manager or supervisor. A famous general once said that 'No one brain can effectively control more than six or seven other brains'. Although this is far too simplistic, it does suggest that there is a limit to one manager's span of control. The actual number depends on circumstances such as:

- The complexity of the work – the more technically demanding the work is, the more supervision will be needed, and the fewer the subordinates that can be controlled.

- The abilities and skills of the subordinates – if this is high, they will be able to work relatively unsupervised, and more can be controlled. A high labour turnover, with new people needing a lot of supervision, will work in the opposite direction.

- The ability and popularity of the manager – if a manager is liked and respected, subordinates will work with less supervision.

The motor trade is certainly highly technical, but most staff are well trained and capable of working without constant close supervision. How many mechanics are controlled by one workshop supervisor in your business? One factor that seems to apply in all organisations is that the span of control decreases the further up the management structure you go. Top managers usually have a handful of department managers accountable to them. A supervisor at shop floor level might control twenty workers if the work is simple and repetitive.

Is there only one sort of authority?

Much of what we have said in this section about authority, control, directing and giving orders, seems to over-simplify many of the fascinating and sometimes contradictory relationships and patterns of behaviour we have discussed in other sections. If people were more like machines and fitted neatly into their boxes on the organisation chart, management might be easier, but it would certainly be dull. How effective such a sterile organisation might be is another matter.

What we have been talking about in this section is **formal** authority – the authority that people get from their position in the management hierarchy. We saw in earlier sections that managers who rely solely on their formal authority are unlikely to be either popular or effective. So what other types of authority are there? In a business there are three, **technical**, **personal**, and **legal**. We shall discuss each in turn.

What is technical authority?

A manager may derive some authority from having expert knowledge, for example the ability to solve technical problems, or knowing how to organise work in a systematic way. Subordinates will more readily accept the authority of a manager if they respect and are dependent on his or her expertise. Even specialists who are not managers may have technical authority because of their expert knowledge. In our everyday life, we accept a lot of technical authority from people who have no formal authority over us at all – doctors for instance.

What is personal authority?

Personal authority tends to come from the individual, rather than the position that individual occupies. It is sometimes called *charisma,* and depends on the popularity and personality of the person involved. You know from your own experience that you accept the authority of managers you like and admire much more readily than of those you do not. You, and your fellow workers, are responding to the personal authority of the manager. In your own progress to becoming a good manager, developing your personal and technical authority is much more important than enhancing your formal power.

What is legal authority?

Managers derive legal authority from the law of the land. For example, a service manager can in certain circumstances retain the vehicle of a customer who fails to pay the bill. The amount of authority is strictly limited to the letter of the law. Managers also of course have certain legal responsibilities to employees, customers and society as a whole. *Motor Trade Law*, The Institute's student guide, covers all aspects of a manager's legal authority and responsibilities.

What is a directive?

A directive is an order to subordinates, usually in writing, to inform them of a decision that the manager has taken. It may give formal and public notice of a change in procedure that a more informal method would not. For instance, if there has been a problem with use of the 'phone which a 'quiet word' does not solve, a manager may have to issue a directive to ban, or to limit, private calls.

What are the limits to a middle manager's authority?

A middle manager's authority is limited in two ways:

- By the amount of authority granted by managers at the top. Some top managers like to hang on to all the power and authority they can, and allow middle managers very little power to take their own decisions. The directive or autocratic leaders that we discussed in Section C are like this. We call this a **centralised** organisation. More participative or democratic leaders encourage middle managers to accept more responsibilities, and with it the authority to act on their own initiative. We call this a **decentralised** organisation.

- By the amount of authority granted to a manager by subordinates. A poor manager may have to rely on formal authority and is unlikely to develop good working relations with staff. Good managers on the other hand will back up their formal authority with technical and personal authority.

What do we mean by delegation?

As soon as one person running a business is no longer able to manage it alone, the process of **delegation** begins. Asking a mechanic to service a car is not delegation. This is just distributing a task. Delegation means handing over a part of a manager's power to manage – a bit of authority in other words. It also means giving someone the responsibility for carrying out that part of the job. Delegation is difficult because it means giving something up. Giving someone a task is easy, but handing over control of some part of your job to someone else is not. In the example we just quoted of a centralised organisation, the autocratic top managers were reluctant to delegate more than the absolute minimum amount of authority and responsibility. Managers like this maintain close control, but it may be at the expense of extra work for themselves and frustration and dissatisfaction for the middle managers. They will certainly not be using their human resources effectively.

Participative top managers who adopt a more democratic style delegate much more. They risk losing close control of every aspect of the business, but reduce their own workload, keep middle managers much happier, and make better use of the talents and abilities of their staff. Staff development depends on effective delegation.

What exactly does a manager delegate?

It is often said that a manager can delegate authority but not responsibility. This is true in the sense that the managing director is, in the end, responsible for everything that goes on in the business. Some brave MDs even have a notice on their desk saying 'The Buck Stops Here'. But this does not help a middle manager trying to sort out what he or she is, in practical terms, responsible for. All members of the management team have some responsibilities – that is what being a manager means. Non-managerial staff carry out tasks and undertake duties – but they do not *manage* the tasks because they do not have the authority or the formal responsibility for carrying them out – this stays with the manager.

A middle manager's responsibilities are delegated by top management in exactly the same way as authority is delegated – in fact, a good rule-of-thumb is that, for any one manager, the amount of responsibility they have should be exactly matched by the degree of authority they are given. This is sometimes called the **principle of correspondence.** For a healthy management structure, this is a good principle to aim for, but there are circumstances when it is not the case, as we shall discover shortly.

What are the responsibilities of a middle manager?

The most reliable guide to a middle manager's responsibilities is included in the job description. This should clearly lay down all the tasks and duties that the manager is responsible for, and for which he or she will be accountable to the next manager up the line. In theory, all the job descriptions of all the managers should add together to constitute all the responsibilities that the business needs to undertake. Of course job descriptions do not always keep pace with reality in a rapidly changing environment, and all managers have to be flexible as the business adapts to new circumstances. But an effort must be made to keep job descriptions (and rewards) in line with actual responsibilities.

What happens if authority and responsibility are not equal?

As a general rule, for a 'healthy' organisation with effective delegation, responsibility and authority should be evenly matched (the principle of correspondence). But what happens in the following situations?

- When authority is temporarily delegated.

- When authority exceeds responsibility.

- When responsibility exceeds authority.

We shall examine each situation in turn.

What happens if authority is temporarily delegated?

This could be when someone takes over a manager's job because the manager is absent, or when a particular task such as conducting a special investigation is delegated. In this case the subordinate is given temporary authority, but the manager still retains the responsibility for the job being done. This sort of delegation causes no difficulties providing the situation does not become permanent. People do not mind taking on temporary jobs of this kind – it does their promotion prospects no harm, and it 'tests the water' in terms of management development.

What happens where authority exceeds responsibility?

We saw above that when this is temporary, there is usually no problem. What happens if the situation becomes permanent? The subordinate will eventually feel exploited, and will quite rightly want to take over formal responsibility (and the extra rewards that go with it) for something that he or she is doing anyway.

What happens where responsibility exceeds authority?

This happens quite frequently when a manager delegates the responsibility for something, but will not give up authority over it. For instance, the service manager may make the supervisor responsible for the timekeeping of workshop staff. This is fine, providing the supervisor can in some way punish late-comers and reward good time-keepers. If not, then the supervisor has the responsibility, but not the authority to carry out the duty effectively. Poor working relations between everyone working in the service department may result.

How serious the effects of all these imbalances are depends on how far out of line things get. No organisation is perfect, but managers should realise that, while delegation is vital to success, to be effective it must be properly thought out.

When should volunteers be used?

Effective delegation involves careful planning to ensure that the right person is given authority and responsibility. Asking for a volunteer is in this case not appropriate.

But we have also said earlier that asking a subordinate to carry out a task is not, on its own, delegation. In distributing tasks, rather than delegating, a manager may sometimes consider asking for a volunteer. If a task is difficult or unpleasant, or involves something out of the ordinary, asking for a volunteer may have some advantages. Volunteers are much more committed to the task than people who are ordered or persuaded into it. They may feel that their co-operation and willingness will not be forgotten when development and promotion is on the agenda.

How does accountability fit in?

Accountability (or 'responsibility to') is quite straightforward. All managers are accountable to their line managers for their actions. Remember that as authority flows down the organisation chart, so accountability flows back up it. The workshop supervisor is accountable to the service manager, the service manager to the general manager and so on. Remember that in a functional relationship a manager may be accountable, in theory at any rate, for one particular area of work. The service manager for instance may be accountable to the chief accountant for providing particular figures.

What other responsibilities does a manager have?

Within the organisation, we have looked at what a manager is responsible for, and who a manager is responsible (or accountable) to. But, using the word in a more general sense, what about the wider responsibilities of a manager? These include:

- Responsibility to the shareholders or owner – to run the business efficiently and responsibly, and to ensure a reasonable return on their investment. This applies particularly to top managers.

- Responsibility to employees – to provide fair pay, good working conditions, security, justice in discipline, and equality of opportunity in terms of recruitment, development and promotion. Managers also have legal responsibilities to employees – health and safety and employment law for example.

- Responsibility to society – to ensure that the business operates safely and does not harm the environment. Many managers like to go farther than is legally necessary, and to consider what the business can contribute to the general well-being of the local area.

- Responsibility to the customer – without sufficient customers, the business will not survive, and in the competitive world of the motor trade, managers must always be aware of their responsibilities to the customer. To begin with there are the legal responsibilities, such as the Sale of Goods Act and the Trades Descriptions Act. Good products and services at a fair price come next, and if the business is to be really successful, managers should ensure that everyone in the business makes the interests of the customer their top priority.

PART 2: FINANCE

Section A

BUSINESS ECONOMICS

Business Structures

What does business structure mean?

When people set up in business, they choose what type of legal form of organisation is most suitable. When panel beater David Morton starts a body repair business in a small lock-up he will obviously need a different legal structure from the Ford Motor Company. What we mean by business structure we can best illustrate by discussing the choices available.

What sort of business structures are there?

There are three common types of business structure:

- **Sole Trader**

- **Partnership**

- **Limited Company**

Sole traders are the simplest and most common form of business. Just over half of all businesses in the UK are sole traders, the rest are evenly split between partnerships and limited companies. It's not just a matter of size, although most sole traders have quite small businesses and almost all very large businesses are limited companies. Most partnerships fall somewhere between the two. All three types are common in the motor industry.

What is a sole trader?

This is a business owned by one individual. It's very simple to start up with few legal requirements and is the type that David Morton would have chosen. In the motor trade, a lot of small garages, workshops and shops selling parts and accessories are sole traders.

What are the advantages of being a sole trader?

- Fast and easy to set up.

- One person in charge.

- Very little red tape.

- Book-keeping and accounts kept to a minimum.

There are also tax advantages, not in terms of how much is paid, but when it is paid. Earnings from the business are subject to personal income tax, but there can be a delay of around two years between earning the money and paying tax on it. Only very simple accounts need to be sent to the Inland Revenue (the Tax office).

What are the disadvantages of being a sole trader?

- Personal liability for all business debts. This means that if the business buys things on credit and cannot pay the bill, or if it borrows money and can't pay it back, then the owner stands to lose his or her personal assets (house, car etc), to pay off the business debts.

- It may be difficult to raise enough capital. As a business grows it may need to borrow large sums of money. Banks and other financial institutions are reluctant to lend large amounts to sole traders.

- Long and unsocial hours. All sole traders complain about long hours, sixty or seventy hours a week being not uncommon. After doing the book-keeping, visiting the bank, chasing people for orders, chasing them for money, preparing quotations and planning for the future, sole traders still have to find thirty or forty hours to do the work for which they get paid.

● The business is dependent on one person. What happens to the business when that person is ill, or on holiday? And if David Morton is run over by a bus, the business ends with him.

What is a partnership?

If two or more people own and run a business, this is known as a partnership. It's very similar to being a sole trader and does overcome some of the disadvantages. Unfortunately it produces problems of its own. The number of partners is normally limited to twenty.

What are the advantages of a partnership?

● Relatively simple to set up. Very similar to setting up as a sole trader, except that a partnership agreement is desirable. We shall discuss this shortly.

● Not much red tape.

● Book-keeping and accounts still fairly simple.

● Taxation is broadly similar to that of a sole trader.

● Resources and responsibilities are shared. The main advantage compared with being a sole trader, is that resources, in terms of money, skills and experience, can be pooled together. The responsibility for all the problems of running the business is also shared out, and the number of hours worked may be reduced.

What are the disadvantages of a partnership?

There's no gain without pain, as they say, and partnerships, when they go wrong, can be very painful.

- Personal liability for all the debts of the partnership. The biggest problem is that a partner is still liable, in the same way as a sole trader, for all the debts of the business. Even if your partner runs off with all the money, you still have to pay all the bills and not just your share of them. This sort of thing happens quite a lot.

- Partners have to share the profits.

- Disagreements may occur. Even if your partner doesn't run off with the contents of the bank account, there will probably be disagreements, usually over money. The best way to avoid all these sorts of problems is to draw up a formal **partnership agreement.**

What is a partnership agreement?

A partnership agreement is usually prepared by a solicitor and covers the following main areas.

- How much money each partner will put into the business.

- How profits will be divided.

- How much partners can draw out of the business.

- What, if any, salaries are payable to partners.

- What happens if a partner wants to leave.

- What happens if a new partner wants to join.

A partnership agreement will certainly not eliminate all disagreements, but what arguments there are may stop short of grievous bodily harm.

What is a limited company?

Sole traders and partners are people who earn money from being in business. If the business can't pay its debts then the individuals are personally liable. In fact the business and the individual can't be legally separated. A limited company is quite different. It is legally separate from the people who *own* it (shareholders), and from the people who *run* it (directors and managers). In law a limited company is a 'person' who can buy things, sell things, enter into contracts, employ people, sue and be sued.

Usually a number of people get together to form a company, sole traders or partnerships who want to expand, or people setting up a completely new enterprise. There must be a minimum of two shareholders and one director. In a small company shareholders and directors are usually the same people. Most large businesses are limited companies.

Why form a limited company?

- **Limited liability** – the liability of the owners (shareholders) is limited to the amount of money they have put into the business. If you as a shareholder invest £1000 in a company, you can lose the whole of that £1000, but not your house and other assets.

- There is no limit to the number of shareholders.

- Shares can be bought and sold without affecting the company.

- Raising money – it's easier to raise funds from a potentially unlimited number of shareholders than from one sole trader or a few partners. The bank and other financial institutions may also prefer to lend to a company.

- Image – a business with 'Ltd' after its name often appears more professional and business-like.

So why aren't all businesses limited companies?

Many small businesses stick to being sole traders or partnerships. This is because in practice they gain little advantage from limited liability. Shareholders will probably not be queueing up to invest, and bank managers will usually demand some sort of personal security from the directors (for example house deeds) before lending money. It's only when the business grows in size and has assets of its own to use as security that limited liability becomes a real advantage. There are also some disadvantages.

What are the disadvantages of a limited company?

- More expensive to set up. David Morton would certainly be put off by the cost of setting up a limited company and would in any case get very little advantage from it in his first couple of years. Setting up a company himself, using the services of an accountant and solicitor would be very expensive. A cheaper alternative would be to buy an 'off the peg' company from a Company Registration Agent. This would keep the cost of registering the company to around £250.

- More record keeping and red tape. Accounts for a sole trader or partnership have to show a true and fair view of the financial affairs of the business, but there are no strict rules about what form these should take. A limited company has to prepare accounts in a particular way, and also must file an **Annual Return** with the **Registrar of Companies**. This return includes details of directors and minutes of shareholders' and directors' meetings. These requirements are all laid down by law in the various **Companies Acts**.

- More money for the accountant. All of this additional work costs money. A large company would have its own accountant, smaller companies would employ a firm of accountants to prepare the annual accounts. All companies, however, have to appoint an outside firm of accountants to act as **auditors**. You may be familiar with the arrival of the auditors in your own business. Their job is to examine the accounts and financial systems of the business on behalf of the shareholders, and to make sure that the accounts show a 'true and fair view' of the state of the company's affairs. The cost of this service is another expense which the sole trader and partnership does not have to pay for.

- Less privacy – the annual accounts and returns can be examined by any member of the public, including employees and competitors.

Choosing a business structure

This is often a straightforward decision based on the individual circumstances. David Morton would obviously choose to be a sole trader. If he wanted to share the responsibility and profit he might take a partner. He might be tempted to go into partnership with his wife (and there could be tax advantages in doing so). A more complicated decision would be whether to form a limited company. David and his wife certainly wouldn't do this at first, although they might after a few years if the business expanded.

A large business setting up from scratch would probably be a limited company straight away. The owners of a growing business have to take a more complicated decision and usually choose to change from being a sole trader or partnership when the advantages of trading as a company begin to outweigh the disadvantages.

It is not a decision that they would take on their own since, apart from the considerations discussed previously, there are complicated issues connected with taxation and National Insurance to think about. For this reason accountants and other business advisors are usually called in for their expert opinion.

Is there only one kind of limited company?

No, there are two possibilities, a **private limited company** and a **public limited company**.

- Private limited company – most companies start off as private companies and all small businesses remain so. There are no restrictions on the number of shareholders but a private company cannot offer its shares for sale to the general public. It is allowed to submit accounts in slightly less detail than public companies.

- Public limited company – or PLC for short. These are larger businesses and must have a minimum **share capital** (the amount of money invested by the shareholders) of £50,000. Shares can be offered to the general public. The British Gas share flotation is an example of this. All major British companies are PLCs.

How is a company registered?

A limited company is registered, or 'incorporated', by filing certain documents with the Registrar of Companies. The main documents are:

- **Memorandum of Association**.

- **Articles of Association**.

- List of Directors.

- Statement of Share Capital.

- Address of the company's Registered Office.

- Statutory Declaration that the requirements of the Companies Act regarding registration have been met.

What is a Memorandum of Association?

This states the objectives of the company in broad terms. Should the company use shareholders' money to exceed these objectives, the directors may be liable for any debts incurred. The Memorandum must also show the number and value of the shares to be issued.

What are Articles of Association?

These set out the internal arrangements of the company and cover such things as the transfer of shares, appointment and powers of directors and the holding of meetings.

Who runs the company?

A company is run by the **Board of Directors**. It must also have a Company Secretary and most large companies have a full-time accountant.

- Company Directors – may be full-time (executive), or part-time (non-executive). Non executive directors only attend board meetings. One of the directors is appointed as managing director, sometimes known as the chief executive. It is also normal to appoint one of the directors to chair board meetings and the Annual General Meeting (AGM) of the company, to which shareholders are invited. Despite the fact that nowadays it is not only men who fill this position, they are almost always known as Chair*men*, whether male or female.

- Company Secretary – every company must have a Company Secretary, appointed by the board of directors. The secretary's main duties are to ensure that the company complies with the regulations of the various Companies Acts.

Are there any other forms of business structure?

The only other legal form of business you may come across is that of a co-operative. There are about a thousand of these in the UK, and many more in the rest of Europe. The main feature is that they are owned and controlled by all the people working in them, irrespective of how much each has invested. There are not many co-ops in the motor trade. The now defunct Meriden Co-op that took over the Triumph motor cycle factory is perhaps the best known.

Wholesale and Retail

What do the terms mean?

A **wholesaler** is someone who buys goods in bulk from a manufacturer, then sells them in smaller quantities and at higher prices to a retailer.

A **retailer** is someone who sells goods or services to the general public. The retailer may buy the goods from a wholesaler or direct from the manufacturer.

How does the system work?

The traditional way in which selling is organised can be illustrated by a simple diagram.

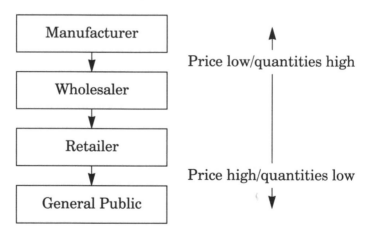

The manufacturer makes the goods, often in very large quantities. The wholesaler then buys direct from the manufacturer in smaller, but still very substantial quantities. The retailer then buys from the wholesaler in still smaller quantities. Finally the general public, or final consumer, buy from retailers in even smaller quantities, perhaps in individual units.

The essential thing to remember is that, as the goods progress down the chain, the quantities bought get lower and the price gets higher. You will be well aware of this as a consumer when you buy a single item in your local shop. An item which only costs a few pence to manufacture may cost a pound or more. Paying for the costs and profits of everyone in the chain helps to explain the mark-up. It doesn't of course help to pay the bill.

Does it always work like this?

This is very much the traditional way in which goods are sold. Independent wholesalers are an important link between a large number of manufacturers located world-wide and an even larger number of retailers spread throughout the country.

Although this pattern still remains there have been a lot of changes in the way that goods are sold over the last few decades. Both manufacturers and retailers have drama-tically increased in size and in so doing have to some extent squeezed out the traditional wholesaler.

Why do some manufacturers cut out the wholesaler?

Manufacturers can expand by making more – more shirts, more teapots, more cars. But they can also expand by tak-ing over that part of the selling and distribution of their products previously done by the wholesaler. As manufac-turers get larger and produce a wider variety of goods, it makes more sense to have their own warehouse and their own fleet of lorries and vans to distribute goods direct to the retailer. It costs a lot to do this but they can pocket the difference between the (low) manufacturing price and the (higher) wholesale price.

Why do some retailers cut out the wholesaler?

The motives are the same – they make more money because they can buy direct from the manufacturer. The reason they are able to do this is that retailers, even more so than manufacturers, have increased dramatically in size. Look at your local high street and try to find a shop that is not part of a national chain. Do you buy your groceries from a supermarket or from a corner shop? This revolution in retailing has given the large retailing chains the power to buy direct from the manufacturer, often at a price even lower than the wholesaler has to pay. Big retailers often have their own warehouse and transport fleet.

Are there any wholesalers left?

Yes there are. Independent wholesalers are still an important part of selling and distribution because there are still plenty of small and medium sized manufacturers and, despite the efforts of the chain stores and supermarkets, still plenty of small retailers finding gaps in the market or hanging on to an endangered way of life. But the most important thing to remember is that, even if there are fewer wholesalers, their job or function still has to be done. Goods still have to be stored somewhere and must still be delivered in the varieties and quantities that the retailer needs. It's not a matter of cutting out the work, but of who keeps the profits.

How does the motor trade fit into all this?

The motor industry is a good example of large manufacturers and comparatively small retail outlets. The car manufacturer also acts as the wholesaler, storing vehicles and parts and distributing them to individual dealerships. The motor trade has not undergone the dramatic changes that we have seen elsewhere. Manufacturers have always been fairly big, and although some garages and dealerships have joined together into small chains, the pattern has remained the same – big manufacturers, small retailers.

Each manufacturer sells its cars through a network of

dealerships all over the country. The dealerships are independently owned, often by an individual or a family, but usually only sell new vehicles from one manufacturer. The way in which this is organised is by a system known as **franchising**.

What is a franchise?

Franchising, like most other ideas in retailing, started in the USA. A franchise is really a licence, bought by a retailer, that entitles a retailer to sell the goods of a particular manufacturer, usually under the trade name of the manufacturer. Fast food outlets (eg MacDonalds, Wimpy), are the most popular, but other types are catching up fast (eg Prontaprint, Bodyshop). Retailers benefit because they get exclusive rights to sell a nationally known and advertised product in the area, but still keep ownership of the business themselves.

The manufacturers benefit because they have control over who sells their goods, they can take a nice percentage of sales or profit as commission, and they do not have to find the money to set up the retail outlets themselves.

The motor trade was ahead of the trend, and franchised dealerships have been common for many years. A Rover dealership will have exclusive rights to sell new Rovers in a particular area, will benefit from national advertising, but of course will buy and sell at prices set by the manufacturer. Unlike in many franchises, the dealership keeps its own name and identity (eg Bristol Street Motors, South Herefordshire Garages).

Are there any alternatives in the motor trade?

In 1995, the Korean Manufacturer Daewoo launched a new method of selling cars in the UK. Daewoo deal directly with the public by eliminating the franchised dealership and setting up their own chain of retail outlets. They also include in the price a considerable number of after-sale benefits such as free servicing. It will be interesting to see how successful this strategy will be and what long term effects it will have on the majority of the motor trade.

What does a retailer do?

We will now look in more detail at what the function of a retailer is. The main functions are:

- To provide goods locally.

- To provide a variety of goods.

- To provide goods in the quantity the customer needs.

- To give a personal service.

- To give information and advice.

- To provide any additional services (eg hire purchase).

- To provide after sales service.

We shall examine each of these in turn.

Providing goods locally

Customers need to be able to buy goods within a reasonable distance of their home. It would be unreasonable to expect a potential customer to visit each car factory when making a choice. A visit to Fiat or Nissan would cost almost as much as the car. And customers, being suspicious people, will also consider how far they must go to return faulty goods.

Providing a sufficient variety of goods

Customers demand choice and it is up to the retailer to provide a sufficient variety of goods to make a sale, and even more important, to keep the customer coming back. A motor factor would expect to keep a range of motor oils in terms of quality and price. An Argos superstore stocks 6500 different items.

Selling goods in the right quantity

One of the main functions of a retailer is to buy goods in large quantities and to sell in smaller quantities, according to the needs of the customer. A motor factor would buy spark plugs in hundreds and sell them usually in fours or sixes. The motor trade is notorious for selling spares in made up units when only one component part is necessary, for example a small crack in one part of the lens of a rear light cluster often means the replacement of an expensive unit, and an angry customer.

A personal service

The retailer is the only person directly in contact with the customer and it's easier to keep an existing customer than to find a new one. A personal service from someone they trust is what maintains a customer's loyalty. A retailer must always think about the customer's needs and put them first, offer good advice when asked and deal with complaints promptly and politely. Think of the reasons why *you* go back to a particular shop.

Of course this personal service is expensive to provide, and some retail outlets deliberately cut out any personal service in order to keep prices as low as possible. Most supermarkets do this, as well as outlets like Argos. It's unlikely, however, that this sort of approach would be helpful when selling pensions or second-hand cars.

At least one car manufacturer is now looking at a complete change in the way that dealerships relate to their customers. Instead of a customer dealing with several different people in the same dealership, there may be just one person who looks after all their motoring needs, from replacing a car to replacing a bulb. Many other organisations outside the motor trade are making similar changes.

Information and advice

Manufacturers rely on retailers to give information and advice about their products, in order for customers to make the right choice for *them*. It works both ways of course and customers often communicate with manufacturers through the retailers over faults or complaints. For instance, claims under a new car's warranty would be dealt with by the dealership.

Additional services

These are particularly important in the motor trade and in other businesses selling expensive items. Providing hire purchase facilities is essential for any dealership or car sales outlet. Large dealerships will usually provide a range of extra services and methods of payment including car hire and leasing cars to business customers.

After sales service

After sales service is important in most trades but nowhere more so than in the motor trade. Good after sales service is one of the most important factors in maintaining customer loyalty and one area that many dealerships could improve on.

What are the advantages of being a retailer?

It sounds, from the list of qualities that a retailer needs, that the retailer has an impossible job. Many retailers, particularly sole traders, will be the first to agree. There are some advantages however. The main one is that they (sometimes) make a profit. They do this by buying at cheap, or 'trade' price, then add a percentage on (often called the 'mark up') when selling to the public. Other advantages are:

- Trade credit is often available, which means that the retailer does not have to pay for the goods immediately.

- Loans and other forms of financial assistance may be available from manufacturers.

- Advertising of the products is usually done by the manufacturer.

- Staff training on products is often provided by the manufacturers.

What does a wholesaler do?

A traditional wholesaler will:

- Buy in bulk and sell in smaller quantities. A manufacturer then saves on selling and storage costs.

- Take a risk. If a product does not sell, a wholesaler may lose a great deal of money.

- Store large quantities and varieties of goods. Wholesalers usually have a lot of floor space in cheap or out of town locations.

- Provide trade credit to retailers. Retailers often have to get the cash in from customers before they can pay the wholesaler.

Wholesaling in the motor trade

As we have said before, the wholesale function is still necessary in the motor trade, even though this is done by the manufacturers themselves. Although dealerships would not normally use a traditional wholesaler, many smaller garages use wholesale motor factors to supply them with service materials, spare parts and many of the non-motor trade products which garages are expected to stock these days, like cold drinks, biscuits and batteries.

Car manufacturers acting as wholesalers have to carry out most of the functions of a traditional wholesaler (risk taking, storage and distribution, providing trade credit) and are also responsible for national marketing of the products. They must also provide training on products for the dealerships and technical assistance when the need arises.

The motor trade in the future

Many people feel that selling cars is going to be increasingly difficult in the next decade. There will be greater competition from the far east, and a demand for cars that will grow slowly, if at all. The revolution that affected retailing in general has largely been ignored by the motor trade which is organised on rather traditional lines. While there are good reasons for some aspects of this, it seems likely that the retailers who will survive and propser will be those who learn lessons from outside the motor trade and who are willing to change to more imaginative ways of keeping the customer satisfied.

Fund Generation

We all need money

You don't need anyone to tell you that you need money to survive. You need it to buy the big things that you keep (house, car etc), and to pay the bills (food, insurance, entertainment etc).

A business is just the same – it needs money to buy the things it needs to keep, like plant and machinery, delivery vehicles etc, and it needs money to buy materials to use, to pay wages and all the other bills.

What does a business need money for?

Think of the business that you work for. It spends money on two very distinct sorts of things. It buys things of a permanent (or semi-permanent) kind that it intends to keep, usually for a number of years. It might buy land and buildings, it will probably have some plant and machinery, fixtures and fittings, and office equipment. It may also buy cars or vans that it intends to keep, to make deliveries or to be used by reps. This sort of expenditure is called **capital expenditure**.

The business will also pay for things of a less permanent nature. Your own wages for instance, the things that it buys to sell to customers (usually as quickly as possible), the rates, the accountant's bill and a whole variety of things that the business consumes, right down to a packet of paper clips. This sort of expenditure is called **revenue expenditure**.

In a supermarket, the shelves where the tins of beans sit are items of capital expenditure. The tins of beans themselves are part of revenue expenditure.

What is capital expenditure?

Most of the money spent in setting a business up in the first place is capital expenditure. How long you intend to keep something is the main test of whether expenditure is capital or not. The general rule is that if the business intends to keep something for more than a year, then it's capital expenditure. In practice we also look at how much things cost. If we buy an office stapler for instance, we have a pretty good idea that it will last for five years. But since it only costs a fiver we treat it as though it will be used up in the current year and call it revenue expenditure.

What is revenue expenditure?

Almost all the day-to-day running costs of a business are revenue expenditure. Everything that will be used up or consumed in the near future is included. The supermarket beans will be sold within a week, the shelves will still be there at the end of the year.

Why is it important to split expenditure like this?

Later in this book we shall be looking at profits and how we arrive at them. For the time being all you need to know is that:

Sales for the year

minus

Costs for the year

equals

Profits for the year

When we split costs into capital or revenue expenditure we are trying to work out what the true 'costs of the year' are. It's obvious that a year's insurance premium is a cost of that year, and that, when you sell a tin of beans, the cost of that tin should also be included in that year's costs.

But what about when a garage buys a hydraulic ramp, for instance? Is it really fair to include the whole of the considerable cost of the ramp in one year's costs? The ramp may last for ten years, and sales will benefit for ten years as a result, not just for the first year. If we do put the whole of the cost into the first year, then profits will be way down in that year and way up for the following nine.

To avoid this, what we do is to spread the cost of the ramp over the ten years that it will help to bring in extra sales. This evens out the profits and shows a fairer picture of what's going on in the business. That's what we do with all capital expenditure and why it's important to distinguish it from revenue expenditure. How we spread the cost of the ramp over its life we shall discuss later in Section B.

Is the cost of a car bought by a dealership capital or revenue expenditure?

This is a bit of a trick question, but it does illustrate the difference between the two types of expenditure. If a dealership buys a car and intends to sell it, then that is revenue expenditure. The dealership has no intention of hanging on to the car, in fact it wants to get rid of it as soon as possible.

If, on the other hand, the dealership buys a car for the managing director to use, or a van in which to collect parts, then that cost is a capital cost, because the dealership intends to keep the vehicle.

We all need money – but where does it come from?

We have been looking at how to spend money, or where the money goes *to*. But we also need to look at where the money comes *from*.

Forget about business for a while and think of your own situation. You can spend money on a car, or on hi-fi equipment which you intend to keep for a few years (your capital expenditure in other words). But you also spend money on food and drink, petrol and parking (your revenue expenditure).

But where does the money come from? It may just come from your wage or salary. Or you may borrow some from a friend, or from the bank. You might buy your car on hire purchase, or blow the whole of Uncle Bert's legacy on a foreign holiday.

When examining your own finances it's important to look at both sides – where the money comes from and where the money goes to. A business is no different.

Where does the money come from in business?

Or you could say, what sources of funds does a business have, or how is it financed? It all amounts to the same thing.

Money, or funds, can come from any one of three places:

- Money *invested* in the business by the proprietors or shareholders.

- Money *borrowed* from banks and others.

- *Profits* made by the business and kept in the business to pay for expansion.

Money invested in the business

This may be money invested by the proprietor of a small business and is often the only source of funds at the start. People invest in a company by buying shares – literally a 'share' of the business. All the shareholders between them own the business.

The main thing to remember about investing in a business is that investors are risking their money and will therefore want a return (or **dividend**) on their investment. The more profit a business makes, the greater return the investors will expect.

What types of share are there?

There are basically two different types of share, **ordinary shares** and **preference shares**.

- Ordinary shares are by far the most common. Shareholders receive part of the profit as dividend, but only after all other business debts have been provided for (bills, loan interest, taxation etc). In most cases, the greater the profit the higher the dividend. Ordinary share capital is often called the **equity**.

● Preference shareholders received their dividend before the ordinary shareholders, but only get a fixed percentage whatever the profit. There is usually no right to vote at the company AGM, and, for reasons connected with taxation, preference shares are no longer popular.

Money borrowed by the business

Almost all businesses have to borrow from time to time and may borrow quite heavily. Sometimes it may be because of weakness that a business borrows money, but it's often quite the opposite. It can be a sign of confidence that customers are going to pay over enough money to repay the loan and leave something over for the proprietors or shareholders. A business may borrow money in a variety of ways, some of them obvious, others not quite so straightforward.

Borrowing from banks

This can be in the form of a **loan**, which is paid back on a regular monthly or quarterly basis. Alternatively it can be an **overdraft** that goes up or down according to what is paid into or out of the bank account. Loans are usually made to buy specific things, like buildings or machinery, and are repaid over the medium or long term (3 to 25 years).

Overdrafts are normally used to purchase stock, pay wages and other bills, while the business is waiting for its customers to pay up. Overdrafts are, in theory at any rate, much more short-term than loans, and can be withdrawn by the banks at very short notice. Some businesses, including many in the motor trade, rely on what has become in effect a 'permanent' overdraft. We shall discuss the services provided by banks in more detail later.

Other sources of loans

Banks are not the only places offering loans. Loans are also available from:

- Investors who require a fixed return. Shareholders usually want a greater return if the business makes more profit. They will also settle for less if profits fall. But some investors are happier with a fixed rate of interest. They won't get more if profits are high, but on the other hand won't lose if they fall.

- Insurance companies.

- Merchant banks. These are banks that specialise in business investment.

- Friends and relatives. This is usually the cheapest form of borrowing, but can end in tears if things go wrong.

What is a debenture?

A **debenture** is simply a piece of paper acknowledging a loan. In normal business use it is a loan to a company at a fixed rate of interest and generally repayable after 10 to 40 years.

What will a lender want?

If someone asked you to lend them £1000, you would be unlikely to hand it over before asking some pretty difficult questions. You would also insist on safeguards to prevent the borrower from failing to repay. People or institutions who lend to businesses are no different. Lenders usually require four things:

- **Security** (sometimes called **collateral**). A loan is

usually secured on some, or all of the assets owned by a business. The lender might for instance hold the deeds to a building. If the borrower fails to repay, the lender can sell the building and recover the amount due. In many small businesses, if the business itself has insufficient assets to offer as security, the bank may insist on holding personal assets, such as the deeds to a family home.

- A **business plan**. All businesses should prepare a business plan showing details of the people involved, the market for the goods or services being offered, and estimated financial details, or forecasts about the future. A lender will want to examine this.

- Financial commitment from the business. If a bank is going to lend money, it will expect to see the proprietors or shareholders risking their money as well.

- Repayment with interest. When the loan is made the lender will want to know when it will be repaid. With interest of course.

Are there any other ways of borrowing money?

So far we have discussed straightforward loans or overdrafts. But there are other ways in which a business can effectively borrow money. The most common are:

- **Hire purchase**.
- **Leasing**.
- **Trade credit from suppliers**.
- **Credit factoring**.

Hire purchase

Anyone working in a dealership will be familiar with hire purchase, although usually when selling cars to customers. Businesses also use HP to buy things, vans or items of equipment for instance. After the final payment the business will own the things outright. It's usually slightly more expensive than borrowing from a bank, but is also much simpler and less formal. Small businesses tend to use this form of finance a lot.

Leasing

This is similar to HP, but the ownership of whatever is being leased remains with the leasing company. The effect is much the same however, the business pays a regular instalment and gets use of the leased equipment.

Trade credit from suppliers

At first sight this doesn't look much like borrowing. Suppliers of goods to a business do not actually lend the money, but they do allow a period of credit before payment is due, which has a similar effect. Imagine you are running a supermarket. You could, if you wished, borrow money from the bank, go out and buy your stocks, then repay the bank when you sell the goods. You could, but it would be pretty stupid. Alternatively you could follow the example of all the big supermarkets and buy your goods on credit. Shoppers fill their trolleys, then fill the till with cash. Tesco's and Sainsbury's remove the cash from the till and then pay their suppliers. They haven't had to borrow money at all, and more importantly to them, neither have they had to pay any interest. Using suppliers' money in this way is a very cheap form of funding for a business.

What is credit factoring?

This is a fast growing form of raising money. Almost all businesses rely on trade credit from suppliers, but not all are in the fortunate position of supermarkets where most of their customers pay in cash (or by cheque, which is usually regarded as the same thing). Motor dealers are in a similar position and will not usually let go of the car keys until payment is made.

But many businesses have to offer trade credit to their own customers and may have to wait two or even three months for their money.

A way of getting over this is by letting a factor chase and collect debts for you. The factor will pay you a large part of the debt straight away and most of the rest when the customer pays up. The factor takes a cut of course, usually around 5% of the total bill. Factoring is particularly popular in a recession when customers are reluctant to pay.

The best source of funds

We stated earlier that funds came from three places:

- Money invested by proprietors or shareholders.
- Money borrowed from banks and others.
- Profits kept in the business.

We have looked at the first two in some detail. Whether to raise finance from investors in the form of shares, or by borrowing the money, will depend on the individual circumstances of each business. But there is one source of funds that any business will make its first choice – profits.

Why are profits important?

The only source of funds that is absolutely free is the profit retained in the business. Shareholders expect a dividend, lenders require interest, but profits 'ploughed back' into the business cost nothing.

Imagine that you go into business in a very small way, buying and selling second-hand cars. You start with funds of £800 in cash. You buy a car for £800 and sell it the same day for £1000. You have made a profit of £200. And what are your funds now? £1000 – with which you can go out and buy another car. You have increased your funds by £200, and it hasn't cost you a penny.

An alternative would be to start with the £800 and borrow the £200, but that would mean paying interest. Expanding your business by using the profits kept in the business is clearly best.

So why not fund a business entirely by profits?

Well, one obvious answer is that when a business starts up there are no profits. There will have to be some initial investment and/or borrowing to fund the business in the first place. Once a business is established, then profits should be available to help with expansion. The problem may be that there just isn't enough profit to go round.

Limits to profit

Profit can be simply defined as sales minus the relevant costs. So you can make more profit by increasing sales or reducing costs. Easy! Except of course that the economic facts of life mean that it's anything but easy.

You can increase sales:

- By increasing the number of units you sell (sales volume).

- By increasing the price of each unit (sales price).

In an intensively competitive market like car sales, if you sell more, then your competitors sell less. They are unlikely to co-operate in this and will be just as determined to sell more themselves. You can put your prices up of course, but a rise in your prices usually means that you sell less than your competitors.

Reducing costs

A good way of making more profit is either to reduce costs, or to keep costs the same but to sell more. The problem here is that suppliers, employees, lenders and investors are no more co-operative than competitors. Suppliers are always putting up their prices, employees and unions demanding more wages. High bank interest rates (the rate at which a business can borrow) can dramatically slash profits. And if there are any profits left over after all this, then first the Inland Revenue will want their slice, and then the shareholders will want a dividend to be paid.

Only the profits that are left over after everyone else has been paid can be used to pay for expansion. If there is not enough, then the business will have to raise money from investors, or borrow it.

Principles of Costing

Why do we need to know what things cost?

In the previous section we discussed the need for keeping costs down. To keep costs down you first have to know what they are. There are three reasons for looking at costs:

- Prices and profits.

- Taking decisions.

- Keeping control.

Prices and profits

A business needs to make a profit and to know how much. It makes a profit if it sells something for more than it costs. It sounds easy enough but in practice a great deal of skill is required in finding out how much things cost. What are the problems?

- Prices are set not only according to how much things cost, but also depend on how much competitors are charging for the same thing.

- You only find how much things cost *after* you have set the price. Prices have to be set in advance. Actual costs are worked out much later. So, in setting prices we have to rely on *estimated* costs.

- If you sell cars, the cost of buying each car should be easy enough to find. But the cost of the car is not the only cost you have to recover. What about salaries of the sales staff? Or of the managing director? Or the general administration costs? All costs have to be covered and passed on to the customer in some way. How we do this in practice we shall come to shortly.

Taking decisions

Successful businesses are the ones that take the right decisions. Decision making is one of a manager's most important tasks and usually involves making choices between different alternatives. For instance, the manager of a car dealership might have to choose between opening a body repair shop or continuing to use the services of David Morton on the other side of town. Part of each decision will be to look at the effect on costs of each alternative.

Keeping control

Costs are like small children. If you don't control them they will get completely out of hand. A business constantly needs to examine how much it is spending on a particular activity and to compare it with how much it *planned* to spend. If the accountant spends too much on running the accounts department, he or she can be held responsible for the overspending. We shall be discussing the control of costs later in the book when we look at **budgetary control**.

The cost of living

We go through exactly the same sort of process in our everyday life. We need to compare our costs with our income in order to live within our means. Do we perhaps need a rise?

We also constantly need to take decisions based on costs. Can we afford a new house? Should we take a holiday in the South of France this year, or stick to camping in Clacton again?

And of course we try to control our costs. Do we spend too much on newspapers and magazines? Was that expensive leather jacket really necessary?

Once again, a business is interested in exactly the same sort of things as you and me.

It all depends on what you mean by cost . . .

Cost is an overworked word and, in an accounting sense, is much too vague and imprecise to use on its own. If you are talking about the cost of a car, do you mean how much it cost to buy at the time that you bought it, how much it would cost to replace it, or how much it costs to run it?

We classify costs in a variety of different ways, and the way we choose depends on what we are trying to achieve. Are we trying to find out how much profit we made in the past? Or are we taking decisions about the future?

We split costs up in different ways according to what we are trying to do.

Fixed and variable costs

An important way of splitting up costs is into **fixed costs**, which stay the same however much is made or sold, and **variable costs**, which change according to output.

Imagine a small business making ice cream in plastic containers. Some costs will change according to the amount of ice cream that is made. The milk and cream for instance, and the containers that the ice cream is sold in. The more ice cream that is made and sold, the more basic ingredients are used. Costs which vary according to the level of sales are called variable costs. Other costs will stay the same whether the business sells 1000 containers a week or 1200. The rent of the premises will not change, neither will the cost of insurance or the accountant's bill. Costs which do not change according to the level of sales are called fixed costs.

How fixed are fixed costs?

Fixed costs do not change whatever the level of output. In practice they are not as fixed as all that. In the ice cream business fixed costs will probably stay the same if output increases from 1000 to 1200 per week, but an increase to 5000 per week might well mean bigger premises, more rent, higher insurance and a larger accountant's bill. But over the increases or decreases in output we would normally expect, we can say that fixed costs will not change.

Fixed and variable costs in the motor trade

The motor trade is like any other business – some costs are fixed and some variable. In a typical dealership, variable costs would include the cost of the vehicles (sell one more and you 'use' one more), the cost of sales staff commission and the cost of pre-delivery check and cleaning. In the spares department the cost of the spares themselves would be variable costs. Service and repair variable costs would include parts used and oil.

The fixed costs of a dealership would include the rent of the premises, the salaries of management and administration staff (and sales staff except for the commission), insurance, electricity and a variety of other costs which will tend to stay the same, at least for the foreseeable future.

In a manufacturing business production wages are usually regarded as variable – the more you make, the more wages you have pay. In a small dealership and over the short term, even workshop wages tend to be fixed. If repair sales fall by 10% the dealership will be reluctant to get rid of highly trained mechanics. If there is an increase in output of 10% the management will also hesitate before taking on extra staff.

Remember, which costs are fixed and which variable depends on what happens in practice, and not necessarily on what you read in a book.

Why bother to split costs in this way?

Splitting costs into fixed and variable is very useful when it comes to making decisions about the future. Managers are constantly asking questions of a 'what if' nature. What if we increase sales by 10%? What if wages rise by 8%? What if we take that order at a discount? What if we close that department? The answers to all these sorts of questions depend on fixed and variable costs.

For instance, if sales increased by 10%, two things would change:

1) Cash coming in from sales would increase by 10%.

2) Cash paid out for variable costs would increase by 10%.

   – BUT, fixed costs would remain the same.

Knowing which costs will change and which will stay the same is a vital part of answering questions about the future.

What are marginal costs?

If output and sales increase by, say 5%, the extra costs that are directly due to this increase are called **marginal costs**.

Marginal costs are often just the variable costs. If output increases from 100 units to 101 units, then the marginal cost of this extra unit will probably be the variable cost. But if output increased to 120 units then the marginal costs of that increase will include variable costs and possibly some extra fixed costs too. Supervisors' overtime, renting additional space, more paperwork, more advertising to sell the extra output might (or might not) be necessary. It all depends on the circumstances and particularly on how close the business is to full capacity.

Capital and revenue costs

We saw earlier how expenditure is classified into capital and revenue according to whether we intend to keep something for a long time (like a machine), or whether we intend to use it up in the current year (like wages, materials or rent). We also saw that it is necessary to divide costs up in this way in order to calculate each year's profit on a fair basis.

It's important to remember that *all* costs, whether capital or revenue, have to be accounted for and in some way passed on to the customer. Capital costs have to be passed on to the customer over a number of years. We calculate the right cost for each year by something called **depreciation**, which we shall cover in Section B.

Direct and indirect costs

Dividing costs into fixed and variable, or capital and revenue, gives a lot of useful information. But when it comes to passing on the right costs to customers, another type of classification is needed. We need to know which costs we can directly identify with a particular job or product. So we also divide costs into:

Direct costs – those costs which we can physically identify directly with a particular job or product.

Indirect costs – those costs which cannot be identified with a particular job or product.

What are direct material costs?

Imagine a small garage involved in service and repair. It should not be difficult to identify the materials used on a particular job. On a simple service perhaps four spark plugs, a filter and four litres of oil. These are the direct material costs that would be booked to that job.

In a factory it might be more complicated with a variety of raw materials going into a particular job or product. A service business often has no materials at all – an accountant for instance.

What are direct labour costs?

In the garage example it should also be possible to record the amount of *time* the mechanic spends on a particular job. This would enable the garage to calculate the cost in wages of each service or repair. This is the direct labour cost.

In a factory it should be possible to determine the direct labour cost of those people who work directly on production. Even an accountant can calculate the number of hours spent on a particular client's books.

What are indirect costs?

Indirect costs are those which *cannot* be identified with a particular job or product. We normally only include manufacturing or production costs in indirect costs. In the garage this would mean the workshop costs that cannot be identified with each job. The supervisor's wages for instance (indirect labour), or cleaning materials (indirect materials). Indirect costs are often called factory or workshop overheads. In a factory it's particularly important to find the manufacturing cost of a job or product.

What other costs are there?

In addition to direct costs and the indirect costs of the factory or workshop, there are also the costs of selling, distribution and administration. These are often referred to as **general overheads**. We usually use 'overheads' as a term that includes factory or workshop overheads as well.

General overheads are really all the other costs of running the business. The rent, insurance, general manager's salary, costs of the accounts department, phone calls, pencils, guard dogs and advertising. It is not of course possible to identify overheads with a particular job because overheads cover *all* jobs.

But we do need to find the total cost of each job, including overheads. How do we do it?

The overhead recovery rate

When a garage carries out a repair it usually charges the customer with a rate per hour and this rate is much higher than the mechanics' rate of pay. This is because the garage has to pass on to the customer not only the direct material and labour costs, but also a little bit of the workshop overheads and of all the other overhead costs.

Material and labour costs can be calculated with a fair amount of accuracy, but with overheads this is clearly impossible. Some arbitrary or estimated method has to be used. In a garage, overheads are usually passed on to customers according to the number of hours spent on the job.

This is how the system works:

A garage estimates that total overheads for the year will be £12,000. The time that all mechanics will spend on repairs is estimated at 3000 hours. The overhead recovery rate is therefore:

12000 ÷ 3000 = £4 per hour.

So, if a job takes one mechanic 6 hours, the amount of overheads charged to that job will be:

6 × £4 = £24.

It's rough and ready, but the fairest and most accurate way of deciding how much each job costs.

The costs of selling cars

We have used car repairs and service to illustrate the different types of cost. A dealership puts a lot of energy into selling cars. What costs are involved in this? The following costs would be incurred by a typical dealership:

- Preparing a new vehicle for sale – cleaning, pre-delivery inspection, fitting number plates etc.

- Used vehicle preparation – cleaning and valeting, plus any parts and labour used in repairs prior to sale, should all be included in the cost of a used car. Errors made in part exchange prices can be expensive.

- First service – if this is 'free' to the customer then the cost will be charged to the sales department.

- Warranty – cost of repairs under warranty for new cars will usually be passed on to the manufacturer.

- **Policy adjustments** – any promotional activities, such as a free sun roof, or a weekend break are additional costs known as 'policy adjustments'.

- Sales staff salaries – the commission can be added to the cost of a particular vehicle. Any fixed salary has to be spread over all car sales.

- Marketing and advertising costs – although a great deal of advertising is done by manufacturers, a dealership still needs to advertise locally and this cost must be covered by car sales.

In addition to the costs that relate directly to selling cars, the sales department will have to bear some of the general dealership overheads in the same way as service, parts or any other department.

Section B

COMPANY FINANCE AND ACCOUNTS

Accounting Terms

Before we look in detail at *why* we keep accounts and *what* accounts we keep, we should first look at a few of the terms we shall be using.

What is a debtor?

A **debtor** is a person or organisation who owes the business money. For example, David Morton may do regular work for a local dealership. Although he would like to be paid in cash, the dealership is unlikely to agree. He will have to provide invoices for the work done and, if he's very lucky he will be paid at the end of the month. More likely he will be paid after two or three months. The dealership will be a debtor of David Morton. Members of the public will probably pay David straight away in cash or by cheque. They will not owe him money and will therefore not be his debtors.

Some businesses have lots of debtors. Most businesses that sell directly to other businesses give them time to pay (or provide them with 'credit').

A business that deals direct with the public (a retail business in fact) will often be paid in cash and will therefore have few debtors. A dealership, for instance, will not usually release the car until payment has been received. It may

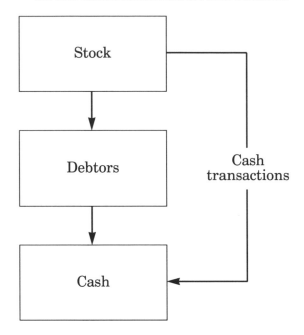

however have to provide credit for its business customers.

We can use a diagram (above) to show how debtors fit in. Stock (of manufactured goods, tins of beans, cars etc.), is sold and turned into debtors, who owe the business money. When the debtors pay up, the money owed is turned into cash. Stock sold for cash can by-pass debtors altogether.

What is a creditor?

A debtor owes the business money. A **creditor** is just the opposite – a person or organisation that the business owes money to. Since David Morton is having to wait for his money from his dealership customers, he will obviously try to delay paying his own suppliers by arranging credit terms.

Although many retail businesses have few debtors, almost all businesses have creditors. Think back to what we said earlier about using trade credit from suppliers as a source of business funds.

Creditors will include amounts due to providers of goods or services. For instance the main creditor of a dealership will be the car manufacturer. But the total of creditors will also include *any* other money owed by the business. Taxation due to the Inland Revenue or dividends owing to share-holders for instance. And what about money *loaned* to a business? The business will have to repay the loan, so the providers of loans are also creditors. Some loans may be due fairly soon, for example a bank overdraft, but some not due to be repaid for several years. Although all money owing is included in the total of creditors, a business will usually split it into:

- Creditors: amounts falling due within one year.

- Creditors: amounts falling due after more than one year.

What is an asset?

An **asset** is something that belongs to a business and which has a value. Assets include such things as buildings, plant, stock, debtors and cash. *Ownership* is very impor-tant – a building that is owned by the business is an asset, a rented building is not. And it must be possible to put a financial value on the asset. You often hear people say something like 'our people are our greatest asset'. While this may be true in a general sense, fortunately accoun-tants have not managed to put a financial value on people.

What is a fixed asset?

Fixed assets are those things which we intend to keep. They are 'fixed' because we have no intention of selling them, at least in the short term. Fixed assets include land and buildings, plant and machinery, fixtures and fittings, office equipment, and vehicles for use, rather than for sale.

Most fixed assets will be sold eventually, because they wear out or become obsolete – but they are not bought with the *intention* of reselling them.

What is a current asset?

Current assets are the ones that we intend to turn into cash in the near future. As soon as possible in fact. Current assets include stock, debtors and cash. Cash of course is cash already, but debtors we hope will pay within a few weeks, and stock we also hope to sell and eventually turn into cash. The cash is used to buy *more* stock, which then turns into debtors, then into cash. While the business continues, the cycle never stops.

What would current assets include?

- Stock: In a manufacturing concern this would include raw materials, work in progress and finished goods. In a retail business usually just finished goods. A service business may have no stocks at all. Stock is normally valued at what it cost the business, but old or obsolete stock may have to be valued at less than this. We shall be covering this later in Section B.

- Debtors – the amount owed at any particular time by customers. The business would have to allow for any customers not expected to pay. These are called **bad debts**.

- Short term **investments** – if the business has surplus cash it may, like you or me, put it into short term investments (shares, or a building society) that can quickly be turned back into cash, hopefully at a profit, when it is needed.

- Cash – this includes actual cash held on the premises in a till or petty cash box. It also includes cash in the bank account, which is being held by the bank on behalf of the business.

What is a tangible asset?

A **tangible asset** is one which you can see and lay your hands on, like land or buildings, machinery or stock. They are assets in a physical sense. 'Tangible assets' is not an expression we use frequently.

Are there intangible assets?

Yes. We use the term to cover those assets which you can't actually see or lay your hands on because they don't physically exist.

If a business buys a trade mark or patent which may benefit the business for several years, this is an asset like any other. Similarly, one business may buy another and pay over the odds because the price includes the **goodwill** value of existing customers. The value of the goodwill that has been bought is also an asset. But because they are not assets in the physical sense they are called '**intangible assets**'.

What is a liability?

A **liability** is the opposite of an asset. A liability is something *owed* by the business, and like assets can be divided into two categories:

● Fixed, or **long term liabilities**.

● **Current liabilities**.

Is there such a thing as a 'fixed' liability?

Well, yes and no. It's a good way of explaining something, but not an expression we normally use. We usually refer to money owed by the business that is not due for more than a year as a long-term liability.

Long-term liabilities would normally include:

- The money invested by shareholders and due to them if the business was sold. This would include the original share capital, plus any profits which have been ploughed back into the business. These profits, in effect, increase the value of their 'share' of the business. (Note: this should not be confused with the value of shares on the Stock Exchange, which depend on rumour, confidence and international pressures, as well as what is actually happening to the company.)

- Long term loans which will have to be paid back at some point. Don't forget that these are also called 'Creditors: amounts falling due after more than one year'. Part of the problem of learning about finance and accounting is that one thing is often called by several different names. Long term loans *are* creditors, but in normal everyday language we would refer to them as loans.

What are current liabilities?

Current liabilities are the amounts which the business owes and which have to be paid within the next twelve months. It is exactly the same as 'Creditors: amounts falling due within one year' that we discussed earlier in this section and which you may see in formal financial documents. 'Current liabilities' is the traditional term we still use in everyday speech. It includes bank overdrafts, trade creditors, taxation and dividends due to be paid in the following year.

Are 'reserves' pots full of cash?

No. You may hear that a company has **reserves** of £65,000. This does not mean that it has £65,000 sitting in a safe or a bank account. Do you remember in Section A we looked at where the money comes from in business? We said that it comes from three places:

- Money invested by the shareholders.

- Money borrowed from the bank and others.

- Profits made by the business and retained in the business for expansion.

This last category is mainly what reserves consist of.

What are reserves?

If a business makes a profit of £100,000, it *could* pay all of it out to shareholders. But usually it pays out some of it (say £40,000) and ploughs the rest (£60,000) back into the business. It's the cheapest source of funds. Now since the £60,000 could have been paid to the shareholders it really 'belongs' to the shareholders and is therefore added to their stake in the business. Although the shareholders cannot get their £60,000 in dividends, the business is now worth more, and they benefit because their *share* of it is also worth more.

But don't forget that this is only looking at where the money comes from. If we look at what the money is used for, it's unlikely to be in wads of used fivers. It might be used to buy fixed assets, or more stock, or to expand the business in any way at all.

What assets would a typical garage own?

Look around your own place of work. What assets can you identify? The most obvious asset is probably the building itself and the land on which it stands (but only of course if the business owns them). The building will normally be shared by all departments who will divide the cost usually on the basis of the amount of space they occupy.

Each department will also have its own fixed and current assets.

New and used car sales

Fixed assets will include:

- Showroom fixtures and fittings.

- Office furniture, desks etc.

- Any vehicles used permanently by sales staff.

Current assets will include:

- Stock of new and used cars for sale.

- Debtors – money owing for cars sold but not yet paid for. This might apply to some trade customers.

- Cash – the bank account would normally be kept in the name of the whole business, although managers would want to know how much cash is contributed by each department. Takings of both cash and cheques would be banked daily, for security reasons, but a small float might be kept in the department to provide customers with change.

Service and repairs

Fixed assets would include:

- Specialist items of plant – ramps, rolling roads, hoists, electronic tuning machines etc.

- Smaller hand tools over a certain value (inexpensive tools would be treated as revenue expenditure and not as an asset).

- Fixtures and fittings – racks, shelves, benches etc.

- Office furniture.

- Computers, typewriters etc.

- Vehicles kept for permanent use.

Current assets would include:

- Stocks of any parts, oils or lubricants kept within the department.

- Debtors – money owed by customers for repairs and servicing carried out but not yet paid for. This would include many trade and some retail customers.

- Cash – a small cash float would normally be kept.

Parts department

Fixed assets would include:

- Fixtures and fittings – racks and shelves where spares are stored, counters and display units.

- Handling equipment for large and heavy items.

- Computers and printers.

- Vehicles kept for permanent use.

Current assets would include:

- Stocks of parts, accessories and lubricants for sale to customers and for use by the service and repair departments.

- Debtors – sales to trade customers not yet paid for.

- Cash – a small cash float.

Administration department

A large dealership would usually have a separate administration department with its own assets. Fixed assets would include:

- Office furniture – desks, filing cabinets, cupboards.

- Computers, adding and accounting machines, typewriters.

- Vehicles kept for permanent use (the general manager's car for instance).

Current assets would include:

- Stocks – stationery, pens and general office consumable equipment.

- Cash – a float of cash for small out of pocket expenses. This is called the **petty cash**.

Because the administration department does not do work directly for customers, there will be no debtors.

Other departments

Other departments, such as a car body shop, car leasing or car rental departments, would have a similar variety of assets. Don't forget that if a garage leases or rents a car to a customer, the garage still *owns* the car. The cars would be fixed assets because they will be kept on a semi-permanent basis.

Accounting Systems

Why keep books at all?

Ask David Morton which part of his body repair business he dislikes most and he will probably say 'doing the books'. He will have become painfully aware that running a business doesn't just consist of knocking out dents. He may well spend up to half his working time preparing quotations, talking to customers, chasing them for money, seeing the bank manager, planning for the future – and of course, doing his book-keeping.

He may not enjoy it so why does he do it? There are two main reasons:

- Because he *has* to.

- Because he *needs* to.

Why does a business *have* to keep books?

- All businesses have to prepare financial statements each year so that the Inland Revenue can decide on how much tax is due.

- All except the smallest businesses have to keep detailed records in order to prepare VAT returns for HM Customs and Excise.

- All limited companies are obliged by law to produce annual accounts in a certain form and send them to the Registrar of Companies.

Why does a business *need* to keep books?

We have seen that a business is obliged to keep books and accounts – it has no choice. But it also needs to keep accounts because it would certainly fail without them. Why?

- One of the major factors contributing to the failure of many businesses is a lack of financial control. It's vital that managers know what is going on so that they can plan and control the business.

- All businesses need to make a profit in order to survive and to expand. Managers need to know the financial implications of their actions, otherwise making a profit will be a matter of pure chance.

- Making a profit is a nice start, but on its own is not sufficient to ensure survival of the business. To survive, a business needs to pay the bills, and for this it needs cash. If a customer pays late, or doesn't pay at all, a business still has to find the cash to settle its own bills. And you can't pay this month's bills with next month's money. A manager not only needs to know how much money is coming in – but *when*.

What sort of accounts does a business keep?

There are three different sorts of accounts that most businesses keep, although to be honest, each sort is closely tied up with the others. In a small business one person will often look after all the accounting functions. The three types, which you will find in your own business, are:

- **Financial accounts**.

- **Management accounts**.

- **Customers' and suppliers' accounts**.

What are financial accounts?

These are the traditional sort of accounts where everything is recorded to the nearest penny shortly after it happens. These accounts show the financial state of the business as a whole, at least annually although sometimes more often. These are the accounts that go to outsiders – the Inland Revenue, the shareholders and the Registrar of Companies. They are often called 'historical accounts' because they relate to what has happened in the past.

What are management accounts?

This is the financial information used by managers to help them in planning and controlling the business and in making decisions. It includes information about costs and prices and about the performance of different departments. Management accounts differ from financial accounts in that:

- Management accounts are for internal use only.

- Financial accounts look at the past. Management accounts are concerned with the past, but even more with the present and the future.

- Financial accounts are balanced to the nearest penny, and this takes time. This level of accuracy is unnecessary for management accounts. It's far more important for managers to have reasonably accurate figures, but to get them quickly. Figures which forecast what will happen in the future are of course estimates and are unlikely to be 100% accurate.

The term 'Management Accountant' has now largely replaced the earlier one of 'Cost Accountant'.

What are customers' and suppliers' accounts?

Keeping track of what customers owe us (our debtors), and what we owe our suppliers (our creditors), is strictly a part of the financial accounting function. But most large businesses will have a separate accounts department which deals exclusively with the accounts of customers (called the **sales** or **debtors' ledger**), and the accounts of suppliers of goods and services (the **purchase** or **creditors' ledger**). Now if all our customers paid in cash, and we paid all our suppliers in cash, there would be no need to keep these sorts of accounts at all. But customers are often allowed time to pay and getting the money out of them is not always easy. Customers are unpredictable, forgetful, sometimes less than honest, and often run out of cash themselves. Making sure that they pay is the job of the **credit controller**. We shall discuss the difference between cash and credit sales later in the book.

Do departments have a role to play in financial accounting?

Looking after the accounts of customers and suppliers and preparing financial reports is the responsibility of the accountant and the accounts department. But they have to rely on each department to provide them with information and to deal directly with retail customers.

What responsibility does each department have?

- New and used car departments have to produce the relevant information so that customer invoices can be prepared. They must also process HP documents and provide details of daily takings to the accounts department.

- Service and repair and the spares department have the responsibility for preparing sales invoices. For credit sales, these will be passed on to the accounts department, who will then take over the task of collecting the money due.

Each department will have to check that cash sales invoices for the day balance exactly with the daily takings of cash and cheques in the till. The details will then be sent to the accounts department.

What is an audit?

If you invest your savings in the shares of a limited company, how will you know that the set of accounts which you receive show a fair and accurate view of the company's affairs? How can you be sure that the directors aren't 'cooking the books' to keep themselves in a job?

This is where the auditors come in. Auditors, as we stated earlier, are a firm of independent accountants who check the books and accounts on behalf of the shareholders. They are appointed by the shareholders, although in practice this is a formality and the auditors are effectively chosen by the directors.

What these accountants do is to check very thoroughly the books and financial accounts (including the sales and purchase ledgers), to ensure that they 'give a true and fair view' of the financial state of the company.

Are they only searching for fraud?

No. They certainly do check that systems adopted are proof

against deliberate fraud. They also look for ineffective and badly designed book-keeping systems that may result in errors. And what about the value of assets? Are they reasonable? We have said that financial accounting systems record transactions with great accuracy to the nearest penny. But when it comes to the annual accounts some assets have to be valued according to the *opinion* of managers. In a dealership for instance, what about old parts stock which may never be sold? Is it worth what we paid for it? Is it only worth scrap value? What about the value of debtors? Does the business adequately provide for any bad debts? Banks lending in the third world sometimes have to write off vast debts that will never be repaid. Garages often have the same problem on a smaller scale. The auditors have to decide whether the estimates and judgements made by managers are reasonable.

If the auditors are not satisfied with the accounts they can issue a **qualified report**. This does not happen very often as directors will normally follow the auditors' advice before the accounts are published.

The Profit and Loss Statement and Balance Sheet

What do you need to know about your finances?

Forget about business for a while and think about your own financial situation. What things do you need to know?

Income and costs

The first thing you would probably think of might be your *income*. What salary do you earn? You might also have other sources of income, building society interest for example.

You would also want to know what your *costs* are – how much is your rent or mortgage, how much do you spend on food, holidays, clothes etc?

If you deduct your costs from your income you may get a nasty shock – but at least you will see whether or not you are living within your means. If your income for the year is more than your costs, then you will be richer at the end of the year. If costs exceed income, then you will be poorer.

Everybody needs cash

Let me make you an offer – two offers in fact, and you can choose between them.

Offer 1 – You can have £1,000 in cash tomorrow.

Offer 2 – You can have £1,000 in cash, payable when you reach 70.

Which would you choose? Well it's not very difficult is it? But why did you choose the first offer? Because you're asking two questions – not just *how much*, but *when* you will get it.

We have just discussed income and costs, but only in terms of 'how much?'. You would also be interested in when the money comes in and when it goes out. Personal incomes, usually in the form of a wage or salary, tend to come in on a regular basis. But costs are much more haphazard. Some costs are regular (food, mortgage etc.) but others are not (a new car, holidays etc.). It's not just necessary to have enough income to cover your costs overall, you need enough cash in the bank to pay for a car or a holiday at the time you need to pay.

How wealthy are you?

We have looked at income and costs and when the cash comes in and goes out. But there is one further thing you will want to know about the state of your finances. How much are you worth? It's the way we often define people – 'he's rolling in it', or 'she's poor'. We are not just thinking about income when we say this but about what people *own*.

We are interested in what we *own*, and also in what we *owe*. The difference between the two is what we are *worth*. What we own of course are our personal assets (car, hi-fi, washing machine, bank balance). And what we owe are our liabilities (phone bill, Access bill, overdraft).

We measure income or costs over a period of time, a month or a year for instance. But wealth, or worth, we can only measure at one particular moment in time. You might say 'I was worth £28,000 on 30th June'. You may not do this in a formal way by putting a value on all your assets and liabilities – but it is something that most people are interested in, without necessarily putting an exact figure on it.

What financial information does a business need?

Exactly the same as you or me. A business is interested in the same sort of things as an individual.

- Income less costs – or sales less costs, shows what profit a business has made. This is shown in a document called the **profit and loss statement**.

- A business is also vitally concerned with when the cash comes in, and when the cash goes out. This is so important that managers put a lot of energy into predicting what will happen to cash in the future. This is shown in a **cash flow forecast**.

- From time to time, and at least once a year, a business will also list all its assets and liabilities to find out how much it is worth. This is shown on a **balance sheet**.

These are the most important accounting documents. A business is of course more complex than an individual and all businesses will need more information than this. But if you can keep in mind these three ways of looking at the financial situation, you will find that most of the complexities you meet in practice will fit into this framework.

The profit and loss statement

We shall start by looking at probably the simplest document – the profit and loss statement. This, along with the balance sheet, is sent to the shareholders at the end of the **financial year**. The financial year is not the same as the calendar year or the tax year, but can be any date (usually a month end) to suit the business – the 1st May to the 30th April for example.

A profit and loss statement looks at history, at what happened last year. Managers will also, for their own use, produce a **profit forecast**, which estimates what the figures will be for the following year. The two documents will have the same layout.

In Section A we said that:

	Sales for the year
less	Costs for the year
equals	Profit for the year

This is what the profit and loss statement shows and the basic layout, even for the biggest company is the same:

	£
Sales	XXXX
less Direct costs	XXX
= Gross profit	XXX
less Overheads	XX
= Net profit	XX

In practice, a profit and loss statement will look more complicated than this, but only because it will be cluttered with lots more figures – taxation, dividends etc. If you look at your own company's, or any other published profit and loss statement, you should be able to detect the above pattern.

How will it look in practice?

Even with a lot more figures it's difficult to disguise that a profit and loss statement is a simple document, giving some pretty basic information. The layout in practice may vary a little, but the 1985 Companies Act recommended a particular type of layout and this has become increasingly popular.

The following is the profit and loss statements of Millington Motors, a car dealership.

Millington Motors Ltd
Profit and loss statement for the year ending 31st October 19XX

	£000	Note no.
Sales	360	1
Cost of sales	(210)	2
Gross profit	150	3
Distribution costs	(5)	4
Administration expenses	(65)	5
Trading profit	80	6
Interest payable	(12)	7
Profit before tax	68	8
Taxation	(17)	9
Profit after tax	51	10
Dividends	(23)	11
Retained profit for the year	30	12

(Minus figures are shown in brackets.)

Note 1. The sales figure is often referred to as **turnover**.

Note 2. **Cost of sales**. This will include all the direct costs of goods or services sold. It would include the cost of vehicles and parts sold and the materials used for service and repair. It would also include the wages and salaries of people involved in selling, servicing or repairing vehicles, and the overheads that relate to those activities.

Note 3. **Gross profit** is a very important figure for most businesses because it shows the profit after deducting all the costs that have been directly incurred in making those sales.

Note 4. **Distribution costs**. A significant figure for some types of business.

Note 5. **Administration costs**. A significant figure for all businesses. The amount spent on general management, preparation of accounts, payments to auditors and other administration costs.

Note 6. **Trading profit**. Sometimes known as **Profit on ordinary activities**, or **Operating profit**. It's the profit from all 'normal' activities and can be compared with the amount of funds being used by the business. The percentage of trading profit to funds being used is called the **'Return on capital employed'**. If the percentage return is too low, the management might consider the funds would be better placed in some other type of business, or even put into a building society.

Note 7. **Interest** paid on loans is shown separately after trading profit. Some businesses borrow a lot of money and have to pay a lot of interest. Others are more cautious and interest payments would be low. During a recession, when sales and profits are low, high borrowers may find it difficult to survive. If interest rates are also high, even more cash must be found.

Note 8. **Profit before tax**. Sometimes shown as Net profit on simpler profit and loss statements. The shareholders are particularly concerned with profit after interest has been paid on loans.

Note 9. **Taxation**. Tax due on the profits for the year. The Inland Revenue has its own complicated rules for calculating the profits for tax purposes. The tax due on company profits is called **corporation tax**.

Note 10. **Profit after tax**. This is what is left for the shareholders after paying all the bills.

Note 11. Some of it is paid out to the shareholders in the form of a dividend (the shareholders' income).

Note 12. The remainder is retained in the business to fund expansion. It increases the 'reserves' of the business (see Section A).

You may come across profit and loss statements which have a slightly different layout. Internal documents for the benefit of management may have the costs broken down much more than this. But providing you have a basic idea of what a profit and loss statement is trying to show, you should have no difficulty in understanding it.

What is a balance sheet?

In Section A we looked at the two sides of the financial situation of a business:

- what the money is used for, and

- where the money comes from,

or, to put it another way:

- what the business owns, and

- what the business owes.

This information is what the balance sheet shows. It lists the assets (what the business owns), and deducts the liabilities (what it owes). The figure that remains is what the business is worth to the owners or shareholders. We have to be careful here with using the word 'worth'. Just because *we* say that our business is worth £250,000 does not mean that someone buying the business agrees with your valuation. Or if the business ceased to trade and all the assets were sold there is no guarantee that buyers will pay what you think they are worth. But, with all these practical reservations, we can say that a balance sheet shows what a business is worth.

What does a balance sheet look like?

Even the most complicated balance sheet is only a list of assets and liabilities. Imagine David Morton's first day in his new business, before he starts trading. What is his financial situation? He puts £3,000 of his own money into the business (his capital). Of this he spends £2,500 on equipment and tools, and keeps £500 in cash.

What are his assets? He has:

Equipment	£2,500
Cash	£500
Total assets	£3,000

What are his liabilities? At first sight you would say that he doesn't have any. He doesn't have a loan and doesn't owe money to anyone. But, in accounting terms at least, David Morton the business is *completely separate* from David Morton the individual. So strictly, the business owes David the individual £3,000. If the business borrowed £1,000 *from* the bank it would owe £1,000 *to* the bank. In exactly the same way, if David puts £3,000 of his own money into the business, then the business 'owes' David the individual £3,000.

His balance sheet on his first day would look like this:

Liabilities		Assets	
Capital	3,000	Equipment	2,500
		Cash	500
	£3,000		£3,000

The balance sheet balances! It shows where the money comes from (David's capital) and what the money is used for.

What if David did get a bank loan?

If on his first day David borrowed £1,000 from the bank to help him over his first few weeks, his balance sheet would look like this:

Liabilities		Assets	
David's capital	3,000	Equipment	2,500
Bank loan	1,000	Cash	1,500
	£4,000		£4,000

The £1,000 has affected both sides of the balance sheet. An increased liability in the form of a bank loan, and an additional asset on the other side in the form of an extra £1,000 in cash.

Is this 'side by side' layout always used?

It was, but this traditional method is rarely used today. Instead we use a *vertical* format which, for all except the simplest business is easier to understand.

Using the same figures for David Morton (including the

bank loan) the vertical format balance sheet would look
like this:

	£
Equipment	2,500
Cash	1,500
Total assets	4,000
less Bank loan	1,000
	3,000
David's capital	3,000

We have just moved the same figures round to show them
in a more sensible way.

What about the assets and liabilities we discussed in 'accounting terms'?

Let us look first of all at how David's balance sheet would
fit into the terms we discussed:

	£
Fixed assets:	
Equipment	2,500
add Current assets:	
Cash	1,500
Total assets	4,000
less Long term loan	
(or Creditors: amounts falling	
due after more than one year)	1,000
	£3,000
David's capital	£3,000

This is the same layout but using the correct terms. Note that the loan would only be classed as due in more than one year providing this was the case. If due back sooner than this it would be shown under 'Creditors: amounts falling due within one year' (or 'Current liabilities').

A full motor industry balance sheet

It's now time to look at an example of a full balance sheet for a dealership. It has more items than the simple balance sheet we have just examined, but still fits into the same pattern. Work through it slowly and try to fit it into the framework we have already discussed. It may help to refer to the section on accounting terms, for a detailed explanation of each item.

Millington Motors Ltd
Balance Sheet at 31st October 19XX

	£000	
Fixed assets:		
Land and buildings	150	
Fixtures and fittings	45	
Plant and machinery	35	
Motor vehicles	12	
	242	(Note 1)

Add Current assets:			
Stock	350		
Debtors	28		
Cash	1		
	379		(Note 2)

Less Creditors – amounts due in less than one year:			
Bank overdraft	60		
Trade creditors	125	185	(Note 3)
Net current assets		194	(Note 4)
Net assets		436	(Note 5)

Less Creditors: amounts falling due after more than one year	85	(Note 6)
	351	
Share capital	100	
Reserves	251	
	351	(Note 7)

(All figures in £thousands)

Note 1. A total of the fixed assets used by the business. Don't forget that motor vehicles are only those kept permanently for use by the dealership, not cars for sale.

Note 2. Current assets. The stock figure is high because the cost of cars and parts is a high proportion of the total assets of the business. Debtors are fairly low because payment for cars is received on, or very close to delivery.

Note 3. Current liabilities due to be paid within the year – although in practice overdrafts often carry on for several years.

Note 4. **Net current assets** – also known as **working capital**. This is an important figure. The dealership has no intention of selling its fixed assets and therefore the cash to pay the creditors *must* come from cash generated from its current assets. Since debtors are very low, this means that creditors can only be paid out of the cash received from selling stock. There is certainly enough money invested in stock to do this, providing of course that the stock can be sold. If stock is slow to sell, the creditors may have to wait for their money and the 'temporary' overdraft may become semi-permanent, or even increase. We shall look more at working capital shortly.

Note 5. **Net assets**. This figure is the total of fixed assets plus current assets minus creditors due within one year. In other words the net assets that are available to the business with which to make a profit. This figure is the same as the **capital employed** in the business. The profit that the business makes can be compared with this figure to see how effectively the managers are running the business with the capital, or funds they have under their control.

Note 6. This figure shows any long term loans being used by the business. It is deducted from the net assets/capital employed figure to show the amount of capital invested in the business by the shareholders.

Note 7. This is in effect the 'other side' of the balance sheet. It shows the amount invested by the shareholders plus the retained profits (or reserves) that have been ploughed back into the business over the years.

Will a balance sheet always look like this?

Not necessarily. A few businesses still use the traditional side by side layout. Others may add long-term loans after the shareholders' funds, instead of deducting it from the other side. In the above example the balance sheet would stay the same as far as net assets:

	£000
Net assets	436
Represented by:	
Share capital	100
Reserves	251
Shareholders funds	351
Long term loans	85
(Capital employed)	436

It's just the same figures shown in a slightly different way. The first layout is the one recommended by the 1985 Companies Act. This format is becoming increasingly popular. But as long as you understand *what* a balance sheet is and what each figure *means*, you need not be put off by a slight change in layout.

What is working capital?

We have just said that the figure for 'net current assets' is also known as 'working capital'. So working capital equals current assets minus current liabilities. In other words, we have to use what current assets we have to pay our current liabilities. Why? Well, we can't use our fixed assets because if we sell those we don't have a business any longer.

Let's examine Millington Motors' balance sheet to see what it tells us about how the capital invested in the business is being used.

		£000
Fixed assets are		242
Current assets	379	
less Current liabilities	185	
Net current assets/working capital		194
Net assets		436

Now net assets equal capital employed, so we could say that:

'Fixed capital' is	242
Working capital is	194
Total capital employed is	436

'Fixed capital' is not an expression that we normally use, but it's useful to illustrate that all businesses have money tied up not just in fixed assets, but also in working capital.

How much working capital does a business need?

Not too little and not too much. If there is too little working capital then the business will be unable to pay creditors and buy new stock. If there is too much, the creditors get paid, but capital invested in the business is being used inefficiently. Stock may be sitting on the shelves for too long, debtors may be taking too long to pay, or there may be too much cash sitting in the bank account and doing nothing.

It's difficult for a business to have just the right amount and the usual complaint, certainly with most small businesses, is that they have too little working capital. This can slow down expansion plans and is a not infrequent cause of business failure.

What can a balance sheet tell us?

A balance sheet gives us some idea of what the business is worth (but don't forget what we said about the use of the word 'worth'). It is also, as we have seen, a rich source of information about all sorts of aspects of a business. Together with the profit and loss account it is a good indicator of the health and profitability of the business. Are the funds invested being used effectively? Can the business pay its bills? Is it too dependent on outside loans and overdrafts? Has it got too much cash? Is it making enough profit?

When you have learned to 'read' the annual accounts of a business, to compare them with those of another business, or of the same business for the previous year, you will find that you can discover a great deal about the business without even moving from your seat.

Are any other accounting statements included in the annual accounts?

Larger companies have to produce a **cash flow statement**. As we shall shortly discover, profits and cash are two very different things. Accountants attempt to measure profits, but it's not a very exact science. The good thing about cash is that you can measure it precisely. The cash flow statement looks at what has happened to cash during the previous year. It shows cash flowing into the company from normal trading activities, from loans received from the bank, or capital paid into the business from shareholders.

The statement also shows cash flowing out of the company to cover interest and dividend payments, payments of tax, repayments of loans or shareholders capital, and the cash paid for new fixed assets.

Although smaller companies (including most in the motor trade) do not have to *publish* a cash flow statement, the managers of any business must be aware of the information that the statement contains. Do you remember the final part of the planning process – evaluation? The statement is one way for the managers to compare their plans with what actually happened to cash. And the most important document in financial planning, the cash flow forecast, is what we turn to next.

Cash Flow

What is cash flow?

The profit and loss statement, balance sheet and cash flow statement are an extremely useful guide to the financial state of the business. They do however only look at what has happened in the *past*. But to manage the resources of a business effectively you also have to be aware of what is going to happen in the *future*.

When we talk about cash flow we are usually referring to what is likely to happen to cash in the future. The document that tries to predict this is called the cash flow forecast.

Why is cash important?

You don't need an accountant to tell you that having enough cash is vital to you as an individual. In the last section we looked briefly at the information that *you* need about your finances and said that *when* you get the money is often as important as how much. A business is no different and needs to plan not only to make the required profit, but also needs to look at when the cash will come in and of course when it will have to be paid out.

The Squib firework company

On 1st January, Squib prepares a forecast of profit for the next twelve months. Things are looking good.

Sales are estimated at	£100,000
All costs at	£60,000
And profits at a healthy	£40,000

So far so good. They then look at when the cash comes in and when it goes out. The costs of £60,000 are spread evenly over each month at £5,000 per month. Sales are of course almost all made in late Autumn, shortly before 5th November. The retailers making the sales finally pay Squib in December. The bank balance 1st January also looks good at £30,000.

What will happen to the bank balance over the year? Let's see how it stands at the end of each month.

Month	Balance start	Cash in	Cash out	Balance end
Jan	30,000	–	5,000	25,000
Feb	25,000	–	5,000	20,000
Mar	20,000	–	5,000	15,000
Apr	15,000	–	5,000	10,000
May	10,000	–	5,000	5,000
Jun	5,000	–	5,000	NIL
Jul	NIL	–	5,000	(5,000)
Aug	(5,000)	–	5,000	(10,000)
Sep	(10,000)	–	5,000	(15,000)

Oct	(15,000)	–	5,000	(20,000)
Nov	(20,000)	–	5,000	(25,000)
Dec	(25,000)	100,000	5,000	70,000

They may be making a profit of £40,000, but in the process will run up an overdraft of £25,000 by the end of November. In view of the profit this may be acceptable to Squib, but will the bank agree? In any case they will have to talk to the bank manager – and the first thing he or she will ask for is a cash flow forecast.

The point of preparing a cash flow forecast is to anticipate these sorts of problems and to discover when the business is likely to run short of cash. You and I will probably make our personal cash flow forecasts on the back of an old envelope – the bank will be more impressed by a neat and orderly forecast prepared well in advance. The manager will be much more likely to grant the overdraft than if Squib announce in July that they have run out of cash.

But isn't Squib an unusual company?

Of course it is. Squib is a **seasonal** business, where demand for the product is limited to a very short period each year. It's an extreme example and very few businesses are quite that seasonal.

But many businesses sell products where demand varies according to the time of year. The motor trade is a good example. New cars sell like hot cakes during January (a new year) and in August (a new registration letter). Sales in August usually make up over 20% of total sales. Demand tails off considerably before these dates. In fact the August 1st new registration letter was introduced purely to spread seasonal demand away from the early part of the year.

When preparing a cash flow forecast, a dealership will have to take into account this big influx of cash twice a year with much lower receipts in between. It will also consider all sorts of incentives and offers to get people to buy cars in the slack periods and to even up the inward flow of cash.

What about cash payments?

We have discussed cash coming into the business – but what about cash going out? Is this always on a regular basis? In the case of Squib Fireworks it was, but for most businesses cash payments are also likely to be unevenly spread.

A lot of costs are paid out on a regular monthly basis – wages and salaries for instance. Other costs are not. Rent for example is usually paid once a quarter, insurance and auditing fees once a year. Taxation is usually paid in two instalments a year. And what about buying expensive capital equipment? Expanding a business, or setting it up in the first place, can involve huge cash payments over a short period. These sort of payments have to be planned and anticipated.

How is cash affected by credit terms?

When the cash comes in and goes out is dependent on how much credit you allow to customers and how much you get from suppliers. A business always has to think carefully about the delay between making a sale and getting the cash.

- A sale made today may result in the cash arriving in two months' time.

- A purchase made today may not have to be paid for until the end of the following month.

It all depends on the **terms of trade** that are agreed with customers and suppliers. It also depends whether you and your customers actually stick to the agreed terms. The average time a company takes to pay a bill is around 75 days – much longer than is usually agreed.

A dealership is in some ways lucky. The cash from a car sale is normally received on the date of the sale, or within a few days if HP is involved. This does not mean the dealerships have lots of cash in the bank, in fact many of them have large overdrafts. The money is usually tied up in large stocks of expensive cars. The cash comes in quickly when the cars are sold – but they may take a long time to sell.

Profits are not cash

– and cash is not necessarily profit. Just because a business makes a healthy profit does not mean it will end up with a healthy pile of cash. It might do, but the point is that any business has to keep an eye on both profits and cash. Rapidly expanding companies are often both profitable and short of cash. They need cash to buy more capital equipment, to buy more materials and to pay additional labour. They may have a full order book but there can be a big delay between paying for what they need, and getting in the extra cash from customers.

What items would be included in a cash flow forecast?

That's simple. Any cash coming into the business from any source, and any cash going out of the business for any reason. Don't forget that 'cash' means actual cash, in notes and coins, and the contents of any business bank accounts. So a cheque is treated as the same as cash for this purpose.

Receipts, or cash coming into the business would include:

- Capital introduced by the proprietors or shareholders.

- Loans received from the bank or others.

- Cash sales.

- Cash received from debtors (the result of credit sales).

- Sales of obsolete or unwanted fixed assets.

Payments, or cash going out of the business would include:

- Wages and salaries paid.

- Commission on sales.

- Cash purchases.

- Cash paid to creditors (the result of purchases on credit).

- Rent and rates.

- Heat, light and power.

- Any other overheads.

- Payments of tax and VAT.

- Loan interest.

- Payments of dividends to shareholders.

- Purchases of fixed assets.

Cash flow in, less cash flow out is often referred to as **net cash flow**.

Paul Hadley's cash flow forecast

Paul Hadley runs a small garage doing service and repairs. On 1st January his bank balance is £300. In the first quarter of the year he estimates that the following transactions will take place:

1) Cash sales will be Jan £6,000, Feb £4,000, March £6,500.

2) In February there will be one large sale on credit, for £1,500. The customer will pay for this at the end of March.

3) Because Paul has a feeling that he may be short of cash he plans to put £500 of his private money into the business bank account in January.

4) He estimates that materials will be bought for cash as follows: Jan £2,300, Feb £2,000, March £2,400.

5) Wages (including Paul's) are paid in cash at £1,600 each month.

6) Rent of £800 is paid quarterly and is due in January.

7) Other overheads are paid in cash at £900 per month.

8) Paul wants to buy a piece of equipment costing £2,000 in cash in January.

Paul's 'feeling' that he may run out of cash is a start but it's not really good enough. He needs to sit down and prepare, before 1st January, a cash flow forecast from the figures he has estimated.

His cash flow forecast for the first quarter would look like this:

	JAN £	FEB £	MAR £	TOTAL £
CASH IN:				
Cash sales	6,000	4,000	6,500	16,500
Credit sales	–	–	1,500	1,500
Capital introduced	500	–	–	500
Total cash receipts (a)	6,500	4,000	8,000	18,500
CASH OUT:				
Materials	2,300	2,000	2,400	6,700
Wages	1,600	1,600	1,600	4,800
Rent	800	–	–	800
Other overheads	900	900	900	2,700
Equipment	2,000	–	–	2,000
Total cash payments (b)	7,600	4,500	4,900	17,000
Net cash flow (a–b)	(1,100)	(500)	3,100	1,500
Bank balance at start of month	300	(800)	(1,300)	300
Bank balance at end of month	(800)	(1,300)	1,800	1,800

Minus figures are shown in brackets ( ).

What does this tell us?

Well, Paul's feelings were justified. But it's even worse than he thought.

- Despite introducing £500 of his own money, the business will have an overdraft of £800 at the end of January, increasing to £1,300 at the end of February.

- The net cash flow out of the business is £1,100 in January, and £500 in February.

- Overall, however, he's not doing too badly. His bank balance will increase from £300 on 1st January to £1,800 on 31st March. The net cash flow into the business in March (when the cash from the credit sale is received) is £3,100.

- It's clear that buying the equipment and paying the rent in January, and the sale on credit in February are the main causes of his temporary financial embarrassment.

What can Paul do?

He has a number of options:

- He can take his cash flow forecast to the bank manager and ask for a temporary overdraft. This will of course mean paying out extra interest.

- He could ask the credit customer to pay up sooner, possibly offering a discount as an incentive.

- He can delay some of his business payments. He buys materials for cash and could surely negotiate trade credit with some of his suppliers. This would delay payment by at least a month.

- He could buy the equipment on extended credit – or wait until March to buy it.

- He may be able to reduce some of his overhead costs.

So, all is not lost. The purpose of a cash flow forecast is not an accounting exercise for its own sake. It's to enable managers to predict these sorts of problems and *to do something about them before it's too late*.

Is it more complicated in practice?

Yes, it is. But *not* because it's more difficult to understand. A cash flow forecast for the Ford Motor Company would include a few more figures, but would not *look* a great deal different. The big problem for any business is that a cash flow forecast attempts to predict the future and this, in any exact sense, is clearly impossible, Estimating when cash will come in and go out is extremely difficult, mainly because you have to predict when customers will buy goods *and* when they will pay for them. Payments out are more predictable but by no means easy. And a forecast is usually for twelve months, rather than three. The further ahead you look, the more difficult it is to predict.

Cash flow forecasts are easy to understand, very difficult to prepare, but because of the valuable information they contain, well worth the effort.

How can a business improve its cash flow?

The easy answer is to get cash in more quickly, and to pay it out more slowly – but how can this be done? The following is not a complete list, but includes some of the important things managers should look at, and all too often ignore.

- Agree payment terms when making a sale.

- Avoid giving credit if you can.

- Consider allowing a discount for cash. It may mean slightly less profit, but you won't run out of cash.

- Chase after customers who have not paid.

- Pay bills when they are due, not before.

- Open credit accounts with suppliers.

- Think carefully before buying in bulk. You may save 10% on the price but end up with an overdraft costing you twice as much.

- Consider buying capital equipment with a loan or on HP. This is easier than trying to borrow money to pay for materials or wages.

- On a regular basis look critically at all your costs and see if you can make any savings.

- Guard against theft. Stolen items will have to be replaced.

- Think carefully before taking on a big order. This may involve paying out huge amounts of cash long before payment is received.

- Plan ahead and forecast your cash position.

- Include the bank manager in your plans.

- Record what actually happens and compare it with your plan.

Depreciation

Nothing lasts forever

We have examined assets at some length and discussed the difference between fixed assets and current assets. Current assets are those things that we don't want to keep, like stock and debtors. We wish to turn them into cash as soon as possible. Fixed assets on the other hand, we *do* want to keep. We use 'permanent' fixed assets like buildings or machines to turn our current assets into sales and profit.

But how permanent is 'permanent'? Nothing lasts forever. Equipment wears out, or becomes out of date. Even buildings are eventually replaced. So fixed assets are not really permanent – it's just that we don't buy them with the intention of selling them and like them to last as long as they do the job that we bought them for.

Your depreciating assets

Forget about business again and think about one of your own 'fixed assets' – your car. If you buy a car for £4,500, you know that in a year's time it will be worth less than this – say £3,700. In general, common-sense terms we would say that it will **depreciate** by £800 over the year.

If a friend asks at the end of the year 'what did your car cost?', you can answer in two different ways. You can say 'it cost £4,500', which it did because that was the cash you paid out. Or you could say 'it cost £800 in depreciation over the year'. 'Cost' is an overworked word which, in accounting terms, always needs to be qualified in some way to make it more precise.

Accountants are as guilty as anyone and often use everyday words when describing very precise technical terms. They also use a lot of jargon when they could use plain language. Like most experts they don't wish their skills to appear *too* simple. Depreciation *is* simple, but is also widely misunderstood.

A sensible purchase

Assume for the moment that you are not a wild and impetuous person and that before buying the car you sit down and sensibly calculate how much the car will cost you in depreciation over its useful life. There will have to be some guesswork involved because you are looking into the future. You know that the price now is £4,500 and you intend to keep it for four years. Because of your vast knowledge of the motor trade, you estimate that after four years you will be able to sell it for about £1,300. What will be the cost of depreciation each year?

		£ value	
Purchase price		4,500	
1st year's depreciation	800	3,700	
2nd year's depreciation	800	2,900	
3rd year's depreciation	800	2,100	
4th year's depreciation	800	1,300	(sale price)

What you have done is to even out the cost of the car over its life. You can see that it will 'cost' you £800 per year. If you think this is reasonable, you can go ahead and buy the car – unless someone else has bought it while you have been working out the figures.

Depreciation in business

If the car were used by a business as one of its fixed assets, it would be unfair to include the whole of the £4,500 purchase price as a cost in the first year's profit and loss account. At the end of Year 1 the car still has a useful life of three years in which to contribute towards profits. So we even out the cost of the car over its useful life, and say that it costs £800 a year. Fixed assets are used to try to make a profit. If they contribute towards profits for four years, then the cost of the assets should be spread over four years.

In order to work out depreciation accurately, a business would need to know three things:

- The purchase price of the asset now.

- How long the asset will last.

- The proceeds of selling the asset at the end of its useful life.

Only the first figure can be known with any accuracy. The other two have to be estimated. When estimating the amount of depreciation to charge to the profit and loss account each year, a business will usually make a decision based on past experience of how long different assets last. We shall discuss the different methods that are used shortly.

What does depreciation do?

Depreciation does *one* thing. It spreads the cost of the fixed asset over its useful life. *That's all*. The effect is to make sure that profits don't rise and fall erratically according to what cash has been paid out for large and semi-permanent assets. If profits *benefit* from the use of a fixed asset, then they should bear the *cost* of that fixed asset.

What does depreciation *not* do?

Confusion about what depreciation is trying to do is very common. The main things to remember are:

- Depreciation does not represent any payment of *cash*. In the example of the car, cash is involved on two occasions – when the car is *bought*, and when it is *sold*. No other cash is involved.

- Depreciation does *not* aim to reduce the cost of the asset to its current market value. It only spreads the cost of the asset over its life.

- Depreciation does *not* provide any cash for replacing the asset. Look at the example of the car again. When you sell it for £1,300, what cash have you got? Only £1,300 – not £4,500. You *may* have been prudent and saved up enough cash to replace the car (which will probably cost £6,000 by now), but this decision has nothing to do with depreciation. A business must plan to replace assets and make sure that there is enough cash to do so. But this is a completely separate exercise and not the job of depreciation.

Where does depreciation appear?

Where would you see depreciation in the documents we have examined?

- The profit and loss statement each year will include the total amount of depreciation for the year for all assets.

- The balance sheet will show fixed assets at the value to which they have been reduced. This is known as the **written down value**, or **book value**. The balance sheet at the end of Year 1 would include the car at a written down value of £3,700. The balance sheet will also show, as extra information, the original cost of each category of asset, and how much these assets have depreciated to date.

What about the cash flow forecast?

Depreciation is *not* cash, so will not appear in the cash flow forecast. What does go into the cash flow forecast? Only the original cost of the asset and the cash received when it is eventually sold.

What fixed assets do we depreciate?

Earlier in the section we discussed in detail what fixed assets are. Which ones do we depreciate?

- Land and buildings. Land is not depreciated because it has an infinitely useful life. Buildings usually are depreciated, but since most buildings have a useful life of sixty or seventy years, the amount of depreciation each year is quite a small proportion of the total cost. If the value of land and buildings goes up, then a business may actually increase the value shown in the balance sheet.

- Plant and machinery/fixtures and fittings. These have a much shorter life than buildings and are usually depreciated over five to ten years.

- Motor vehicles kept as fixed assets may be depreciated over much shorter periods.

What methods are used?

There are a few methods of calculating depreciation, but by far the most common are:

- The straight line method.
- The reducing balance method.

What is the straight line method?

This is the method we have used in the example of the car. It's very simple to calculate. We take the original cost of the asset, *minus* the estimated selling price at the end of its useful life. Then we divide this by the number of years of expected use:

$$\frac{\text{Original cost minus eventual sale value}}{\text{Number of years of expected use}}$$

For example: David Morton buys a compressor costing £2,000. He plans to keep it for five years by which time he reckons that he will be able to sell it for £500. What is the annual depreciation using the straight line method?

Annual depreciation will be:

$$\frac{2{,}000 - 500}{5} = £300 \text{ per year}$$

Each year the written down value of the compressor will be

reduced by £300. The amount by which the asset has been depreciated – called the **accumulated depreciation** – increases by £300 per year:

Year	Depreciation per year £	Accumulated depreciation £	Written down value £
Original cost			2,000
1	300	300	1,700
2	300	600	1,400
3	300	900	1,100
4	300	1,200	800
5	300	1,500	500

The straight line method very simply spreads the net cost of the asset (2,000 – 500) over its useful life at an even £300 per year. This is the most widely used method of depreciation in this country.

What is the reducing balance method?

The reducing balance method calculates depreciation as a percentage of the written down value at the end of each year. As this figure reduces, so the annual depreciation charge gets smaller. There are two advantages to using the method:

The depreciation charge is high in the early years when repair bills are low. In later years repair bills will increase, but by then depreciation will be lower.

In practice it's not necessary to calculate the life and eventual sale value of each asset when calculating depreciation. An estimated percentage, based on past experience, is applied to each different type of asset.

How does the reducing balance method work in practice?

David, being a sophisticated manager, decides to compare the two methods of calculating depreciation on his compressor. In reality he hasn't got a clue how long he will keep the compressor, or what value it will have when he eventually sells it. But, based on his previous experience he decides that a reasonable percentage to knock off the written down value each year is 25%. He calculates depreciation as follows:

		£
Original cost		2,000
Year 1:	Depreciation 25% × 2,000	500
	Written down value at end of Year 1	1,500
Year 2:	Depreciation 25%× 1,500	375
	Written down value at end of Year 2	1,125
Year 3:	Depreciation 25% × 1,125	281
	Written down value at end of Year 3	844
Year 4:	Depreciation 25% × 844	211
	Written down value at end of Year 4	633
Year 5:	Depreciation 25% × 633	158
	Written down value at end of Year 5	475

The book value at the end of Year 5 is very similar under both methods. But the regular amount charged under the straight line method (£300) becomes £500 in Year 1, and falls to £158 in Year 5 under the reducing balance method.

Which method is best?

Both methods are widely used and both have their merits. But as you can see, both also rely on looking into the future and making informed guesses.

How does depreciation arise?

The fact that an asset has a limited life and therefore has to be depreciated is due to two different factors: *physical factors* and *economic factors*.

The physical factors that affect depreciation are *use* and the *passage of time*. If you use an asset, it gradually wears out. And over a period of time it also physically deteriorates, by rusting for instance. A motor vehicle is a good example of both processes happening at the same time – it wears out mechanically, and rusts mainly due to age.

Economic factors are *obsolescence* and *inadequacy*. An asset which is still in good condition may become obsolete if it goes out of date. Computers become out of date every few years. Changes in Government regulations might affect depreciation. For example a change in MOT testing some years ago made all existing brake testing equipment obsolete overnight. A machine might also become obsolete because it *makes* something that becomes obsolete. When a car manufacturer stops making a particular model, the plant used to make it may still be in good condition but will become obsolete.

Inadequacy is a result of changes in a business whereby a piece of equipment just cannot cope any more. If David Morton's business expands, his compressor may just not be big enough to handle the demands made on it.

What happens if you calculate depreciation wrongly?

It would require someone much cleverer than the average accountant to estimate depreciation with 100% accuracy. Even if an asset is sold at the expected time, it is unlikely to sell for the estimated written down value. If an asset is sold for less than the book value then, in effect, a bit more depreciation has to be charged to the profit and loss statement in the year it is sold. For example:

David Morton uses the straight line method to depreciate his compressor. After five years the written down value is £500, but he sells the compressor for only £400.

Written down value	£500
Sale proceeds	£400
'Loss' on sale	£100

This 'loss' on sale is the extra bit of depreciation that will have to be **written off** in Year 5. It will not be shown as depreciation, but separately as 'Loss on sale of fixed assets'. If the compressor was sold for £600, then the 'profit' would be shown as 'Profit on sale of fixed assets'.

Does depreciation only apply to fixed assets?

We have assumed so far that only fixed assets are depreciated. Current assets after all we don't keep for long enough to depreciate. But there is one type of current asset that we may keep for longer than we would like – stock. In an average dealership, a glance in the remote and dusty bins at the back of the parts department may reveal a few antiques. They may have deteriorated or become obsolete and be worth less than the original cost. They may be worth only scrap value.

These sorts of items should be depreciated in the same way as fixed assets. As a general rule stock should be valued at '**the lower of cost or net realisable value**'. Net realisable value is the amount for which the items can be sold, less the cost of selling them. If this figure is *less* than the business paid, then this is the value the business should place on them. The advantage of depreciating stock is that the balance sheet will include the stock at the reduced and more realistic value. The profit will also be reduced by the amount written off. This will also be more realistic and should reduce the tax bill.

Banking

What types of banks are there?

When we refer to 'the bank', we usually mean the high street banks that we use either as individuals or as a business. These are called the **clearing banks** because they 'clear' cheques for payment. Other types of banks you may hear about are:

Merchant banks, which mainly raise capital for industry.

The **Bank of England**, which acts as the government's banker.

In this section we are referring to the activities of the clearing banks, which are the National Westminster, Barclays, Lloyds and the Midland, operating mainly in England and Wales. The Bank of Scotland, the Royal Bank of Scotland and the Clydesdale are found mainly in Scotland.

What services do banks offer?

Banks offer a variety of services to individuals and to a business. These include:

- Payment by cheque – a simple and secure way to make and receive payment.

- Lending money to customers in the form of a loan or overdraft.

- Taking deposits of surplus cash and paying interest on them.

- Issuing **cheque cards**, **cash cards** and **credit cards**.

- Arranging **standing orders**, **credit transfers** and **direct debits**.

- Issuing foreign currency and travellers cheques.

- Giving advice on investment and taxation.

Some of these we shall deal with in greater detail shortly.

Are there additional services for a business?

Some services are provided particularly for business customers:

- Advice, from the bank manager or business adviser, on a range of business problems and opportunities.

- Arranging finance through factoring, HP or leasing (see Section A).

- Providing a **night safe** for secure overnight banking of takings.

What types of bank account are there?

There are two basic types of account, a **current account** and a **deposit account.**

- Current account. This is the most common type of bank account. No interest is paid by the bank for money kept in the account, but a customer can get at the money immediately by writing out a cheque or using a cash card.

- Deposit account. Unlike a current account, a deposit account pays interest, but it's not so easy to withdraw money from the account. A cheque book is not issued and with some accounts there is a penalty for withdrawing money without sufficient notice. A deposit account is useful to a business with surplus cash.

How does the cheque system work?

You are probably familiar with the cheque system from your own experience. Using a cheque offers a safe and secure way of transferring money between individuals and businesses without resorting to the hazardous procedure of moving round large quantities of cash. The bank makes a charge for each cheque processed.

Drawers and payees

- The person or business who makes out the cheque, and whose bank balance will decrease, is called the **drawer**.

- The person or business to whom the cheque is made payable is called the **payee**.

What is a crossed cheque?

Cheques can either be **open** or **crossed**. An open cheque can be turned into cash at the bank issuing the cheque. This can lead to forging of signatures and fraud. For this reason most businesses use crossed cheques. Two lines are printed on the face of the cheque and this means that the cheque has to be paid into a bank account, rather than cashed. The addition of the words 'Account Payee Only' means that the cheque can only be paid into the account of the person or business named on the cheque.

Using a cheque card

Customers who pay by cheque are usually asked to show a cheque card. Also known as a service card, this will guarantee that the bank will honour the customer's cheque up to the limit shown on the back of the card. The card contains a code number which should be written on the back of the cheque. It also shows the customer's signature, which should be compared with signature on the cheque. A cheque card can also be used to withdraw money from cash dispensers.

Examining a cheque

Any cheque that a business receives should be examined carefully before acceptance.

- Look at the date – is it today's date? A post-dated cheque, dated some time in the future will not be credited to your account by the bank until that date. A cheque more than six months old is no longer valid.

- Is the cheque made out to the correct business name?

- Do the figures and words agree?

- Has it been signed?

- Are there any alterations? There must be a signature next to any alterations.

- Has the customer produced a valid cheque card?

What is a dishonoured cheque?

A **dishonoured** cheque is a cheque that the customer's bank refuses to pay. This can be for a number of reasons:

- Insufficient funds in the customer's account. This is usually referred to as a 'bouncing cheque'. The bank will return the cheque to you, usually marked 'Refer to Drawer', and it is then up to you to try to get payment from the customer.

- Because you have not examined the cheque carefully enough and there is an error (e.g. unsigned alterations).

- The signature differs from the bank's records.
- The customer has '**stopped**' the cheque.

What is a stopped cheque?

Anyone making out a cheque may instruct the bank to stop payment (unless the cheque is covered by a cheque card – see below). A cheque may be stopped for a variety of reasons, honest and otherwise.

- A cheque may have been lost in the post. In this case a new cheque can be made out and the old one can be stopped.
- The customer is unhappy with the goods purchased and wishes to return them, or negotiate a lower price.
- The customer is happy with the goods but is dishonest and just doesn't want to pay for them.

A business can avoid these sorts of problems by:

- For cheques under the cheque card limit – make sure that the customer presents a valid cheque card. A customer using a cheque card cannot stop a cheque.
- For cheques over the cheque card limit – unless the customer is known and trusted, do not release the goods until the cheque has been cleared. This is particularly important in the case of high value items like cars.

What about other ways of transferring money?

The use of cheques and hard cash has been declining for some years, as advances in electronics and banking have made possible more convenient methods of moving money around. We shall look at:

* Standing orders.

* Direct debits.

* Credit transfers.

* The 'BACS' system.

* Credit cards.

* Debit cards.

* Telephone banking.

* PC banking.

What is a standing order?

Anyone with a bank account can order the bank to pay out money on a regular date to a business or any other individual or institution. Rent, insurance premiums, or any other payment which stays the same for a reasonable time can be paid like this.

The advantage of a standing order is that payment happens automatically, without invoices, reminders, cheques and postage being involved.

What is a direct debit?

A direct debit is similar to a standing order except that the payee, and not the drawer, informs the bank of the amount to be paid. This has the same advantages as the standing order and the drawer does not have to inform the bank of any increases. The drawer must of course agree to this arrangement by signing a **mandate form** for the payee. The system works well for annual subscriptions which tend to rise each year and for payments like water rates, where there is no competition and no alternative but to pay.

What is a credit transfer?

The credit transfer system can be used by customers and non-customers of the bank. A gas or telephone bill for instance can be taken to the bank, who will then credit the payee with the money. Non-customers would of course have to hand cash over the counter, but would save on postal orders and postage.

What is the 'BACS' system?

This is a form of credit transfer that is becoming increasingly popular for businesses making routine payments. Instead of making out many cheques, a business can fill out a largely pre-printed form with details of payment amounts to regular suppliers, along with one cheque to cover all the payments. Each bank markets this service under a different name, e.g. 'Autopay', and it is frequently used for the payment of salaries and commission.

Payment by credit card

People nowadays carry less cash around in purse or pocket due to the popularity of credit cards. The most widely used are MasterCard and Barclaycard and both companies are controlled by the banks.

A huge number of retail businesses, including garages, now accept payment by credit card. Each card holder is given a credit limit, which is the total amount that may be owed at any one time. When a purchase is made the card is pressed onto the voucher machine. The customer signs the voucher and takes one copy. The retailer can then take one of the retained copies to the bank, who will pay the money due into the retailer's account, less a small percentage commission.

Increasingly, even the smallest garage or retailer uses a computerised card reader. The computer adds the total credit card takings for the day and sends the information via a telephone line to the bank. This is all done automatically and saves the retailer a great deal of time and effort.

What are the advantages for a customer?

- Convenience – purchases involving quite large sums of money can be made instantly and without the need for cash or a cheque.

- Credit – the purchaser does not have to find the money for around four to six weeks. If payment is made to the credit company within 25 days of the statement date, no interest is payable. Payments after this date incur interest payments.

- Only one cheque per month has to be made out for all credit card purchases.

What are the advantages to the retailer?

- Because customers don't have to find the cash when they buy, they are inclined to spend more and to buy on impulse.

- Guaranteed payment – the credit card company guarantees payment, less their percentage of course.

- Payment doesn't have to be collected from lots of different customers.

What is a debit card?

An increasingly popular method of payment is a **debit card**, usually better known by a brand name such as 'Delta' or 'Switch'. This can be incorporated into a cheque card and is acceptable in an increasing number of retail outlets, including garages. It is *not* a credit card, but works in a similar way to a cheque. Instead of writing out a cheque, a customer can hand over the card, sign a voucher, and his or her current account will be debited in about three working days. The advantage for retailer and customer is that, unlike with a cheque, there is no particular limit. Providing there are sufficient funds in the account, payment up to any amount is authorised immediately by the bank's computer system.

Telephone and PC banking

As banks attempt to become more flexible, there are increasing options for all of us to gain access to our bank accounts. Most banks now allow customers to transfer money by telephone, using passwords to maintain security.

As computers become a normal part of equipment in the home and in business, most banks now offer **PC banking**. By dialling into the bank's computer, customers can have access to the same screen of information as the bank staff and can move money around accordingly. Security is effective but not obstructive, and this is an option that is proving extremely popular with business customers.

Bank statements

A record is kept by the bank of all transactions and a business will receive a copy of this in the form of a **bank statement** at least every month. A business keeps its own records of course, but the bank statement is a very useful check. At the end of each month the business will compare the bank statement with its own cash book to highlight any errors in its own records, or that the bank may have made.

Bank lending

One important service which banks provide for business is to lend money. We have already discussed the funding of a business in Section A, and said that a business may borrow money from the bank in the form of a loan or an overdraft. We have also looked at what the money is used for – to buy fixed assets or to finance things like stock. And how the balance sheet examines both sides of the equation – where the money comes from, and what it is used for. If the money comes from the bank, what is it used for?

What is a bank loan for?

A loan, as distinct from an overdraft, is most often used to buy the fixed assets of a business. The agreed amount will be credited by the bank to a special loan account, and this amount will be repaid over a period of time, usually between two and ten years. Banks may also provide much longer term loans, repayable over ten to thirty years. Security will have to be provided, and bank managers prefer land and buildings to less 'permanent' assets.

What is an overdraft used for?

A loan is usually used for fixed assets. An overdraft is used for the other thing that a business needs money for – working capital. Because cash flows into and out of the business at different times, there may be a time when there is no money left in the current account. At these times, by prior agreement with the bank and up to a certain limit, a business may be allowed to overdraw, or go 'into the red'. The Squib Firework Company is a good example of a business using a temporary overdraft while waiting for customers to pay. A car dealership will often go into the red just before the January and August peak sales periods, which will put them back 'into the black'.

An overdraft is strictly temporary (in theory at any rate) and for smaller overdrafts, security may not be necessary.

What is the bank rate?

You often hear, on the national news, that the bank rate has risen or fallen by say, a half of one per cent. This is known as the **bank base rate**, and is the figure on which banks base their charges for lending money to businesses and individuals. A bank will not lend money at this rate, but at so many per cent over the base rate. Interest on a loan is charged at between 1% and 4% over base rate, depending on the size of the loan, the size of the business, and the risk involved. Overdraft interest is usually slightly higher, varying between 3% and 5% over base rate.

How does a change in the rate affect a business?

A change in interest rates affects the whole of the economy, not just a business borrowing money. Lower interest rates mean lower costs, lower prices, more expansion and more demand from customers. Higher interest rates mean higher costs, higher prices, lower output and less customer demand. The motor industry, selling high priced goods, is particularly affected by high interest rates, in a way that a supermarket may not be. People don't have to buy a new car, but they do have to eat.

For the individual business, we have seen earlier how loan interest has to be paid out of profits. If interest rates go up that means much less profit for the shareholders' dividend and for expansion. Profits may also be low because customers are just not buying. The shareholders may be willing to forgo a bit of dividend, but the bank will always insist on its percentage, however much profits are down. High interest rates are therefore bad news for business.

Banking in the future

Banking has changed out of all recognition over the last few decades. Plastic cards are becoming the dominant feature of payment in retailing and as cards become 'smarter' and electronics and telecommunications increase in sophistication, this trend seems likely to continue.

There is intense competition between banks and from other institutions like building societies. Banks now adopt very aggressive marketing strategies, many of them aimed at the business market, and the sort of services offered will change and expand over the next few years. Keeping in touch with these developments and using them effectively in the financial management of a business will become increasingly important.

What is 'Mondex'?

Mondex is an example of a change in technology that will radically affect the way in which transfers of money will take place in future. Mondex is a **smart card**, which can electronically store cash on a microchip. Mondex is an international company, but the system in this country is being developed by a number of the major banks and BT. It was introduced in Swindon on a trial basis in 1995 and is planned to go nation-wide in the late 1990's. Some of the features are:

- Users will be able to download cash from their bank (or pay in) using a special telephone or their PC.

- Retailers will have a small device to 'swipe' the card which will download the exact amount paid directly to their bank account.

- An 'electronic lock' gives complete security unless unlocked by a personal code.

- Transactions will be faster, with no pin number, signature or change.

- Secure payments by phone or via the internet.

- Suitable for transactions of any size, from pence to the price of a new car.

Mondex, or similar systems, seem likely to revolutionise cash transactions and should result in benefits for retailers. Cash will be transferred quickly and securely, and the costs of counting, securing and transporting notes and coins should be reduced.

Insurance

Why insure?

None of us enjoys paying for insurance. After all, we are trying to cover ourselves against disasters which we desperately hope will never happen. But there are risks attached to all businesses, and insurance against at least some of these risks is vital. What risks should a business insure against? Taking the wrong decision could be costly, or even result in the collapse of the business.

How does insurance work?

The idea of insurance is simple. Say for example that 1,000 people want to insure their houses against the risk of fire. They all pay a small premium to an insurance company, which holds the 'pool' of money until one of the houses burns down. They then pay out a large sum to the person making the claim. None of the 1,000 by themselves could bear the huge loss, but by insuring they spread the risk. Everyone pays a little but only a few claim a lot.

Should a business insure against all possible risks?

No. It's not possible to insure against absolutely every risk, but even where it is possible to insure, the cost may make it prohibitively expensive. A business has to be selective and decide which risks it can take itself, and which should be covered by insurance. Some risks have to be insured against by law and we shall discuss these shortly.

What is an insurable risk?

You can only insure against risks which, if they happen, will involve you in some sort of loss. For instance, you can insure your own premises against fire, but not the premises of the business down the road. Even if it burnt down, you would suffer no loss. You must have an **insurable interest**.

What does the 'utmost good faith' mean?

All insurance contracts are subject to special conditions. They are called (in Latin) **contracts uberrimae fidei**, which means 'of the utmost good faith'. This means that you *have* to tell the insurance company of any factors which might make them increase the premium, or refuse to insure you, even if the insurance company fails to ask. These sort of contracts are covered in detail in The Institute's Student Guide to Motor Trade Law.

What is indemnity?

Insurance contracts, except for personal insurance, are also **contracts of indemnity**. This means that an insurance company will pay out enough money (but not too much) to compensate the insured for the loss involved. In other words the business should be restored to the position it was in before the event took place, but should not make a profit out of it. You know from your own experience that if you insure a new car for £7,000 and write it off two years later, the insurance company will only pay out the value of a two year old car, not a new one.

What types of insurance are there?

There are two main categories of insurance that a business needs:

- Statutory insurance, which means insurance that a business must have by law.

- Optional insurance against risks and disasters.

What statutory insurance must a business have?

A business must have insurance cover by law for the following:

- Employers' liability.

- Motor insurance.

- Engineering equipment insurance.

What is employers' liability insurance?

This is to cover any accidents or illness to an employee as a result of working for the business. Employers would be covered against claims for injury or death to employees. This would apply during the normal course of employment whether the employee was on or off the premises. This is particularly important in the motor trade where employees are in potentially dangerous situations while driving in the course of their work.

What motor insurance must a business have?

Any vehicle used on a public road must be insured for injury caused to other people, including a passenger. This is known as **Road Traffic Act** insurance and is compulsory. It is very rare to stick to such basic cover and most businesses have at least **third party, fire and theft** cover. This covers the statutory insurance but also includes damage caused to other people's property and some legal costs. To cover accidental damage to vehicles, whoever is to blame, a business would need **fully comprehensive** insurance.

A dealership using large numbers of constantly changing

vehicles would usually opt for **block vehicle insurance**, which allows any authorised person to drive company vehicles. While this is expensive, effective motor insurance is obviously a high priority in the motor trade.

What about engineering equipment?

By law, certain plant and machinery such as air compressors and lifting equipment has to be inspected and tested at regular intervals. This can be combined with an insurance policy to cover the business against the risk of accident or explosion.

What optional insurance does a business need?

Statutory insurance is the absolute minimum, but a business that failed to take advantage of at least some of the insurance policies available would be risking disaster. This non-compulsory insurance is often called 'catastrophe' insurance, and the following are the most common options:

- Fire and other perils – covers destruction and damage to buildings and contents due to fire, flood, storms etc. Vital to all businesses.

- Loss of profits – if the business cannot operate due to a fire for example, this sort of policy would cover payments to staff and normal profits. Useful to dealerships where it would be difficult to move, but unlikely to tempt a smaller business like David Morton.

- Theft – covers loss or damage to contents or premises. Vital in the motor trade.

- Loss of money – covers theft of cash or cheques from premises or while in transit (except theft by employees). Vital in the motor trade where large quantities of cash are involved.

- Theft or fraud by employees – called **fidelity guarantee insurance**. Important in the motor trade.

- **Credit insurance** – protection against your customers failing to pay. Expensive and not very useful in the motor trade where most payments are in cash or on delivery.

- Glass breakage – plate glass windows in showrooms are very expensive and a dealership would normally have this cover.

- Vandalism – damage to premises. May be useful in high risk areas.

- Business equipment – damage to signs, petrol pumps and tanks etc. May be useful.

- **Public liability** – covers injury or illness to members of the public or damage to their property caused by your business. Vital in the motor trade as claims can be very high.

- **Product liability** – covers the same things but specifically as a result of your products. This would normally be the responsibility of the motor manufacturer, rather than the trader.

- **Keyman insurance** – if the business would suffer badly in the event of a key person dying (like a partner), it is possible to take out life insurance on them.

How does a business choose which policies to buy?

Most people in business like to think positively and do not enjoy anticipating all the disasters that might occur in the future. But it has to be done and the decisions are not always easy to take.

Some decisions are straightforward. Fire, and public liability insurance for instance, are not very expensive, but the result of *not* having them can be disastrous. Insurance for loss of profits is much more difficult to assess. A business will consider three things when making decisions:

- What is the *risk* involved?
- What are the *consequences* if the worst happens?
- How much is the *premium* to be paid?

The business has to strike a balance between the three. In effect the manager is asking 'can we afford to have it, and can we afford *not* to have it?'.

A yearly review of insurance?

All too often a business will just carry on paying for the same insurance policies year after year. Even worse, it may forget to renew a policy. Circumstances change, both within the business and in terms of the kinds of policy on offer. The value of items may also increase considerably. For these reasons it is essential for all businesses to sit down and thoroughly assess their insurance needs every year.

What factors affect the size of insurance premiums?

Premiums are fixed by the insurance companies according to the risks involved and the number and size of claims likely to be made. They will have access to a variety of statistics and will closely monitor any changes in society which affect claims made. For instance an increase in car thefts and thefts from cars has recently resulted in a substantial increase in motor insurance premiums.

For the individual the size of the premium may also depend on geographical location. The incidence of crime in cities means that premiums are usually higher than in country areas. Policyholders who claim frequently are also likely to face increased premiums. When taking out insurance it is also possible to choose the type and amount of cover you want, and therefore how much you can afford to pay. Any personal insurance premiums will depend on the age, occupation and health of the person involved.

What happens if you over insure?

You will pay more in premiums but receive no extra benefits. The insurance company will only pay out what they consider to be the value of the item insured.

What happens if you under insure?

This is much more likely to happen, particularly without an annual review to assess the value of items insured. In this case the insurance company will not pay out the full value but only the value shown in the policy. With a fire policy it may only pay out a proportion of this value.

A building should be insured not for its market value, but for the cost of replacing it, including the cost of clearing the site and building new premises.

Where should you buy insurance?

The usual answer to this is through an **insurance broker**. Insurance brokers are independent advisers and not attached to a particular insurance company. They can therefore shop around for the best deal, give you information about what is on offer, and have to behave in accordance with a code of conduct.

Insurance companies have their own representatives and offer standard policies for the motor trade. The **Motor Traders Combined Policy** for example covers a wide variety of insurance from which a trader can make the appropriate choices

Section C

PROFIT PLANNING

The Company Profit Plan

Why plan for profit?

We have seen in previous sections why a business needs to make a profit – to pay interest on loans, to pay a reasonable dividend to shareholders investing in the business, and to provide the cheapest source of funds for expansion. Unfortunately, profits do not happen automatically. Working hard and carrying on the way we did in the past is not enough. A business needs to adapt and change, to use flair and imagination, and to *plan* ahead.

Looking at the past

The past is not a foolproof guide to what is likely to happen in the future, but it certainly cannot be ignored. The first step in the planning process is to look at past results and see what can be learned from them. What sales did each department make last year? How much profit? And how did these figures compare with last year's plan? What did we do right? And where did we go wrong? A business is no different from an individual – it can learn from its mistakes.

Where are we now?

The next stage is to examine the present position of the business. What are our strengths and weaknesses? What financial resources do we have? What fixed assets do we have and in what condition? What about stock – is it too high or too low, or of the wrong sort? What about the order book? How much money are we owed? How much cash do we have? How much money do we owe? And what about the people who work for the business – any weak points, or promotion candidates? What about the competition – who are they and what are they up to?

An assessment of all these questions, together with a long hard look at the general economic situation both nationally and locally, is a firm foundation for the next and most important stage – planning for the future.

Where do we want to go?

Examining past performance and the present position is comparatively easy. Predicting the future is not. When running a business there is always a tendency to get bogged down in day to day affairs and to ignore the problems and possibilities of tomorrow. A business that ignores planning leaves its future prosperity to chance.

The one thing that is predictable is that things will not stay the same. There will be changes in what we buy, what we sell, and in the way we sell. Remember the changes in retailing that we discussed in Section A? The successful businesses have been the ones that anticipated the changes and got in ahead of the competition. It's not enough to react to the changes you see around you – you have to make the changes first.

Managing the future

You will remember from Section B of Management, that planning is a part of attempting to manage the future. The steps involved are:

- The mission statement – the overall aims of the business.

- Objectives – some of which will be expressed in financial terms.

- Planning – both short and long-term, and involving strategy and tactics.

- Evaluation – comparing what actually happens with the plan.

Are all plans financial?

Not all plans are expressed in financial terms, but almost all have some financial implications. Sales, costs and profit have to be planned, in addition to the replacement of worn out assets and plans for expansion. We have also seen that managers have to plan out when the cash comes into the business and when it goes out. Detailed financial plans are usually shown in the form of budgets, which we briefly discussed in Management, Section B.

Evaluation through budgets

It would be foolish to devote so much time and effort to the business plan and then to put it into a drawer and forget about it. It's vital that what happens in practice is compared with the plan – are the strategies and tactics producing the desired objectives? Budgets not only express the plan in financial terms, but also enable managers to control the business by showing where things are not going according to plan in time for corrective action to be taken.

We shall cover budgetary control in detail shortly, but in the meantime we shall concentrate on an essential part of the planning process – planning for profit.

How can profit be improved?

Business plans will of course be shown in great detail and will include marketing strategies, personnel details and product information. But in business, the 'bottom line' is always profit, and a manager is unlikely to say 'Our strategy worked brilliantly but we made a loss'. A plan centres on making more profit. How can this be done?

At the end of Section A we briefly discussed the limits to profit, and suggested that the ways to increase profit were to:

- Increase the volume of sales.

- Increase sales price.

- Decrease costs.

We shall investigate each of these in turn.

How can the volume of sales be increased?

This is the key question in the motor trade where the market is very sensitive to increases in price. For the individual dealer, selling more cars, more parts and more services than its competitors is the best way to increase profits. It can do this by:

- Getting the sales staff to sell more – greater incentives, more supervision, training.

- Improve the product – largely up to the manufacturer, although dealers have control over the way in which the product is sold.

- Policy adjustments – offering better incentives to customers, finance deals, sunroofs and other promotions.

- Reducing the price – this is only popular with customers, but sometimes happens in a recession.

- Increasing output of service and repair departments by using the facilities and staff more efficiently, or by extending and increasing them.

Some of these options will cost money and would have to be assessed carefully as part of the planning process.

How can sales prices be increased?

Sales prices do increase, all too often if you are a customer. Regular price increases apply to all manufacturers and are usually fairly similar. The individual dealer is not in a position to increase list prices and would be committing commercial suicide if it tried. The only options are to:

- Try to sell profitable 'extras' – accessories, expensive radios etc.

- Tighten up on discounts allowed.

- Reduce part exchange allowances – but this may lower the volume of sales.

A more realistic option would be to concentrate on selling the products that make most profit. This is one of the reasons why costing products is so important.

How can a business reduce costs?

There are very few businesses that could not cut out a few unnecessary costs, or do things more efficiently. The areas that can be investigated for savings are:

- Materials – is it possible to use less, to reduce scrap, to reduce obsolescence, to guard against theft, to control stock more effectively? Is the buyer doing a good job? Could we pay less, subcontract some jobs, buy some things in bulk?

- Labour – do staff have the right skills, is it possible to increase productivity by offering a bonus or incentive? Do we pay some staff too much? Is extra training needed, what about time keeping and absenteeism and overtime? Are the staff reasonably happy and are they kept informed about the business?

- Overheads – is spending on overheads closely monitored and controlled? Who decides what will be spent? How effectively is space used? Could clerical procedures be streamlined?

All costs tend to creep up unless managers are constantly vigilant. The most successful businesses are those where any member of staff can ask 'why do we spend money on this?', or 'why do we do it that way?' Most people are more likely to make suggestions if they feel they will share in the benefits. A way of creating this sort of atmosphere is by introducing **profit related incentives**.

What is a profit related incentive?

An incentive is a reward, usually of money, for working harder or more effectively. Sales staff commission is a form of incentive and shop floor wages often have an element of incentive in them. A profit related incentive means that some part of the earnings of staff depend on the amount of profit made, either in their department or for the whole business. The idea is that people will be encouraged to make the link between how hard they work, how much profit is made, and the amount they earn.

How well does it work?

Not particularly well. The problems are that:

- There is a very long gap between the effort put in and the reward. People may not connect the two.

- To affect profits significantly a whole group of people have to work together. But single individuals may feel that they have little influence over the performance of the group.

- Profit is affected by many factors and not just the efforts of staff. They may work hard but find that profits are down for some other reason beyond their control.

How can better customer relations improve profits?

We said earlier that in the motor trade, the best way to increase profits is by increasing the volume of sales. Increased sales means new customers, but also not losing old customers. Dealerships are lucky in that many customers remain loyal and will keep coming back. But that loyalty is also very fragile – one serious row and they are gone forever. Remember that what may be just another car to you is probably the customer's second most valuable possession.

The customer is the single most important part of a business and *must* come first. Remember what we said in Section A about keeping the customer satisfied in the retail trade? Honest straightforward dealing, promises kept, friendliness, courtesy and competence will help to keep customers coming back for more. They may also help to increase profits by recommending you to new customers.

How can good knowledge of the product increase profits?

The motor trade is not dealing in baked beans. It's dealing in technically complex and expensive equipment that most people own or use, but few people understand in any depth. A dealership has to match a customer's needs with the products available. Since many customers, for cars, parts, service or repair, are unsure about their needs, it's doubly important that you have an expert knowledge of your product.

Knowing your own products, and those of your competitors, means that you can point out the features of your own product that will fulfil a customer's needs and solve their problems. In order to keep customers, rather than just make a sale, this advice and help has to be genuine and not just a sales technique. Know your products, put them over well, and you can increase sales, improve customer relations and contribute to a growth in profits.

Credit control and profit

In the section on accounting systems, we looked at the accounts kept for customers (the sales or debtors' ledger) and the role of the credit controller, who is responsible for getting customers to pay up on time. Then in the section on cash flow, we saw how there is a big difference between cash and profit, and how waiting for money to come in can cause problems. We also said that dealerships are in some ways lucky, because sales are often paid for immediately. But in order to encourage certain types of customer, such as other businesses, most dealerships and garages offer credit, and therefore cannot afford to be complacent.

If credit control is poor and customers pay late, then too much of the funds available to the business will be tied up in debtors. These funds would be better used to buy fixed assets or more stock, either of which should eventually result in higher profits. And if there is a shortage of funds, if the business has an overdraft for instance, the situation is even worse. The customers fail to pay, the overdraft increases, and extra interest will have to be paid – which of course will reduce profits.

How can self-service improve profits?

Section A discussed the changes in retailing that have revolutionised our high streets. Many of these changes are connected with the increase in supermarkets and self-service shops. In the motor trade, sales of cars and parts have been largely unaffected, but petrol sales are now largely self-service and forecourt shops tempt petrol buyers with a wide variety of goods from chocolate bars to coal. Some of the advantages to the trader are:

- Savings in the number of staff employed.

- Customers may buy things on impulse.

- Increased custom due to the greater range of goods on offer and possibly lower prices.

- High profit margins on some items.

There are also advantages to the customer:

- Easy parking compared to most shops.

- Lower prices on some items.

- Longer opening hours than many shops.

- Time to browse.

Petrol and forecourt sales are well suited to self-service, but it's unlikely that cars will ever be sold in this way. Some dealerships sell a limited amount of parts by self-service, although personal service will always be needed for many sales. But looking at accessory shops such as Halfords, and seeing the sort of changes made in other trades (builders' merchants for instance) there seems to be scope for a greater role for self-service in parts sales.

How might changes in the environment affect a profit plan?

A business does not operate in total isolation from its environment. Changes in national and local economic conditions and other changes in society may affect profit plans.

- National economic conditions – we have already discussed the impact of high interest rates on a business. Not only do costs increase, but customers are also much less likely to buy. Changes in government transport policy are also important. Subsidising public transport or increasing taxes on petrol are likely to reduce motor industry profits.

- Local economic conditions – boom and recession some-times happen on a national scale, but the effects are often distributed unevenly, some areas suffering from high unemployment and depressed sales, others faring better. Building developments, new roads and motor-ways can all have an impact, good or bad, on the profits of an individual business.

- Fashion and taste – your products may just go out of fashion. It is the job of marketing to try to ensure that this does not happen.

- Consumer demand – consumer organisations are now very vocal and may make demands over safety, quality and reliability.

- Environmental concerns – the public is becoming in-creasingly aware of the damage which is being caused to the environment, and the car is in the front line. Demand for more environmentally friendly vehicles may increase the demand for a particular make, and reduce it for another.

What difficulties might a department have in achieving the company's profit plan?

Shortly we shall be looking at the profit plan for each department. We shall discuss the difficulties that a depart-ment might face and see that most of the problems are the same as those faced by the business as a whole. There are particular difficulties, however:

- The results that one department achieves may be depen-dent on the success of another. If new and used car sales do not reach expected levels, then the number of services performed may also drop.

- If the profit plan is imposed on a department by senior management, the staff may not feel that the required profit is attainable. Planned profit must be agreed by those people expected to achieve it. The way in which this is done is what we shall turn to next.

The Departmental Profit Plan

A profit plan for each department?

So far we have discussed the profit plan for the business as a whole. Is it necessary to break it down to show the contribution of each department? Yes it is. In fact in arriving at the final company plan, the figures will have been built up from the profit plans of each separate department.

How is the plan arrived at?

There is a two way process in arriving at the final profit plans. A month or so before the end of the financial year, the management will set about the task of preparing the detailed plans for the following year. The directors will decide on the objectives, strategy and tactics for the whole business, and then in discussion with individual managers will see what contribution each department will make. The final plan will be the result of negotiation. There may be good reasons why individual departments cannot achieve the required profits. As we stated in the previous section, the results of one department may also depend on the performance of another. Arriving at the final figures is a difficult and lengthy procedure involving disagreements and compromise. But it's important to get it right, and that all departments are committed to carrying out their part of the plan.

What form will departmental profit plans take?

The basic form of any profit plan or forecast will be very similar to that of the profit and loss account we described in Section B. A profit and loss account looks at what has happened in the past, a profit plan tries to predict what will happen in the future.

A profit plan will therefore estimate sales for the coming year, then direct material and labour costs, to arrive at gross profit. Departmental overheads are then deducted to show net profit. All the net profits for each department added together should equal the total net profit forecast by the whole business.

The way in which sales are expressed will be different for each department:

- New and used car sales – number of cars expected to be sold (possibly broken down into each type) and total value.

- Parts sales – total value, or may be broken down if appropriate.

- Service and repair – number of labour hours charged out to customers and total value.

- Forecourt sales – litres of petrol sold and value. Value of other forecourt sales.

What happens next?

Preparing the profit plan is only half the battle. Remember what we said earlier about evaluation and control? The profit plan for the year will be broken down into months, and at the end of each month the accounts department will prepare figures for what actually happened. This will be better or worse than the plan, and the management will meet to discuss the differences. This is known as **management by exception**. Where things are going according to plan, or very close, everything is fine and there is no point in spending time on it. The management team will concentrate on those areas where things have not gone according

to plan. Where profits are up there will be praise and con-
gratulations. Where they are lower than expected then it's
more important to find out why, and to try to put it right.
The problem may be beyond the manager's control (a rise
in interest rates affecting sales for instance) in which case
there is no point in blaming the manager.

How can a department improve profitability?

In exactly the same way as the business as a whole – the
rules are just the same. An individual department can
increase sales volume, increase sales prices, or reduce
costs:

- Increase sales volume – a department has a lot of control
  over the number of products or hours of work that it
  sells and can influence sales volume by its own efforts.

- Increase sales price – a department does not usually
  have much influence over sales prices which are normally set by manufacturers or by top management. New and
  used car sales do have a certain amount of leeway over
  trade-in prices. And the manager of a department can
  choose to promote sales of those products which give the
  biggest profit.

- Reduce costs – all departments have a responsibility to
  control and reduce costs and we shall see in the next section how budgets help to do this.

What about the other factors which affect profit?

All the other factors that we talked about for the business
as a whole apply to each department – the giving of credit,
product knowledge, customer relations and different ways
of organising sales such as self-service. The way that customers see the business as a whole is through their dealings with each individual department. A row with the

service manager can affect not just the future profits of the service department, but the profits of car sales as well.

What factors can adversely affect profit?

There's an easy answer to this – exactly the opposite of all the things which improve profits. Reduced sales volume or prices, increased costs, poor product knowledge and customer relations, badly organised ways of selling, inefficiency and broken promises. If, as many people suggest, sales of new cars are likely to be depressed for many years to come, the businesses that fail to come up to scratch and make the necessary improvements will suffer from much more than reduced profits and are unlikely to survive.

Improving profit from capital equipment

A business invests money in capital equipment (fixed assets) in order to try to make a profit. There is no point in spending hundreds of pounds on a specialist tool if it's only used once and then sits gathering dust and taking up valuable space. Look around your own place of work. Can you see any items that fit this description? Most businesses have them. It may be because a bad decision was taken in the past and that there is no customer demand for its use. But it's often because the management is not actively promoting the asset.

A small garage buys or leases an expensive diagnostic tuning device. It will be used during the course of normal service and repair work, but this may not be enough to pay for its keep. The manager would also need to make potential customers aware that the garage is able to offer an additional service. This could be done by local press advertising, or by drawing it to the attention of existing customers (on letters, invoices, by notices on the forecourt etc.).

Managers should regularly assess what assets they have under their control and whether they are being adequately utilised. If not, is there some way of marketing them more effectively?

How can a department prevent the loss of materials and equipment?

Every piece of equipment or item of stock that goes missing has to be replaced. This costs money and reduces profit. In the building trade losses from pilfering are quite considerable. The motor trade does not suffer to the same extent, but you will all be aware of things that have quietly disappeared from your own place of work. Parts, tools and self-service items are most likely to be stolen, and staff and customers are the most likely suspects. How can these sorts of losses be prevented?

- Good security – parts and all except the most frequently used tools should be kept under lock and key. Only the staff responsible should have access to these areas.

- Close supervision – the use of these items should be under the guidance and control of the work supervisor.

- Control of customers – customers should not be allowed in any secure area and if possible should be (politely) discouraged from entering work areas.

- Surveillance of self-service areas – this can be done in smaller areas by a beady-eyed cashier. Large displays may mean using closed circuit television, which is quite expensive and may give offence to some customers.

- Vehicle parks – these should have a locked barrier and must have good lighting at night.

The best way of preventing the loss of equipment and materials is to have a practical and effective way of issuing them from stores to the workshop. This is what we turn to next.

Why is a stock control system necessary?

An efficient stock control system is important from a financial point of view. Too little stock means that customers will go elsewhere and jobs will be held up. Too much stock means that customers will be satisfied, but more capital than necessary will be used to finance it. Either way profits will be reduced. A business can also lose money by failing to control the use of materials.

How is the use of materials controlled?

An inefficient method of issuing materials and parts to a workshop is an open invitation to dishonesty. The larger the organisation, the more formal the system will have to be. A typical arrangement would be:

- An order is raised by the service or repair manager who deals directly with the customer. This is given to the workshop supervisor.

- The supervisor will assess what parts are needed and raise a material requisition. This will be taken to the stores and exchanged for the actual parts. The storekeeper will raise the paperwork to be sent to the accounts department so that they can prepare an invoice.

This sounds like a long and tedious procedure, but larger garages will have a computer system that should reduce the amount of time involved, if not the quantity of paper. With so many people involved, and so many expensive parts, the system has to be foolproof. The use of multi-part documents is covered in Section D.

How is the issue of equipment controlled?

Expensive specialist tools will soon 'walk' if they are left lying around in the workshop. They should be issued only when needed and returned immediately after use. The most effective way of achieving this is to keep equipment of this sort in the parts stores. They can be issued at the same time as parts needed for the job and signed for by the mechanic, who will then be responsible for them until they are returned.

Budgetary Control

What is a budget?

A **budget** is a detailed financial plan for the future, and we have already come across two examples, although we did not call them budgets at the time. The profit plan that we have just looked at, and the cash flow forecast are both budgets, and the most important budgets at that. In fact we have already covered much of what we need to know about budgets, particularly how we prepare them, in the sections on planning. We do, however, need to look at financial plans in more detail, to see how we use budgets to control the business, and to discuss the advantages and problems of budgets.

It's part of the plan

The budget is really the financial part of the business plan. A business plan, as we have already said, will cover objectives, strategy, tactics, marketing, personnel matters, product information, technical changes and a whole host of matters that will be described in words. But the result of all these words will have to be translated into figures – into projected sales, material and labour costs, and estimated overheads, for the business as a whole and for each department. All these detailed figures make up the annual budget.

What about control?

Budgetary control is about more than just preparing budgets. As the name suggests it's also concerned with control. This is done by comparing what *actually happens* with the plan, or budget. It means that we can concentrate on the areas where things are going wrong – or management by exception.

All businesses use budgetary control. David Morton may only do it in the most informal way, on a scrap of paper or even in his head. Large concerns have to use a more formal system of reports and meetings. But the basic rules are the same – setting out the plan, and comparing this with what actually happens. Most individuals do this as well.

A holiday in Taramasalata

Few of us can afford to have a holiday without considering the cost. Most people set a budget for what they can afford. Whether they can face up to comparing their budget with what they actually spend is another matter, but they may have to when next month's bank statement arrives.

David Morton, having survived his first year in business, decides that he deserves a holiday. Money is tight so he works out how much he can spend. Travel £300, accommodation £200, meals £150, car hire £100, entertainment £120, presents £50, and sundries (ice creams etc.) £80. He adds this up to £1000 and decides he can just about afford it, providing he lives on bread and cheese for a month when he gets back. He books a holiday in Taramasalata, has a wonderful time, but on the way home begins to count the cost. He prepares a budget statement which compares his actual spending with his budgeted figures. He's horrified to see that it looks like this:

	Budget	Actual	Variance
	£	£	£
Travel	300	320	+20
Accommodation	200	190	−10
Meals	150	170	+20
Car hire	100	220	+120
Entertainment	120	170	+50
Presents	50	40	−10
Sundries	80	170	+90
Total	1,000	1,280	+280

He's overspent by nearly £300, but by preparing his budget statement at least he can see where he went wrong. Travel, accommodation and meals went more or less according to plan and can be ignored. He even saved money on presents for the family. But look at the big differences. £50 too much on entertainment (too many discos), £90 on sundries (he can't have eaten that many ice creams), and his plan to hire a car for a few days seemed to turn into most of the holiday. By looking at the exceptions he can see where the problems are and (just maybe) do something about it next time.

Does it work like this in a business?

More or less. A business would prepare a budget in the same way, show actual spending alongside, and then work out the difference, or **variance**. It would not only have budgets for spending, but also for sales. David Morton waited until his holiday was over before preparing his statement, but a business cannot afford to wait until the end of the year to see how things have worked out. The annual budget will be divided into months, or sometimes quarters for a smaller business, and actual sales and spending can be compared very quickly with the plan. In this way something can be done about poor performance or overspending before it's too late. If David had looked at his spending half way through the holiday, he might have been able to do something about it. But would he have enjoyed it so much?

What are the advantages of budgetary control?

All but the smallest businesses will operate a budgetary control system for the following reasons:

- It gives the business as a whole, and each separate department a co-ordinated plan to work to.

- It should give each department a goal to aim for – although it's important that the budget set should be attainable. If sales figures are set too high, or costs impossibly low, then staff may give up before they even start.

- It allows management to control the business more effectively by looking at where actual results are different from the plan. Management by exception becomes more useful as a business gets bigger and managers become more remote from the day to day running of things. Instead of trying to keep an eye on everything, they focus their attention where it's needed.

There may be savings to be made even at the preparation stage. This is what we turn to next.

How should budgets be prepared?

Preparing the annual budget can be a valuable exercise in which department managers get together to plan the future of the business. Alternatively it can be a time of conflict, hostility and argument. It depends to some extent on how the process is handled, and there are some important ground rules:

- As many staff as possible should participate in setting budgets. The people who will be involved in carrying out the plan should be involved in making the plan in the first place. Too often in practice a budget is imposed on a department without even the manager who will be responsible for it having a say in what a reasonable target might be.

- Successfully integrating all the departmental plans together is a lengthy and complicated process and sufficient time should be allowed.

- Genuine conflicts of interest have to be faced. There will be disagreements between different managers, particularly over levels of spending. The sales manager will want to keep every model in stock and in every colour. The accountant and managing director will be aware that this will encourage sales, but also that high stock-holding will tie up too much capital. Sorting out disputes like this can be an opportunity for managers to appreciate the difficulties of others and to see how their department fits into the business as a whole. Handled in the wrong way, the budget can become a focus of resentment and bad feeling, and have the opposite effect to the one intended.

- Preparing budgets can itself be a valuable exercise. Taking a long hard look at sales, costs and cash is a useful discipline. Why do we do things this way? Why do we spend so much on that? By asking questions like this it may be possible to save money even before the year starts.

How are staff involved in the control of budgets?

We have seen that it's important for staff to be involved in the preparation of budgets, but it's equally important that they are involved in the control aspect. The most important things to consider are:

- Who is in control?

- How much information do they need?

- How often do they need it?

- When should they take action?

Who is in control?

This is possibly the most important question. The organisational structure (who is in charge of what) should be clear and well understood. One particular budget should be the responsibility of one person, who can then be held accountable for any differences, or variances from the budget. If there is an overspending on parts, or on any costs over which the parts manager has control, then he or she will have to attempt to justify it. After all, they will get the praise if they save costs, or exceed their sales budget.

How much information does a manager need?

Not too little and not too much. Managers need sufficient information to manage their departments effectively, but it is important not to provide too much information so that managers are overwhelmed. Computer systems are now capable of supplying vast amounts of figures and statistics and the temptation to drown a manager in paper has to be resisted. Budgets are important but managers have other work to do as well.

How often do they need it?

This depends on the circumstances. Most larger businesses produce budget reports monthly, but smaller concerns may consider that once a quarter is sufficient. On the other hand there may be some information, the number of new cars sold for instance, that a manager will want to keep up to date with on a daily basis.

When does a manager need to take action?

The business where everything goes exactly according to plan has not yet been invented. There will always be differences between the budget and what happens in practice. But when does a variance become big enough to take action? It's a matter of judgement – a thousand pounds overspending on the advertising budget for Rover may be insignificant, but not for a small dealership. Differences can also come about because the budget was wrong in the first place. Budgets can be altered in this case, but if they are changed too frequently they will soon be ignored altogether.

Are all costs controllable?

Unfortunately not. There may be many reasons why actual results are not in line with the budget and not all of them are within the manager's control. World oil prices for instance can affect petrol sales. The forecourt manager can hardly be held responsible for a war in the Middle East. Changes in economic conditions cannot always be anticipated – a surprise increase in VAT, or an increase in interest rates will depress sales and are outside the control of the sales manager. Blaming managers for problems they have no control over is a waste of time and will soon destroy the credibility of the budgetary control system.

What *is* within a manager's control?

Most managers would prefer to blame high costs or low sales on somebody else. The performance of a department is however greatly influenced by the staff involved, and particularly by the actions of the manager. The main point of a budgetary control system is to discover when things are not going according to plan, and to find out quickly enough to do something about it. It should not just be concerned with praise or blame, but with putting things right. If costs are up, then action will have to be taken to reduce them. If sales are down then extra effort will have to be put into getting more customers to buy.

What does a budget statement look like?

Each business will design its own statements to fit its own particular circumstances, although manufacturers sometimes provide standard forms to supplement these. A typical budget statement for the used car department of a small dealership might look something like this:

Used car sales – Budget statement for May 19XX			
	Budget	Actual	Variance
Sales:			
No. of cars sold	20	17	3 U
	£	£	£
Value of cars sold	80,000	69,700	10,300 U
Direct costs:			
Trade-in allowances	60,000	51,500	8,500 F
Repairs/preparation	1,900	1,700	200 F
Salaries	1,800	1,800	–
Commission	700	580	120 F
	64,400	55,580	8,820 F
Gross profit	15,600	14,120	1,480 U
Overheads:			
Advertising	1,100	1,050	50 F
Promotions	800	950	150 U
Entertainment	250	340	90 U
Telephone	150	230	80 U
Stationery	100	80	20 F
	2,400	2,650	250 U
Profit before charging general overheads	13,200	11,470	1,730 U

Note: You will see the letters '**U**' and '**F**' after the variance column. Instead of using '**+**' and '**–**', which can be confusing when dealing with sales and costs, many statements use 'U' for a variance that is *unfavourable* to a business, and 'F' for a *favourable* one.

What does all this mean? It's not necessary for you to understand the finer points of budgetary control at this point, and the above example is merely to give you some idea of what a typical statement might look like. The main points are that:

- Actual sales are down on the budgeted level.

- Some direct costs show a favourable variance, but this is only because costs have fallen in line with the reduced sales. Some more sophisticated businesses would take this into account when calculating the budget figures.

- Gross profit is down, as you would expect.

- The overheads are expenses that can be directly charged to the used car department. There has been some over-spending that the manager will have to explain, and do something about in the following month.

- The final profit figure is the profit that the department is contributing towards the business as a whole. It will go towards paying for the general overheads shared by all departments and to provide its share of the overall profits, if any.

What are the main things to remember about budgets?

Budgetary control is an essential part of the planning process, and of the financial control of a business. Used in the right way it can motivate staff by setting goals that they can achieve, and provides a means of communication between departments. A poor budgeting system can have the opposite effect. What makes a good system?:

- A regular review of each budget. Targets and spending need to be justified each year – there is little point in taking last year's figures and 'adding a bit on'.

- Departments depend on each other. When the budget is prepared there must be the maximum *consultation* between departments if the overall plan is to fit together.

- Consultation is essential but not enough. There is a real need for departments to *collaborate* with each other, to understand their different needs and problems, and to co-operate in achieving the objectives of the business as a whole.

- Using budgets as a means of control has to be done wisely. Blaming managers for things beyond their control, and using unfavourable variances as a big stick with which to beat them is a recipe for disaster. The aim should be to find out where things are not going according to plan and to put them right.

Marketing a Department

'Our products sell themselves'

You may have heard something like this before, probably just before the business in question collapsed. One thing is certain, no matter how good the product, unless it is brought to the attention of potential customers in the right way, the product will not sell itself. This is where the role of marketing comes in – in the distribution, presentation and promotion of products or services to potential customers, and in looking after customers before, during and after a sale has taken place.

Many people within the motor industry are now acknowledging that although their own products are good, there are now very few bad ones. Cars within a particular price range are similar in appearance and in technical specification. Competition is intense and the search is on for what is called 'added value', that something extra that will convince a customer to buy your product, rather than your competitor's.

What is market research?

To begin at the beginning, you can't start marketing your product until you know what your market is. To do this you need to find out about two sets of people:

- Customers – who are they, where are they, and what do they need? In order to direct your marketing efforts to the right people in the right places and to offer them what they want, it is necessary to find out everything you can about your potential customers, or your 'market'.

- Competitors – who are they, where are they, and what have they got to offer? How big are they and how do they operate? Do they have any weaknesses? Do they have any advantages over you? You can't decide how to market your own products until you know what the opposition are up to.

Market research is not just about people with clip-boards in city centres, it is more to do with managers trying to find answers to these questions before spending scarce resources on marketing the product itself. Market research is not something you do once at the start of a business, it should be a continuous process of monitoring changes in the market. The needs of customers will change, as will the strategy of your competitors.

What is marketing?

Having done your market research, you can now turn to marketing your product with more confidence. One common way of looking at marketing is to consider the 'four Ps' of marketing – **product, price, promotion** and **place**:

- Product – what are we trying to sell, and is it good enough? A poor product is unlikely to succeed, but even if the product is a good one, what about the 'added value' that we talked about earlier? What about our customer care arrangements?

- Price – are we selling at the right price to encourage customers? A dealership has limited scope for changing prices in new car and spares sales, although trade-in prices allow some flexibility. Other prices may be easier to alter. It's sometimes better to sell two things at a low price than one (or even none) at a high one.

- Promotion – you can have the best product and the best customer care and not sell a bean until customers are aware of your products. How are they to be promoted and advertised? What is the best method of getting the message across and can we afford it? Dealerships rely to a great extent on the efforts of manufacturers in marketing their products, but still have a lot of control over their own destiny.

- Place – the physical location of a garage or dealership will have a critical effect on its success. How easy is it for customers to get to and to park? Is it a high cost town centre site, or a low cost site in a run-down area? There has been a recent tendency for dealerships to relocate in modern out-of-town developments with good services and customer facilities.

The marketing plan

Each year the managers of each department will get together to work out the business plan for the following year. We have already discussed the financial aspects of this in great detail. An equally important part is the marketing plan. Difficult decisions will have to be taken about the product and how it can be improved, and the pricing policy to be adopted. A lot of the time will be spent on deciding how to promote and advertise the product and how much this will cost. Can we afford to spend this much on advertising, and can we afford not to? A decision to change site has enormous consequences, but is not one that is taken very often.

How can a department's services be marketed?

An individual department has quite a lot of scope to market itself, within the overall marketing plan. Manager and staff will have the major influence over how a customer experiences a department. We shall discuss customer care later in this section.

Where and how goods are displayed is an art in itself, as you can see on a visit to any supermarket. Have you ever been to a supermarket and come out with exactly what you went in for and no more? A parts department or forecourt shop can be laid out using similar techniques to encourage the customer to buy. In order to buy what they do want, customers should have to walk past eye catching displays of items that they may want – but didn't realise when they came in!

Making customers aware of what you have to offer is hard work, but by far the easiest time to do it is when they are in the department. Whenever customers are on the premises, they should be made aware of services on offer and any current promotions, including clear information about prices.

Using the manufacturer's publicity

It's a fact of life that motor manufacturers are large and powerful, and that dealerships have limited resources in comparison. National advertising is done almost exclusively by manufacturers, and advertising budgets are enormous, particularly for television campaigns. Dealerships should tie in their own marketing strategy to that of the manufacturer by:

- Planning a local advertising campaign to coincide with the national one. Pull together in order to reinforce the message.

- Making sure that stock levels of a particular model are sufficient. A customer who is inspired by the latest Renault advert will be less than impressed to be told 'Sorry but we're out of stock'.

- Making a big splash locally over the launch of a new model. Plenty of local press advertising and features, open days and launch parties to create a 'buzz' around the event.

- Using images and displays from national campaigns in a local setting so that customers make a connection with your business when they see a national advert.

How do promotions help?

You may have a good product at the right price, it may be well advertised, and you may have a good reputation. So might your competitors. To gain an advantage you may also need a little bit of magic to tempt the customer to buy, particularly at periods of low demand. Good finance deals or free tax and insurance are promotions that appeal to the customer's pocket. Free sunroofs or weekend breaks do not reduce the price, but do offer something extra, and for nothing. All these ideas have been used effectively in the past – but it is up to you to use your flair and imagination to think of new and original promotional activities to give you the slight advantage that may make all the difference. These are all sales incentives, but there are other ways of promoting your business.

Getting people onto the premises by offering wine, cheese or free advice is often cost effective, and one area of promotion largely ignored by the motor trade until recently is sponsorship. Sponsoring a local football team, or a sporting or charitable event is a powerful and simple way of bringing your name to the attention of the local public.

The art of advertising

Advertising is not always effective, but can be expensive if not properly planned. People in advertising often quote the initials 'AIDA' in explaining what an advert should do. It should:

A: grab the Attention of the potential customer.

I: get them Interested in the product.

D: create a Desire for the product.

A: get them to take Action and buy the product.

That's all very well in theory, but how does it work in practice?

Designing the perfect advert

Motor traders sometimes advertise on local radio, and even on regional television, but the bulk of their advertising is in local newspapers. How do they design an advert that will work?

- The advert should be eye-catching, to draw the reader's attention. Use a symbol or logo that will identify the business.

- Get over the essentials of what you are trying to convey, but don't drown the advert in too much detail.

- Be honest in your claims – make sure you can deliver what you promise.

- Make sure that the customer is aware of the benefits and advantages of buying from you, including sales incentives.

- Include prices wherever possible.

- Make sure that customers who do respond to the advert know what action to take next – who to phone, where and when to call etc.

It's worth spending time and effort on getting an advert right and it may be cost effective to enlist the help of an outside professional. If you are involved in advertising you should also be aware of the Code of Practice for the Motor Industry which covers advertising standards.

Where to advertise

Where you advertise depends on who you are trying to sell to and how much it costs. There is no point in a local garage advertising on national television, even if they could afford it. The potential customers of an average dealership are spread over a comparatively small geographical area, and the most common places to advertise are:

- On the premises – an opportunity that should not be wasted. Also on vehicles sold ('Another car from Millington Motors'). Cost is very low.

- Local press – evening and weekly newspapers and free papers often cover about the same area as your potential customers. Cost is moderate.

- Local radio – may cover about the right area and could be worth it, particularly for promotional events. Cost depends on timing and frequency.

- National press – covers a much wider audience than necessary. May be suitable for some specialist dealers who supply cars not available locally. Cost is quite high.

There are many other places to advertise – from the side of a football pitch to the side of a bus. It's a matter of using your imagination while staying within your advertising budget.

What is a press release?

A **press release** is a form of free advertising. Journalists are always looking for news and you can help them out by providing it. 'Local garage to open new premises', 'Apprentice wins award'. 'Open day at Vauxhall dealership' – any newsworthy event can get your name into the papers. Press releases should be brief, and written in a journalistic style to avoid rewriting. They may not always be used, but you can't get cheaper publicity.

How do you compete with your competitors?

We have already discussed the process of market research, in which the activities of competitors are continuously monitored. But it's not sufficient to react to what competitors are up to – you need to be in there first with new ideas and innovations. Where do these ideas come from? Make use of your human resources and try to create an atmosphere in your department that encourages staff to make suggestions. Look at retail outfits outside the motor trade – can you use any of their ideas? Can you compete on price? Make sure that all your advertising stresses your strengths (and by implication your rivals' weaknesses).

Creating an image

An image or publicity identity is about how your department or business is seen by the public. Cheap and cheerful, expensive and refined, old-fashioned and reliable, or modern and full of new ideas. You can to a large extent choose your image according to the sort of customers you are trying to attract. A garage specialising in exhaust replacement will want to appear inexpensive, fast and efficient. A Rolls-Royce dealer will wish to appear efficient, but not speedy and definitely not inexpensive.

You can choose some parts of your image, but other aspects are merely common-sense and apply to all businesses.

Clean, tidy, efficient, courteous, reliable, caring. These sort of things sound obvious, but we all know places where not all of these descriptions apply.

All advertising should contain something strong and recognisable to identify the business. It could just be the name, or a simple logo. Remember that for most people, most of the time, this is the only part of your advert they will read. They may not buy this time, but at least they will remember your name.

What is an 'ongoing' marketing scheme?

An ongoing scheme is one that never stops. The marketing scheme, or plan may be set out in broad terms at the start of the year, but it's important that the plan is also updated, revised and improved continuously. Market conditions may change, competitors may gain an advantage, or someone may come up with a brilliant idea. Always doing the same thing leads to stagnation. The aim of an ongoing marketing scheme is to ensure that there is always something going on to attract customers.

What about displays?

Displays of goods, posters and other display materials are a powerful way of marketing a particular product or brand. It's part of ensuring that there is always something going on, and gives a customer something to look at while waiting. Many retailers use displays to promote 'loss leaders' – or goods sold at a loss or at cost to encourage customers into the premises.

There are dangers with displays, however. Too many displays can look fussy and overwhelming. And displays which remain too long begin to get dusty, tatty and boring. The secret to effective display is to keep it simple and keep it changing.

Do-it-yourself or use an external agency?

The advantage of using an external advertising agency is that they will be much better at it than you are. Adverts will be more likely to work if you engage the services of a professional. Should you decide on a DIY approach, you will not be entirely on your own as all newspapers have staff who will help in the design of an advert.

In terms of your image or publicity identity it may well be worth using the services of a design consultant. Your name and logo, letterheads and leaflets, and the whole appearance of your business from showroom to service reception has a dramatic effect on the way in which customers see you. The cost of putting right a poor decision is far greater than the cost of a good designer.

Seasonal promotions

Sales staff will always tell you that selling cars is very difficult at any time. But as we have pointed out before, it's much less difficult around the new year and August 1st. The time to really go to town on special promotions and all the other marketing ideas that we have discussed, is in the slack periods of demand leading up to these dates. After all, the sales staff will have more time to devote their energy and imagination to the task of tempting customers to buy.

What is a mail shot?

A **mail shot** is a letter and/or leaflet sent through the post to prospective customers. The most significant thing to remember is that well over 90% of the letters will end in the dustbin unread. A few people in every hundred may respond, and if you get it right, about one in a hundred will end in a sale. This may not sound a particularly successful method of selling, and it's certainly an uneconomic use of paper, but many businesses use this method because it targets likely customers more accurately than general advertising. To be successful a mail shot should:

- Use a good mailing list. This can be made up of past customers, or a more general list which can be purchased or rented. Make sure that it's up-to-date. It's a waste of time writing to people who have moved, and people who have died will be unlikely to need a car.

- Letters should be short and to the point and should attempt to grab the readers attention in the first line, before the whole thing is consigned to the bin.

What is a co-operative promotion?

Promotional ideas and displays can be very expensive. One possible way of getting round this is to share the cost of a promotion with another business. This will not work with competitors, but may be possible with different sorts of business. Large department stores will sometimes incorporate a car into a fashion display. And what about your business customers? If they are planning a promotion, is there some way of incorporating your products into it? Part of your on-going marketing plan is to react to opportunities like this.

What is customer care management?

We mentioned right at the start of this section that the search is on for 'added value', that extra something that will give you an edge over your competitors. Many of the things we have discussed have been ways of trying to achieve this. But adverts, displays and promotions have a limited life, and in any case your competitors are all trying to do the same thing. The motor trade deals with what is often a customer's second most valuable possession, and real and lasting added value can be gained by treating both customer and car in the right way. Care for your customers properly and not even the most spectacular display or sales incentive of your competitors will tempt them to take their business elsewhere.

What does a customer expect?

What a customer expects and what a customer gets are often two entirely different things. Customers today expect a far higher standard of service than they did in the past, but they don't always get it. **Customer care management** aims to put this right. Customers are the people who pay your wages and provide your profits – and giving them what they want is the only way of increasing both. So what do they expect?

- A good product – not just the car, or the service or repair, but everything surrounding the product. Vehicles should be returned clean and tidy, invoices should be clear and detailed, courtesy transport should be provided where necessary.

- Good surroundings – clear directions to departments, a comfortable waiting room with facilities like a telephone and a coffee machine.

- A personal service – perhaps most important in providing added value. The managing director may understand the importance of customer care management, but does the clerk on service reception, or the mechanic who describes a problem to a customer? The staff who meet customers directly are often the lowest paid and least trained in the business – but your reputation depends on them.

Providing a personal service

Customer care is not having a fixed smile and telling customers to 'have a nice day'. It's not an instant and easy solution, a 'bolt-on accessory' to staff behaviour, but something much more deep seated, and affecting all staff from the boss to the cleaner. It's a realisation by everyone that the customer is the most important part of the business, and not just an interruption to their work.

To create this sort of atmosphere takes time, training and money. The benefits are unlikely to be felt immediately, but if you want a healthy business in ten years' time, customer care management could be your most profitable investment.

Section D

DEPARTMENTAL FINANCE

Financial Paperwork

Why does fast paperwork make financial sense?

One advantage of the motor trade is that most customers pay up fairly quickly, which improves cash flow and increases profit. Customers buying a car usually pay for it on delivery, and service and repair bills are often paid for on collection. This means that bills have to be ready and waiting when the customer calls in, and for service and repair work in particular, this requires some pretty speedy paperwork.

How do multi-part documents help?

Most of you will be familiar with **multi-part documents** both inside and outside of the motor trade. The main advantage is that, where more than one copy of a document is needed, most of the information can be recorded once rather than two or three times. Multi-part documents can be hand-written, or produced by a till or computer. There can be anything from two to five copies.

We shall be concentrating on the financial aspects of multi-part documents. For a more detailed view, including illustrations of the sort of documents used by a modern motor trader, you should consult The Institute's Student Guide to Administration and Organisation.

Where are multi-part documents used?

It would be quicker to list where they are not used. Most

departments will produce multi-part documents of some sort, and all departments will handle individual documents from each multi-part set after they have been split. The parts department, accounts, and the forecourt will all make out different sorts of document sets, but service and repair presents the most complex problems to solve, and we shall start with this.

Job cards and customer invoicing for service and repairs

A customer brings in a car for a service or repair. A few hours later the customer will expect to pick up not only the car, but an invoice itemising what materials and parts have been used, what labour has cost, and the charge for VAT (particularly important for business customers). How can all this be done in such a short time? Individual garages use different systems. Smaller outfits may use hand-written or typed documents, larger dealerships will use a computer. But the basis of the system is usually something like this:

- When a customer arrives, an order is raised by service reception. This consists of a three part set of documents.

- Copies 1 and 2 go to the spares department and details of any parts used on the job are entered, together with prices.

- The third, harder copy, usually called the **job card**, goes to the workshop supervisor and then to the mechanic who does the work. The mechanic will enter the time spent on the job, the parts used and the repairs made.

- When the job is finished, all the copies will be sent to the accounts department so that the job can be costed, and an invoice, including VAT, can be prepared (with a computer, invoices may be produced in service reception).

- All documents will then go to the service manager for approval, and then to service reception to await the arrival of the customer, who will be given the top copy of the invoice.

- The multi-part set, having been split up and then brought together again, is now split up yet again. One copy is filed in job number order, another is kept by the service department in the owner's file as a record of work done on a particular vehicle. The final copy may be kept by the accounts department.

This procedure may sound complicated at first, but it works very well in practice and ensures that invoices are produced accurately and quickly and that cash flows into the business as fast as possible. Individual garages will adopt a system to suit their own needs. The main thing to remember about multi-part job cards is that the set is split up, processed in various ways, brought back together again to prepare the invoice, and then split up again for future reference.

What other multi-part documents are used?

The other multi-part documents that a motor trader would use are much simpler. The most common are:

- Parts sales – cash and credit sales will be treated differently. Cash sales need an immediate invoice including VAT. One copy will go to the customer, a copy will be needed by accounts, and a copy will be retained by the parts department for stock control purposes. For credit sales, a more elaborate set is used. The customer will sign for the parts taken and keep one copy of the set as a delivery note, which will not include prices. The invoice will be priced later and sent to the customer as soon as possible. A copy will be needed by the accounts department, and another by the parts department. This is an ideal application for a computer which can keep a record of prices and stock.

- Car sales – the preparation of invoices for customers would usually be done by the accounts department. Both sales and accounts departments would keep a copy.

- Forecourt – cash sales would be recorded on a till. The top copy would be given to the customer, and the other copy, or till roll, would be used to check on the amount of cash taken for the day, and then sent to the accounts department. Credit cards are frequently used and these also require multi-part sets. The top copy goes to the customer, another is taken to the bank for payment, and the final copy is retained.

- **Credit notes** – these should not be confused with credit card slips. A credit note is the opposite of an invoice and has to be raised when a customer is overcharged. A customer with a monthly account will then deduct the amount of the credit note from the next payment. A cash customer may demand to be repaid in cash. Credit notes are sometimes given to customers who are not entirely satisfied with the service they have received. Copies are kept in the same way as invoice copies.

How does a time sheet system work?

We have seen how a job card is used to record time spent and materials used on a particular job. This ensures that a customer's invoice is prepared when the vehicle is collected. The information contained on the job card has another financial function – to record each mechanic's hours so that the correct amount of wages is paid at the end of the week. This can be done in one of two ways:

- In a large dealership where job card sets are processed by computer, all the information on time spent and any bonus earned will be held on a computer file. At the end of the week the wages can be prepared and a statement given to each mechanic showing the relevant details. (Details of wages and bonus schemes are covered later in this section.)

- In a smaller garage, each mechanic will have a daily or weekly **time sheet** to record time spent on each job, the standard time allowed for the job according to the manufacturer (particularly if there is a bonus scheme), and any waiting time or other delays. At the end of the week, wages can be prepared from these details.

What is a service loading chart?

The function of a **service loading chart** is to help in the organisation of jobs passing through the workshop. It's essentially a list of jobs to be done. Unlike all the other documents we have discussed, the service loading chart does not usually contain any direct financial information. Without it, however, it is unlikely that a garage could function efficiently, and customer service and profits would deteriorate.

A smaller garage might operate a weekly service loading chart, a larger one would use a series of daily charts. The sort of information shown would be:

- Order number – when a customer books in, the job will be given an order number, or job number.

- Customer name and telephone number, model and registration number.

- Details of job, approximate time required, and details of how payment will be made (in cash or on account). Jobs done under warranty will also be noted.

- Time at which the customer wishes to collect.

From this information the service manager and workshop supervisor can organise the flow of work through the department and the order in which jobs should be done.

Prices and Costs

How are prices set in the motor trade?

We shall be looking in this section at the relationship between costs and prices. In order to make a profit, a business must sell things for more than they cost. But this does not mean that you can work out your costs and then just add a bit on for profit. Some prices are set by the manufacturer and others are influenced by what your competitors are charging. It's vital to know what your costs are, and to cover them, but you can't depend on them in setting your prices.

A reminder about costs

In Section A we looked at different types of cost and discussed, among others, the following categories:

- Variable costs – which change according to output. The more you sell, the more you use.

- Fixed costs – which stay the same whatever the level of output. Costs like rent and the general manager's salary will not increase if our sales go up by 10 per cent.

- Direct costs – which can be identified with a particular job or product. A mechanic's wages, or the parts used on a particular job for instance.

- Indirect costs – or costs that cannot be identified with a particular job because they relate to all jobs in general. The service manager's salary and costs of heating the department would be included in this category. These costs are overheads, but are normally restricted to departmental overheads only.

- General overheads – are those costs which cannot be charged to a particular department because they relate to all departments and have to be shared between them.

The general manager's salary, interest payments and auditor's charges would be included.

These are the main cost categories we shall be dealing with in this Section.

Costs, prices and profits

In order to look at how costs relate to prices and how both relate to profit it's necessary to split costs up into variable and fixed costs. Don't forget that for an individual department, fixed costs are made up of:

- The indirect costs of that department (the department overheads).

- The department's share of the general overheads of the business.

Costs and prices in the sales department

Prices of new cars are set by the manufacturers, although the amount of money coming into the business is also affected by part-exchange allowances. Used car prices are much more under the control of the department, although the major influence is still the marketplace, or in other words what all your competitors are charging.

The costs involved in car sales we have already covered in some detail at the end of Section A. It's important for what we are going to do next to divide these costs into variable and fixed costs:

- Variable costs – the cost of the car itself, including getting it into a saleable condition, plus any promotional extras. Sales staff commission will also be variable.

- Fixed costs – these will include the departmental overheads (heat, light, advertising, the fixed part of staff salaries), and a share of the general dealership overheads.

Costs and prices in the parts department

Prices of manufacturer's spares will be set by the manufacturer, although the dealership will have some control over discounts allowed to customers. The price of other parts and supplies can be set by the trader. Parts department costs are:

- Variable costs – the cost of the parts themselves (the more you sell the more you have to buy). For most dealerships and over the normal range of sales, wages will probably not be a variable cost as an increase in sales of say 10 per cent might well be handled by existing staff. Multi-part stationery is usually a variable cost.

- Fixed costs – departmental costs including wages (probably), and depreciation of fixtures, fittings and computers. Plus a share of general overheads of course.

Costs and prices in service and repair departments

All prices are under the control of the individual trader – but if they are too high, sales will drop and profits will fall. If they are too low, the quantity of sales will be fine, but profits will again fall. To get prices right, it's necessary to look at the competition and at costs:

- Variable costs – in a large dealership wages are a variable cost (increase the number of services and you have to pay out more in wages). For a smaller garage, wages may be nearer to a fixed cost. In practice it's necessary to look very carefully at what will happen to wages costs if output goes up or down. For the remainder of this section we shall be assuming that wages costs are variable. Multi-part stationery tends to be variable, as do consumable items such as grease, seat covers etc. The parts used in repair and service are usually regarded as sales of the parts department and are ignored in calculating the costs, prices and profits of the workshop.

- Fixed costs – departmental fixed costs include any non-production salaries (the service manager, reception engineers, supervisors etc), and depreciation of tools and equipment. Plus a share of the general overheads.

Which overheads are departmental and which general depends on the circumstances. For instance if a garage is all under one roof, rent and heating are general overheads which will have to be shared out between departments on some agreed basis. If a department is in a completely separate building, then these costs can be worked out exactly.

Why have we split costs like this?

We have mentioned this briefly before, in Section A, when we said that dividing costs into fixed and variable was very useful when taking decisions about the future. We gave an example that is worth repeating, and said that if sales increase by 10%, two things would change:

1) Cash coming in from sales would increase by 10%,

2) Cash paid out for variable costs would increase by 10%,

  – BUT, fixed costs would stay the same.

And think what would happen if the reverse happened, and sales fell by 10%. What would happen now:

1) Cash coming in from sales would decrease by 10%,

2) Cash paid out for variable costs would decrease by 10%,

  – BUT, fixed costs would stay the same.

This is a very important concept to grasp and it has implications for all sorts of decision making about prices, marketing, expansion and contraction. The clearest way of showing how all these things fit together is on a chart.

How do you plot costs on a chart?

Millington Motors has a service and repair workshop employing ten mechanics who each earn £5 per hour. Sales are charged out at £20 per hour of labour time spent on the job. Total yearly sales are 15,000 hours at £20 = £300,000. Total variable costs (including wages) are £105,000. Fixed costs are made up as follows:

Department overheads	=	£60,000
Share of general overheads	=	£85,000
Total fixed costs	=	£145,000

How do we plot the fixed costs on a chart? We can plot costs on the vertical scale, and output, in terms of hours sold, on the horizontal one, like this:

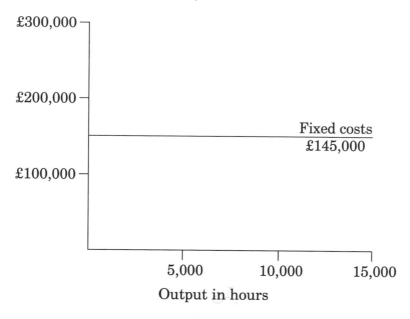

Using the same chart we can also plot variable costs:

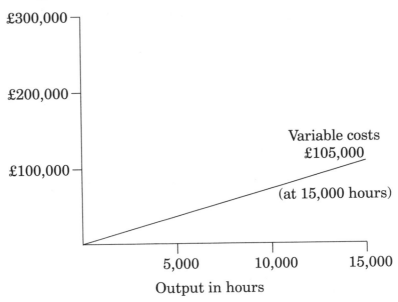

If we add the two charts together, we can show total costs. Don't forget that if we didn't sell a single hour of service or repair we should still have to pay the fixed costs of £145,000. So we just add the variable cost line on top of the fixed costs to show the total costs.

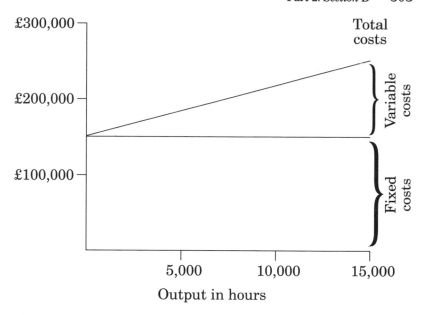

If we read off the number of hours sold along the bottom scale, we can see at a glance the total cost involved. We can see the total cost of selling 13,000 hours, or of selling 16,000 hours. The cost of 14,000 hours, for example, we can read off at approximately £245,000 (in fact the exact figure works out at £243,000, which you can see if you plot the chart on graph paper).

Remember something that we said in Section A about fixed costs not being as fixed as all that. It's pretty obvious that if sales hours dropped to 8,000 hours, some fixed costs would be saved, and that if sales increased to 20,000 hours, some additional fixed costs would be incurred. But over the levels of activity that we normally encounter in practice, we can assume that fixed costs will not change a great deal.

Why stop there?

Predicting costs is a useful exercise, but isn't there something else we can do with the chart having got this far? By putting in a line to show sales we can do much more – our chart will then show costs, sales and profit. It will also show the point at which the department is neither making a profit nor a loss. This is called the **break-even point**.

The break-even chart

If we add a line to show sales at £20 per hour, the chart will look like this:

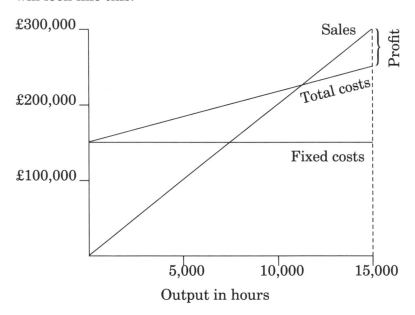

What we have prepared is a **break-even chart**. What does it tell us? Take a line vertically upwards at the normal output level of 15,000 hours. We can read off fixed costs of £145,000, total costs of £250,000, and sales of £300,000. And if we look at the difference between sales and total costs, we can see that the profit is £50,000. But we knew these figures already, so what's the big deal? Well, if we can read off sales, total costs and profit for output of 15,000 hours, we can also read off what will happen at *any* level of output. And if we can do that, there must be one particular level where the money coming from sales exactly equals the money going out on costs – the break-even point in other words. What is the break-even point in this case? It's the point where the sales line crosses the total cost line – where sales and total costs are the same. If you draw a line vertically downwards from that point, it crosses the output scale at about 11,150 hours. So we know that if we sell this many hours we shall neither make a profit, nor make a loss.

What is 'the contribution'?

About 11,150 hours is okay, but is there some way of calculating the break-even point exactly? We shall turn to this shortly, but first we must look at what basic information we have to work with. We have seen that when 15,000 hours of work are sold, the figures look like this:

Sales are 15,000 × £20		=	£300,000
less Variable costs		=	£105,000
		=	£195,000
less Fixed costs		=	£145,000
Profit		=	£50,000

Now variable costs vary according to output, so if we divide the total variable cost by the the total of hours, we should arrive at a variable cost per hour:

$$\frac{\text{Variable cost}}{\text{Total hours}} = \frac{£105,000}{15,000} = £7 \text{ per hour}$$

We know that sales are charged out at	£20 per hour
and we know that variable costs are	£7 per hour
and that the difference is	£13 per hour

This difference is known as the **contribution**. What this means is that for every hour of output we sell at £20, we shall have to pay out £7 in wages and the other variable costs. This leaves us with £13 that will go towards (or contribute to) paying off the fixed costs, and when these are paid to giving us a profit. Contribution is really short for 'contribution to fixed costs and profit'. In strict accounting terms, contribution is close to, but not quite the same as, gross profit. If it helps to get the idea across, think of it as gross profit for the time being. Or you can think of it as the profit after paying for variable costs, but before paying for fixed costs.

Selling garden gnomes

In order to illustrate how to use the contribution and the break-even point we shall leave the motor trade for a moment and look at a much simpler business. Imagine that you are trying to buy a garden gnome and discover that there is no local supplier. You therefore decide to start a part-time business supplying them yourself. The gnomes cost £3 each to buy in bulk, and you can sell them for £5. Your only other cost is £200 per year to rent a lock-up garage to store your stock. How many gnomes must you sell per year to break-even?

Selling price per gnome is	£5
Variable cost per gnome is	£3
The contribution per gnome is therefore	£2

So for every gnome you sell you make £2. Your first target is to make enough £2s to pay for the rent of the lock-up. The rent is a fixed cost of £200. How many gnomes do you have to sell to cover this? It's £200 divided by £2, or 100 gnomes. You can check it out if you want to:

	Sales would be 100 × £5	=	£500
less	Variable costs 100 × £3	=	£300
therefore	Contribution 100 × £2	=	£200
less	Fixed costs	=	£200
equals	Profit	=	–

You have just broken even, and the way in which you calculated the break-even point was:

$$\frac{\text{Fixed costs}}{\text{Contribution per unit}} = \frac{£200}{£2} = 100 \text{ units}$$

In fact you expect to sell much more than this, an estimated 250 gnomes per year. What would be your profit now? Having discovered the secret of the contribution we can take a short cut:

250 gnomes at a contribution of £2 each	=	£500
Deduct fixed costs	=	£200
And your profit will be		£300

You can of course do this calculation for any level of sales. What if there were a slump in the gnome market and you only sold 80?

Contribution 80 × £2	=	£160
Fixed costs	=	£200
Loss	=	(£40)

You can see that using the contribution, or 'contribution analysis', gives us a really quick way of calculating these sorts of figures. But does this apply only to garden gnomes? Surely it must be much more complicated in the motor trade?

The break-even point at Millington Motors

Yes it *is* more complicated – but only because there are a lot more costs, and it's difficult to decide on which are the truly variable ones. The principle is exactly the same. Let's go back to the workshop at Millington Motors. We discovered that:

Sales are charged out at	£20 per hour
Variable cost is	£7 per hour
and that the difference or unit contribution is	£13 per hour

Our 'units' are hours, rather than gnomes, because hours of work is what we are selling. We also know that our fixed costs are £145,000 per year. We now have the same sort of information that we had for our gnome business – and we can work out our break-even point in the same way. All we have to do is to find out how many hours at £13 contribution will it take to pay off our fixed costs:

$$\frac{\text{Fixed costs}}{\text{Contribution per unit}} = \frac{£145,000}{£13} = 11,154 \text{ hours}$$

Look again at the break-even chart. We said that the break-even point was around 11,150 hours, and now we have an exact figure. We can check it out:

Sales	= 11,154 hours × £20 =	£223,080
less Variable costs	= 11,154 hours × £7 =	£78,078
Contribution	= 11,154 hours × £13 =	£145,002
less Fixed costs	=	£145,000
Profit	=	£2

(The £2 difference is due to rounding up the break-even calculation to the nearest hour.)

That's all there is to it. Once you get used to seeing costs and prices in this way, you will find that you can use contribution analysis in a variety of business decisions.

How is contribution analysis used in pricing?

Contribution analysis can be used in setting prices – or at least in looking at the effect of using different prices. For instance Millington Motors might decide that £50,000 profit is not enough, and they would like to make £65,000. What price would they have to charge if hours sold (15,000) remain the same:

Fixed costs are	£145,000
Profit required is	£65,000
So they need a contribution of	£210,000

– and they have 15,000 hours in which to earn this, so the contribution per hour will have to be:

$$\frac{£210,000}{15,000} = £14 \text{ per hour}$$

This will put the selling price up to £14 + £7 = £21 per hour. As we have stated before, however, the motor trade is very competitive, and it's extremely unlikely that prices will be set in this way, without reference to what competitors are charging.

Can we work out a break-even rate?

It's just as likely, in view of the competition, that we might have to think about reducing profits and cutting prices. Before we decide on an actual rate, is it possible to work out a rate per hour to charge that would reduce profits to nil – to break-even in fact? We should know then that if we go below this rate we shall be making a loss. We can do it by using the same figures (and assuming the same 15,000 hours sold). To break-even we know that our contribution must just equal our fixed costs, so:

Our fixed costs are	£145,000
So our contribution must also be	£145,000

The contribution per hour is therefore:

£145,000 ÷ 15,000	=	£9.67 per hour
Add on the variable cost of		£7.00 per hour
And the break-even rate is		£16.67 per hour

We can check if this works out:

Sales are 15,000 × £16.67	=	£250,050
less Variable costs, 15,000 × £7	=	£105,000
Total contribution	=	£145,050
less Fixed costs	=	£145,000
Profit	=	£50

Which proves that, to the nearest penny, £16.67 is our break-even rate. We shall of course want to charge more than this, but's useful information to know.

How can it be used in other decisions?

Contribution analysis is very useful in answering 'what if' questions. What if we want £70,000 profit? What if we sell 16,000 hours instead of 15,000? What if variable costs increase to £7.50 per hour? What if fixed costs go up by £10,000? By changing the figures, we can see very quickly what will be the effect on profit. It can also answer more complicated 'what if' questions. For example, what if a large local firm offered us all their repair work if we would reduce our rate to £18 per hour? Would it be worth accepting the contract?

Although you will not be expected to perform these sorts of

calculations, it's important to realise the potential of using contribution analysis in managing a modern dealership.

What problems are there in using these techniques?

The main problem is that costs do not always behave in the way we would like them to. It's often difficult in practice to decide which costs are fixed and which variable. Fixed costs are less 'fixed' than we think, and even variable costs per hour can change if output goes up or down.

Remember that break-even charts and contribution analysis are useful and powerful tools you can use in managing the business, but not ones you can rely on absolutely. A break-even chart may help you to make a decision – *but don't let it make the decision for you.*

What is the labour utilisation rate?

If you look back at the original details of Millington Motors given at the start of this section, you will see that ten mechanics are employed at a rate of £5 per hour. A normal working week is 39 hours. How many hours of labour per year does the garage pay for?

10 mechanics × 39 hours × 52 weeks = 20,280 hours per year.

But we already know that the garage only sells 15,000 hours per year. The missing hours have disappeared for a variety of reasons. Holidays, tea-breaks, training courses and a certain amount of sick leave are all unavoidable. Waiting for work, or for parts is to some extent inevitable, but there is often room for improvement by better organisation and workshop loading.

The **labour utilisation rate** shows what proportion of hours paid for are recovered from customers in hours sold. In this case the rate is:

$$\frac{\text{Number of hours sold}}{\text{Number of hours paid}} \times 100 = \frac{15,000}{20,280} \times 100 = 74.0\%$$

Which means that for every 100 hours paid, only 74 hours are sold. Is there any room for improvement? Let's see how the difference is made up in more detail:

Paid hours
10 mechs × 39 hrs × 52 wks   = 20,280 hrs

less Holidays
10 mechs × 39 hrs × 4 wks   = (1,560) hrs

less Tea breaks
10 mechs × 2.25 hrs × 48 wks   = (1,080) hrs

= 17,640 hrs

less Other contingencies at 15%
(rounded down)   = (2,640) hrs

Hours available for sale   = 15,000 hrs

The management will want to look very closely at the 15% contingency allowance, for sickness, waiting time etc., as this is where savings may be made. It should also be possible to include the labour utilisation figure in reports on a weekly or monthly basis to see if the workshop is doing better or worse than the 74% expected.

What is a 'levy'

In the motor trade, a **levy** is an additional charge on a customer's bill, made for the use of a particular piece of equipment. The cost of most tools and equipment is eventually recovered from customers through the normal pricing system that we have just examined. The cost of a hydraulic ramp for instance, is spread by depreciation over a number of years. Each year's depreciation charge will be included in the workshop's fixed costs, and those fixed costs will be recovered from customers, along with the variable costs and a bit of profit, through the retail rate charged (e.g. the £20 per hour of Millington Motors). So, even if a customer's car has been on the ramp, there will be no separate charge for using it. A customer would not be impressed to see a bill including items such as 'Use of ramp £4', or even worse, 'Use of 7/16" A/F spanner 25p'.

But there are occasions, with specialised machines, when this sort of procedure is adopted. Imagine a garage that wishes to buy a wheel balancer, but is finding it difficult to justify the expense. One way of getting round the problem is to get the customers to pay for it in a slightly less round-about way than usual. It can do this by including a levy, or additional charge, on a customer's bill every time the wheel balancer is used. The bill will show materials and labour in the usual way, and then show an item for 'Wheel balancing £2'. All the £2 charges added together will eventually recover the money paid out for the capital equipment.

Cash Sales and Credit Sales

What is a cash sale?

We have said that motor traders have a high proportion of cash sales, and that in general this is a good thing in terms of cash flow. But what exactly do we mean by cash sales? A cash sale is where payment is received in one of the following ways:

- In actual cash – notes and coins in other words.

- By cheque – which will take a few days to be 'cleared' by the banking system, but is generally regarded as cash.

- By switch card – which also takes a few days before the money is credited to your bank account.

The advantage of cash sales is of course that cash in the hand, or the till, is better than waiting for the customer to pay in thirty days, or sometime, or possibly never. There are some disadvantages as well – notes and coins have to be counted and all daily cash receipts have to be balanced to the till roll. Wherever there is cash there is always the problem of security, and of danger (and temptation) to staff.

What is a credit sale?

There are three basic types of sale where credit is involved, or to put it another way, where the customer is given a certain amount of time to pay:

- By opening a credit account – the customer signs for the goods, is sent an invoice, and agrees to pay within say, 30 days.

- By using hire-purchase – the customer pays for the goods over an extended period.

- By using a credit card – the customer signs for the goods, and can then choose over what period to pay.

We shall examine each type of credit sale in turn.

Why offer to open a credit account?

Since cash sales are preferable to credit sales, why bother with credit accounts at all? Because if you don't one of your competitors will, and they will get the sale. This does not mean that you have to open a monthly credit account for all customers, but it may be a good idea for trade and high-spending retail customers, particularly for service, repair and petrol sales.

When making a sale on a credit account, it's important to adopt the correct procedure:

- Always obtain a signature – the customer must sign to acknowledge that they have received the goods or service.

- Make sure an official order is presented – this is particularly important for trade parts sales. Trade customers may provide an order for service and repair, retail customers with accounts will not. Care should be taken with petrol sales to ensure that only people authorised by the customer are allowed to sign.

Sales on hire-purchase

Sales of new and used cars frequently use hire purchase as a means of payment. The agreement is made between the customer and the finance company, and payment is made in a series of monthly instalments. From the customer's point of view, the sale is on credit. The dealer, however, will obtain from the finance company, full payment for the car within a few days. The considerable costs of allowing credit are therefore entirely passed on to the customer.

Sales using a credit card

We have already discussed in the section on banking the advantages of using a crdit card from the point of view of the trader and of the customer. Credit card sales are in some ways similar to sales on hire purchase, in that some of the risks and costs involved in offering credit are avoided by the trader. Providing the correct procedures are adopted, once the customer has signed the credit card slip, the credit card company (MasterCard, Barclaycard etc.) will then take over responsibility for obaining payment from the customer.

As far as the customer is concerned, if payment is made in full by the due date, no additional cost is incurred. If the choice is made to pay over a longer period then interest will be added to the amount due.

From the trader's point of view, certain risks and costs have been avoided – they are sure of getting the money, and it will be credited to their account even more quickly than a cheque. The credit card slips are taken to the bank, along with cash and cheque takings, and are credited to the trader's account immediately. The only cost involved is that a small percentage commission is deducted from each payment.

What are the costs of allowing credit?

We can see from the above that with hire purchase and credit card sales, many of the costs and risks involved in giving credit are avoided. But what about the ordinary monthly accounts for trade and some retail customers? What costs are involved here?

- Accounts department staff – a great deal of time has to be spent preparing and sending out invoices, preparing and sending out statements at the end of the month, and dealing with payments when they come in. And if they don't come in, reminders will have to be sent, phone calls will have to be made, and eventually solicitors may have to become involved. These sorts of cost can increase overheads considerably.

- Bad debts – some customers will be unwilling or unable to pay. Using the legal system to recover debts is very expensive, and if a customer is unable to pay, will not in any case produce the desired result. All businesses offering credit suffer from a few bad debts, but if one or two major customers fail to pay, the effects on profit, and even on the future of the business, can be disastrous. This is why it's important to adopt the correct procedure when a customer asks for credit. We shall deal with this shortly.

- Interest charges – allowing credit means waiting for cash. We have seen the importance of cash flow and the

cost of waiting for money. If the business has an overdraft, then waiting for money will increase it, and extra
interest will have to be paid. Even if there is no overdraft, the resources of the business will be tied up in
debtors. Cash could be used more profitably, invested in
fixed assets or in stock.

Cash versus credit

In Section B we gave examples of the effects on cash balances of allowing credit. Here we can show a direct comparison between two new businesses, identical except that
one allows credit and the other deals only in cash. Both
businesses make sales of £3,000 per month, and both pay
out costs of £2,000 per month. On 1st January, both start
with a bank balance of £500. The cash business, shown on
the left below, makes all its sales in cash. The credit business, shown on the right, is paid on average two months
after the date of the sale – by no means an unusual delay.

	CASH BUSINESS			CREDIT BUSINESS		
	JAN £	FEB £	MAR £	JAN £	FEB £	MAR £
Cash in	3,000	3,000	3,000	—	—	3,000
Cash out	2,000	2,000	2,000	2,000	2,000	2,000
Net cash flow	1,000	1,000	1,000	(2,000)	(2,000)	1,000
Opening bank balance	500	1,500	2,500	500	(1,500)	(3,500)
Closing bank balance	1,500	2,500	3,500	(1,500)	(3,500)	(2,500)

You can see at a glance that the cash business has a
healthy bank balance with which to buy extra stock or
equipment. The credit business is immediately in trouble,
and has run up a £3,500 overdraft by the end of February.
In fact the credit business has permanently to finance two

months' sales, or £6,000 of debtors. And interest payments on the overdraft will put up costs to more than the £2,000 shown – so profits will be reduced. All this gloomy news does not mean that credit should never be allowed. The choice may not be between credit or cash – it may be between credit and no sale at all. But it is important to be aware of the implications of allowing credit and of the effect on cash and profits.

What procedure should be adopted if a customer requires credit?

For all the above reasons it's important that if credit is given, it should only be given to the right customers. How do we find out if a customer is creditworthy? There are a number of ways of finding out:

- **Bank reference** – the customer's bank manager will supply a reference, but will not give much away.

- **Trade references** – far more useful can be references from other traders who deal with the customer.

- **Credit ratings** – from agencies who specialise in this area, like Dun & Bradstreet.

- Analysing the customer's accounts – if the customer is a company, its annual accounts will be available for inspection and should give some idea of its financial position.

- Personal opinion – the opinion of sales staff and others who have dealt with the customer should not be ignored.

Discounting

Why offer a discount?

Why should a business offer a discount? After all, if you accept less money, surely you must be making less profit? Well, not necessarily – discounts can have two effects:

- It's true that you will make less profit on each item, but because the price is cheaper, you may increase the *number* of items you sell. Total profit may even increase.

- Discounts are usually to encourage customers to pay in cash. A business has to keep an eye on both profits and cash, and offering a discount may be a way of getting things moving and improving the cash flow into the business.

How does discounting work?

Discounts work on a rational and logical level by allowing the customer to buy at a lower price than normal. But they also work at a 'psychological' level, encouraging the customer to feel they have got a better bargain than is necessarily the case.

Imagine two firms selling roughly the same sort of product. Firm A offers a straightforward deal of £95, payment in thirty days. Firm B offers a similar product for £100 – but then adds 'pay in cash and you can have it for £90'. The customer thinks (or is supposed to think) that it's a better product (it costs £5 more), but they are getting it for £5 less. Firm B makes the sale and gets the cash in immediately.

What are the advantages of discounting?

Discounting should be approached with caution, but there are a number of advantages:

- The cash flow into the business improves.

- The quantity of goods sold may improve. This also applies to services – if for instance the workshop is under-utilised, it may be worth considering a special offer on service or repair. Discounts may be offered for bulk purchases of parts.

- Discounting may bring in new customers who, providing they are looked after, will then stay with the business.

- Customers who come onto the premises to buy the discounted items may also buy items that are not at a discount.

What are the disadvantages of discounting?

Most retailers would prefer to sell a large quantity at a high profit. They may be prepared to settle for a large quantity at a lower profit, but what they don't want is the situation of a small quantity at a low profit. One major problem of discounting, and particularly in the motor trade, is that introducing discounts is a reaction to difficult times and low demand. Most retailers introduce discounts at the same time, and instead of gaining an advantage over competitors, everyone is in the same boat, chasing the same low volume of sales. The effect of a price war of this sort is to reduce the number of retailers, rather than to maintain profits.

If discounts are too high, there will not be a big enough margin, or contribution, to pay off all the fixed costs, never mind produce a profit.

When should discounts be offered?

There are particular times when discounting is appropriate:

- Getting rid of old stock – this the traditional basis of January and summer sales. Space may be needed for new stock and cash can be injected into the business at a slack time.

- Drawing attention to new stock – if a new product is not doing well, offering a discount may get demand moving.

- If the business has cashflow problems – offering discounts may be a way of reducing an overdraft. As we have seen, in times of low demand there may be dangers involved in this.

In some areas of retailing, businesses have been very successful in using discounting as a continuous marketing strategy. Instead of offering reduced prices only in times of low demand, firms like B&Q or Argos have been far more aggressive and used discounting when demand is high as well as low. Building up customer loyalty when times are good can help to sustain a business when times are bad.

How will discounting affect a departmental budget?

It depends of course on whether the discounting was part of the departmental plan in the first place. If it was, then the budget will not have to altered. The difficulty is often that discounts may have to be offered at short notice, either because an opportunity has been spotted, or because of an unforeseen problem. The amount of cash flowing into the business will change, and the budgets will have to be examined to see what effects this will have. An increase in cash flow is unlikely to cause any problems, but if demand and cashflow *in* is down, then planned cashflow *out* must also be reassessed:

- Costs may have to be cut – from overheads to trade-in allowances. If reduced demand is likely to last for a long time, redundancies may have to be considered.

- Capital investment projects may have to be delayed or cancelled.

What alternatives are there to discounting?

We examined in Section C the ways in which a department can be successfully marketed, and many of the ideas discussed there – advertising, promotions, special offers and customer care management – are alternatives to discounting. There are two particular financial incentives that can be compared in a very direct way to discounting:

- Interest free credit – few customers can pay for a car in cash, and the cost of borrowing money from a bank or paying interest to a finance company, may put them off buying at all. Offering interest free credit is therefore a powerful inducement and a big saving. The problem from the retailer's point of view is one of cashflow. Although the money starts to come in immediately, it will take a long time before the vehicle is fully paid for.

- Buy now, pay later – this may suit some customers who will get to use the car for, say, three months without paying a penny. At the end of three months the money is due in full. This also presents problems in cashflow as the dealer will have to find the cash to replace the car long before the customer pays.

Wages and Salaries

What is the difference between a wage and a salary?

- A **wage** is the payment made to an employee, normally expressed as a rate per hour, per day, or per week. It is usually paid in cash at the end of every week.

- A **salary** is payment made to an employee, normally expressed as so much per year. It is usually paid by cheque, or credit transfer (direct into an employee's bank account), on a monthly basis.

What responsibilities does an employer have?

Employers have certain responsibilities in connection with the payment of wages and salaries. All employees must be given a statement of their gross pay, of any deductions made, and of net or take-home pay. This should include:

- Gross pay – this is made up of basic pay (the hourly,

weekly or monthly rate), plus any overtime or shift payments, plus any bonus or incentive payments.

- Deductions – income tax and national insurance are deducted, as are contributions to a pension scheme and any voluntary deductions such as trade union subscriptions.

- Net pay – the amount left after all deductions. This is the cash in the pay packet, or the amount on the cheque.

Employers also must act as collector of taxes for the government. Deductions of income tax and National Insurance contributions must be regularly paid over to the Inland Revenue. Other deductions must also be paid to pension schemes, unions, etc.

What is a code number?

Everybody is allowed to earn a certain amount of money before they have to pay tax. The amount they are allowed to earn depends on their status – single, married, over 65 etc. Each employee is given an allowance in the form of a **code number**, and the amount of tax deducted from each employee's pay will depend on this number.

Small garages will calculate the amount of tax to deduct from tax tables. Larger businesses will use a computer to prepare wages and salaries.

What are a P45 and a P60?

- **P45** – when an employee leaves a job, the employer prepares a form called a P45 showing pay and tax deducted for the current tax year. One copy goes to the Inland Revenue, the other to the employee. The employee should then hand this over to a new employer on the first day of the job.

- **P60** – at the end of each tax year (5th April), all employees are given a P60 form which shows details of pay, tax and National Insurance for the year. Copies of this form are sent to the Inland Revenue.

What are fringe benefits?

Fringe benefits, called 'benefits in kind' by the Inland Revenue, are any part of an employee's pay that is not received in money. Examples are the use of a company car, private health insurance, or the provision of cheap loans. Although not paid in cash, they are taxable, and employers have to notify the Inland Revenue of the value of these fringe benefits paid during the year. The Inland Revenue will then adjust each employee's code number to take account of the additional 'income'.

What are the advantages of monthly pay?

Some years ago, all manual workers were paid weekly and could be hired and fired at very short notice. Today there is relatively more job security and payment on a monthly basis is becoming increasingly common. What are the advantages:

- A monthly salary system is much cheaper to operate. Pay and deductions have to be calculated once a month instead of once a week. Making out a cheque or credit transfer slip takes much less time than counting out and balancing up notes and coins.

- There used to be a big difference in status, security and conditions of employment between weekly and monthly paid employees. To some extent this is broken down when all employees have the same rights, hours and entitlements such as pension schemes and sick pay.

There is still reluctance by some employees to accept monthly pay because:

- A regular weekly wage is easier to manage.

- There is still some unfamiliarity and distrust of banks and payment by cheque, although this is gradually reducing.

- There is a long gap between working overtime or earning a bonus and actually receiving the money.

What are the disadvantages of cash payments?

The payment of wages in notes and coins presents a business with a number of problems:

- Security – collecting a large amount of cash from the bank on the same day each week, and keeping it on the premises, means increased danger to employees.

- Insurance – additional insurance premiums will have to be paid in case of loss.

- Administration costs – making sure that exactly the right amount of cash gets into each pay envelope, and that there is not cash short or left over at the end, is a very time consuming exercise to carry out every week. Any mistakes made are difficult to rectify.

From the individual employee's point of view, receiving a large amount of cash in a pay packet also presents problems of security and of accidental loss.

Control of overtime

We saw in Section C how department spending is controlled through budgeting. One cost that can very easily get out of control is spending on overtime. It is the manager who must decide on what overtime is to be worked, because the manager will be held responsible if spending goes over budget. Efficient methods of workshop loading should ensure that overtime is kept to a minimum. This does not mean that overtime is always a sign of inefficiency

– it may be a sign of effective marketing that brings in more sales, increases the amount of work to be done, and justifies the additional cost.

What is the National Joint Council?

The **National Joint Council for the Motor Vehicle Retail and Repair Industry** (or **NJC**) is the body which negotiates rates of pay, working conditions and other industrial relations matters in the motor trade. The NJC consists of 24 members, 12 representing the employers, and 12 from trade unions. It has been in operation since 1943, and has produced an agreement covering pay and conditions in great detail. Although the agreement is not legally enforceable, in practice motor traders feel bound by its provisions.

What does the NJC agreement cover?

Anyone employed in the motor trade, either as a manual worker or a manager, should make themselves familiar with the contents of the agreement. The full agreement is included in the NJC Handbook, copies of which will be available at your place of work. As a manager with responsibility for staff, it is essential to be aware of, and to comply exactly with the rules and procedures laid down.

The agreement covers manual workers and some clerical staff, but does not apply to managers or sales staff. The main provisions include:

- Minimum rates of pay, agreed annually. Individual employers can pay more than this, but not less.

- Job classification (e.g. Motor Mechanic (General), Auto Electrician).

- Hours of work, shift and overtime pay.

- Procedure to adopt in industrial disputes.

- Holiday entitlement and sickness benefit.

- Apprenticeship contracts.

National agreements of this sort are useful for employers because they avoid lengthy and potentially damaging local negotiations over pay and conditions. Employees benefit because they have greater bargaining power at a national level.

What is a bonus scheme?

A **bonus scheme** provides workers with an incentive to work harder and more effectively. The incentive is usually in the form of more pay, and the scheme will normally be agreed at a local level. If the bonus system is well thought out, there can be a dramatic increase in productivity. A poor bonus system can result in an unhappy workforce and quite the opposite effect. The best recipe for good productivity and industrial relations is probably an interesting job, a reasonable rate of basic pay, good working conditions and effective supervision. The motor trade does, however, have the right sort of conditions for a fair and workable bonus scheme.

What makes a good bonus scheme?

A bonus scheme works properly where the following conditions apply:

- The work can be measured.

- The pace of work must be largely controlled by the worker.

- There must be a steady flow of work.

- Tasks should not be subjected to frequent changes of methods or equipment.

(Recommendation of National Board for Prices and Incomes.)

A workshop in the motor trade fits in well with these conditions. Manufacturers usually supply estimates of the time it takes to complete a particular job – for example, replace gearbox 3 hours. Providing the management can keep the work flowing, a bonus scheme can be based on these 'standard times'. The mechanic is set 3 hours in which to replace the gearbox. If the job is done in 2½ hours, the mechanic will still be paid for 3 hours. Fast and efficient workers will therefore be paid for more hours than they actually work.

What are the advantages of a bonus scheme?

A well-designed scheme is to the advantage of employer and employee. Individual mechanics have some control over their earnings, and will receive more pay. But what is in it for the employer?

- They will pay out more in wages, but will also sell more hours of work. Sales will increase, variable costs (wages) will increase, *but fixed costs will stay the same*. Profits will therefore be up.

- All staff will have an interest in developing more efficient working methods.

- Less direct supervision of the amount of work done is necessary.

What are the disadvantages of a bonus scheme?

A badly thought-out bonus scheme will be seen as unfair, will create ill-feeling and resentment, and will probably be difficult to remove. Even a good scheme has some disadvantages:

- Working quickly and efficiently is one thing, cutting corners on a potentially lethal machine is quite another. Hospital surgeons are not paid extra for working more quickly, and mechanics have a serious responsibility to drivers and passengers in the vehicles which they service. The most important part of any bonus scheme is to ensure that *quality is not compromised in any way*. Supervision and inspection of the standard of work done is absolutely vital.

- The paperwork involved may be quite complex and even, in a large dealership, require more staff to operate.

- There will always be disputes over the time allowed for particular jobs.

- Managers have to ensure a constant flow of work and materials. Delays will reduce earnings.

Leasing

What is a lease?

A business needs to use assets, but does not necessarily need to own them outright. In the same way that you or I can either buy a TV set or rent one, a business can buy an asset or **lease** it. Payments are made in regular instalments over the working life of the asset. During this time the total amount paid will be much greater than the cost of buying outright. The big advantage is that the business does not have to find or borrow a large amount of capital. It's quite common for a business to obtain the use of plant and machinery, vehicles and office furniture in this way. And where a machine or tool is needed for a short time, leasing is the only practical option.

How is leasing different from hire purchase?

On the face of it, leasing seems very similar to hire purchase (HP). The business does not have to find a lump sum of money, it has immediate use of the asset, and pays in regular instalments. Legally, however, the two are quite different.

- With HP, the asset is hired for a period at the end of which the business *owns* the asset. For tax purposes, the Inland Revenue presumes that the asset is owned immediately, and gives certain allowances (called 'capital allowances') which reduce the amount of tax payable.

- With a lease, the business *never* owns the asset, although at the end of the period of the agreed lease it may extend the lease for a very small rental. The whole of the payments may be set against tax, but there are no capital allowances.

One form of hire purchase is called 'lease purchase'. As with HP, the asset can be purchased outright for a nominal sum at the end of the agreement. The business taking out the lease (the 'lessee') has the responsibility of maintaining and insuring the asset.

What types of lease are there?

Two types of lease are available – a **finance lease** or an **operating lease**. Under both systems a rental is paid, and ownership is retained by the leasing company.

- Finance lease – the lessee is responsible for servicing and maintaining the asset.

- Operating lease – commonly known as '**contract hire**'. This is a more expensive arrangement as the hire company takes responsibility for service and maintenance. It is most popular in the motor trade and used by car hire firms and some dealerships. The hirer also takes responsibility for providing replacement vehicles.

Lease or buy?

We have seen that there are certain advantages to leasing,

to having the use of an asset without finding a large cash sum. But are there any advantages to buying an asset outright? If a business has cash to spare, spending it on an asset that will produce profits may be a sensible thing to do – the business will certainly pay out less money overall. Even if the business has to borrow the money to buy the asset, and therefore pay interest, it may still be appropriate to buy rather than lease. The cost of the asset plus interest payments may be similar to the cash paid out on a lease. But the advantage of buying is that the business will own the asset – and can therefore include it in the balance sheet. The business will then appear to be larger and stronger because leased assets are not owned and therefore cannot be included.

Whether to buy, to borrow money from the bank, to use hire-purchase, or to lease, is a complex decision which depends on the financial situation of the business. Management will take into account the cash situation, the present level of borrowing, the cost of borrowing, the effects of taxation and a number of other factors in taking the decision.

The effect of leasing on cash flow

The real difference between buying and leasing can be seen in the effect on cash flow, shown of course in the cash flow forecast. Take for example a small garage that wants to acquire a machine which costs £5,000 to buy. On 1st October it has £1,200 in the bank, so would need to borrow money to buy it outright. An alternative is to lease the machine for payment of £150 per month. What would be the effects on cash flow of the two alternatives? The forecast on the left shows what happens if the garage buys the machine, the one on the right the effects of leasing. All other relevant figures are shown on the forecasts.

We can see from the 'Buy' forecast that the purchase price will result in an overdraft that will last for some time to

CASH FLOW FORECAST

	BUY			LEASE		
	OCT £	NOV £	DEC £	OCT £	NOV £	DEC £
Cash in:						
Sales	2,000	2,400	2,400	2,000	2,400	2,400
Cash out:						
Materials	700	900	900	700	900	900
Wages	500	600	600	500	600	600
Overheads	300	300	300	300	300	300
Capital equipment	5,000					
Bank interest		40	35			
Lease				150	150	150
Total	6,500	1,840	1,835	1,650	1,950	1,950
Net cash flow	(4,500)	560	565	350	450	450
Opening bank balance	1,200	(3,300)	(2,740)	1,200	1,550	2,000
Closing bank balance	(3,300)	(2,740)	(2,175)	1,550	2,000	2,450

come. This in turn will mean paying bank interest until it is cleared. Looking at the 'Lease' forecast, however, we can see that there is still plenty of cash left in the bank account, and of course no interest to pay. If you look at the net inflow of cash, however, you will see that in November and December, the net cash flow into the business is much lower under the leasing option.

Looking at the first three months is useful to illustrate the immediate effects on cash, but it's also a little misleading. Over the life of the asset, the amount of cash paid out will be much more than the purchase price. In order to take a proper decision to buy or lease, it is necessary to look at the likely cash flows in and out of the business for the full term of the lease.